J. F. DiMarzio

SAMS
Teach Yourself
Routing
in 24 Hours

SAMS

201 West 103rd St., Indianapolis, Indiana, 46290 USA

Sams Teach Yourself Routing in 24 Hours

Copyright ©2002 by Sams Publishing

International Standard Book Number: 0-672-32364-8

Library of Congress Catalog Card Number: 2001097519

Printed in the United States of America

First Printing: April, 2001

04   03   02   01   4   3   2   1

Trademarks

Warning and Disclaimer

ACQUISITIONS EDITOR
Jenny Watson

DEVELOPMENT EDITOR
Mark Renfrow

MANAGING EDITOR
Charlotte Clapp

PROJECT EDITOR
Andy Beaster

COPY EDITORS
Seth Kerney
Kitty Jarrett

INDEXER
Ken Johnson

PROOFREADER
Abby Van Huss

TECHNICAL EDITORS
Sally Miller
Mark Hall

TEAM COORDINATOR
Amy Patton

INTERIOR DESIGNER
Gary Adair

COVER DESIGNER
Aren Howell

PAGE LAYOUT
Rebecca Harmon

Contents at a Glance

Introduction   1

Part I   Routing Basics   5

Hour 1	Introduction to Routing	7
2	Routers, Protocols, and the OSI Model	15
3	Routing Algorithms	31
4	Understanding Routed Protocols	39
5	Understanding WAN Protocols	51
6	Understanding Routing Protocols	61
7	Understanding How Routers Move Data	71

Part II   Basic Protocols   89

Hour 8	Introducing IP	91
9	Discovering IP Router Configurations	101
10	Understanding Segmented Networks	111
11	Using CIDR	129
12	Understanding IPX Basics	139
13	Dynamic Versus Static Routing	153
14	Understanding ISDN	167
15	Learning X.25	179
16	Learning Frame Relay	189
17	Understanding RIP	197
18	Routing with IGRP	217

Part III   Advanced Routing and Protocols   229

Hour 19	Learning EIGRP	231
20	Exploring OSPF	237
21	Exploring PNNI	253
22	Using IS-IS	283
23	Understanding BGP	323
24	Basic Router Security	349

Part IV Appendixes   **355**

    A   Using NAT   357

    B   Access Lists   361

        Index   367

Contents

Introduction   **1**

PART I Routing Basics

HOUR 1 Introduction to Routing   **7**

Routing and the Internet 8
    A Brief History of the Internet 8
Routing in Everyday Life 10
Summary 13
Q&A 13

HOUR 2 Routers, Protocols, and the OSI Model   **15**

The OSI Model 16
    The Application Layer 17
    The Presentation Layer 18
    The Session Layer 20
    The Transport Layer 20
    The Network Layer 21
    The Data Link Layer 22
    The Physical Layer 24
Router Interaction with Protocols and the OSI Model 25
    Network Maps, Protocols, and Protocol Addresses 26
Summary 29
Q&A 29

HOUR 3 Routing Algorithms   **31**

Routing Algorithms Within Routing Protocols 32
    Distance Vector Algorithms 35
    Link State Algorithms 36
Summary 37
Q&A 37

HOUR 4 Understanding Routed Protocols   **39**

How Routed Protocols Work 40
Routed Protocol Divisions and Classifications 41
    Connection-Oriented Versus Connectionless Protocols 41
    Classful Versus Classless Protocols 44
Protocol Encapsulation 46
Summary 48
Q&A 49

Hour 5 Understanding WAN Protocols   51

The Purpose of WAN Protocols 52
Understanding the Difference Between Public and Private Networks 54
WAN Protocols and the PSN 56
   ISDN and T-Lines 57
Summary 58
Q&A 59

Hour 6 Understanding Routing Protocols   61

The Big Picture 63
Dynamic Route Updates 65
   Convergence 68
Summary 69
Q&A 69

Hour 7 Understanding How Routers Move Data   71

Routers and the Network Layer 72
Protocol Routing 74
   Protocol Headers 74
   Data Packeting 78
The Mechanics of Routing 78
   Simple Network Routing 79
   Complex Network Routing 82
   Routing Tables 84
   Achieving Convergence 86
Summary 86
Q&A 87

Part II Basic Protocols   89

Hour 8 Introducing IP   91

TCP (Transmission Control Protocol) 91
IP (Internet Protocol) 92
Network Subnetting 96
Supernetting an IP Network 99
Summary 100
Q&A 100

Hour 9 Discovering IP Router Configurations   101

Router Interfaces 102
ICMP (Internet Control Message Protocol) 104

Using ICMP and ICMP Tools 105

The ping Utility 106

traceroute 108

Summary 109

Q&A 109

HOUR 10 Understanding Segmented Networks   **111**

Learning the Basics of Subnetting 112

Subnetting IP Networks 113

Placing Routers Within Segmented Environments 122

Configuring Static Routes Between Subnets 125

Summary 127

Q&A 128

HOUR 11 Using CIDR   **129**

The Problem: Classful IP 130

The Solution: CIDR 133

Summary 137

Q&A 137

HOUR 12 Understanding IPX Basics   **139**

Introducing IPX 140

IPX Addressing 140

Sample IPX Router Configuration 143

IPX Encapsulation 144

Ethernet Encapsulation Fields 145

IPX Routing 148

Summary 150

Q&A 151

HOUR 13 Dynamic Versus Static Routing   **153**

Dynamic Routing Basics 155

Problems with Dynamic Routing 159

Static Routing Basics 161

Problems with Static Routing 163

Summary 165

Q&A 165

HOUR 14 Understanding ISDN   **167**

The History of ISDN 168

ISDN Technology 168

ISDN Terminology 169

ISDN Protocol Terminology 171

        ISDN Functionality 172
        Configuring ISDN 174
    Summary 178
    Q&A 178

HOUR 15 Learning X.25   179

    X.25 Terminology 181
    X.25 Concepts and Functions 182
        PVCs 182
        SVCs 184
        LAPB 185
        PLP 185
    Summary 187
    Q&A 187

HOUR 16 Learning Frame Relay   189

    Frame Relay Technology 190
    Frame Relay Configuration Basics 194
    Summary 195
    Q&A 196

HOUR 17 Understanding RIP   197

        RIP Technology 198
    How RIP Works 207
        Routing Updates in RIP 209
    Configuring RIP 211
        Setting RIP Timers 212
        Working with Multiple Versions of RIP 213
    Summary 214
    Q&A 214

HOUR 18 Routing with IGRP   217

    IGRP Versus RIP 218
    IGRP Technology 221
        IGRP Metrics 221
        IGRP Routing Updates 223
    IGRP Configuration Information 223
        Modifying Update Timers 224
        Enabling/Disabling Split Horizon and Hold-down Timers 225
    Summary 226
    Q&A 226

Part III Advanced Routing and Protocols

HOUR 19 Learning EIGRP **231**

EIGRP Technology 232

Configuring EIGRP 234

Summary 235

Q&A 235

HOUR 20 Exploring OSPF **237**

OSPF Technology 238

    The Link-State Algorithm 242

    OSPF Updates 242

    OSPF Areas 244

    Route Redistribution 247

OSPF Configuration 248

Summary 251

Q&A 251

HOUR 21 Exploring PNNI **253**

ATM Architecture 255

    ATM Network Layout 257

The UNI Signaling Protocol 260

PNNI Hierarchy 263

    PNNI Peer Groups 264

    PNNI NSAP Addressing 265

PNNI Routing Protocol 270

The Relationship between PNNI and QoS Metrics 273

PNNI Signaling Protocol 275

PNNI Crankback 278

Configuring PNNI 280

Summary 281

Q&A 281

HOUR 22 Using IS-IS **283**

IS-IS and DECnet 283

    DECnet Areas and Nodes 285

    DECnet Nodes 287

    DECnet Routing Basics 291

    DECnet Phase V 292

How IS-IS Relates to CLNP 293

IS-IS Link-State Routing 294

    Controlling Link-State Floods 298

IS-IS Metrics and Algorithms 302

Exploring IS-IS Addressing, Areas, and Domains 304

    IS-IS Areas 305

    IS-IS Addresses 308

Examining IS-IS Packets 309

    Inside IS-IS Hello Messages 312

    Uncovering Link-State Packets 313

    Sequence Number Packets 314

IS-IS Routing 315

    Designated IS 316

    Examining IS-IS Pseudo-Nodes 316

    Routing in an IS-IS Environment 318

Sample IS-IS Configurations 321

Summary 321

Q&A 321

Hour 23 Understanding BGP   **323**

Defining BGP Autonomous Systems 324

    Obtaining an Autonomous System Number 326

    Public Versus Private ASNs 327

    ASNs and IP 329

    Autonomous System Terms 330

Routing with the Exterior Border Gateway Protocol (EBGP) 333

    BGP Route Maps 335

    BGP Route Flapping and Flap Dampening 337

    Some BGP Metrics and Attributes 338

Interior Border Gateway Routing 343

    BGP Confederations 343

    BGP Synchronization 345

    BGP Route Reflection 346

Summary 347

Q&A 348

Hour 24 Basic Router Security   **349**

Hardware-Based Router Security 350

    Physical Router Security 350

    Physical Port Security 351

Software-Based Security for Routers 352

    Introduction to NAT 352

    Introduction to Access Lists 353

Summary 353

Q&A 353

Part IV Appendixes

A Using NAT **357**

Behind NAT: The Concepts and the Technology 358

B Access Lists **361**

Examining IP Access Lists 362

Index **367**

About the Author

J. F. DiMarzio is a network engineer with 10 years of experience in system design and administration. He has worked as a consultant since 1991 for companies such as the Walt Disney Company and the United States Department of Defense.

Currently a technical consultant for a large financial institution in central Massachusetts, Mr. DiMarzio has achieved the certifications of MCP, MCP+I, MCSE, and CCNA. He is also a GOLD member of the IEEE, serving on the IEEE Computer Society Task Force on Virtual Intelligence and the Task Force on Information Technology for Business Applications.

About the Technical Editor

Sally Miller is a network administrator for a manufacturing company in Minnesota and maintains a WAN with links in Indiana and Mexico. She holds a B.A. from Wayne State University in Detroit, Michigan, as well as the MCSE and CCNA professional certifications. Formerly, Sally has worked as an assistant technical writer, a software support analyst, and a trainer in the computer software industry.

Dedication

To my family: Suzannah, Christian, and Sophia.

Acknowledgments

I would first like to thank William E. Brown, Jenny Watson, Mark Renfrow, Sally Miller, Seth Kerney, Kitty Jarrett, Mark Hall, and the team at Sams Publishing.

My sincere thanks also go to my wife, Suzannah, and my two beautiful children, Christian and Sophia, for brightening my life; Jerome and Agnes (my parents), my brother Matt, and my mother-in-law, Diana, thank you.

I would also like to thank my agent Vicki Harding at Studio B, Walt Adams and Darby Weaver of Double Eagle Services in Central Florida, and everyone who made this book possible. My sincere apologies go to anybody I forgot or left out.

Tell Us What You Think!

As the reader of this book, *you* are our most important critic and commentator. We value your opinion and want to know what we're doing right, what we could do better, what areas you'd like to see us publish in, and any other words of wisdom you're willing to pass our way.

As an Associate Publisher for Sams, I welcome your comments. You can e-mail, or write me directly to let me know what you did or didn't like about this book—as well as what we can do to make our books stronger.

Please note that I cannot help you with technical problems related to the topic of this book, and that due to the high volume of mail I receive, I might not be able to reply to every message.

When you write, please be sure to include this book's title and author as well as your name and phone or fax number. I will carefully review your comments and share them with the author and editors who worked on the book.

E-mail: feedback@samspublishing.com

Mail: Mark Taber, Associate Publisher
            Sams Publishing
            201 West 103rd Street
            Indianapolis, IN 46290 USA

Introduction

Sams Teach Yourself Routing in 24 Hours is focused on providing readers with the basic building blocks of knowledge needed to successfully learn the concepts and technology behind routers.

The examples and subject matter contained in this book are derived from my years of networking and routing experience. I've structured this book to be a concise primer for those who desire a base from which to build a career in networking, or who simply want to keep on top of the latest in technology.

How This Book Is Organized

The lessons contained within this text are divided into 24 one-hour exercises designed to give you the most important information in one sitting.

The 24 hours of lessons are as follows:

- Hour 1: Introduction to Routing—This lesson introduces basic concepts of routing technology and sets the tone for the remaining lessons.
- Hour 2: Routers, Protocols, and the OSI Model—This lesson discusses the correlation between routing, protocols, and their interaction with the OSI model.
- Hour 3: Routing Algorithms—The core of every router is the routing algorithm. In this hour you will be introduced to the different algorithms that exist in routing today.
- Hour 4: Understanding Routed Protocols—This lesson will examine the function of routed protocols in the routing process.
- Hour 5: Understanding WAN Protocols—Used for WAN connectivity, WAN protocols can play an important part in many routed environments.
- Hour 6: Understanding Routing Protocols—Hour 6 will focus on the protocols that aid in the movement of data from network to network.
- Hour 7: Understanding How Routers Move Data—After having been introduced to the major pieces of the routing puzzle, this lesson will cover the concepts behind how protocols, algorithms, and routers combine to move data.
- Hour 8: Introducing IP—This lesson will introduce you to the most important protocol in use today—most of the world's interconnected systems use IP.
- Hour 9: Discovering IP Router Configurations—After being introduced to IP, this lesson will examine configuration examples for the functions of IP.

- Hour 10: Understanding Segmented Networks—One commonly misunderstood property of IP is the ability to subnet networks. Hour 10 will discuss this process and teach you several tips for segmenting IP networks.
- Hour 11: Using CIDR—Also known as supernetting, CIDR is an important tool for today's IP environments.
- Hour 12: Understanding IPX Basics—This short lesson will introduce you to the properties of another routed protocol, IPX.
- Hour 13: Dynamic Versus Static Routing—Routing can take on one of two characteristics, dynamic or static. This lesson will provide you with the pros and cons of each.
- Hour 14: Understanding ISDN—Hour 15 covers an important WAN protocol, ISDN. This protocol forms the basis for many of the WAN communication advances seen today.
- Hour 15: Learning X.25—This hour focuses on X.25, one of the first widely used WAN protocols.
- Hour 16: Learning Frame Relay—This lesson discusses the functionality of one of the most popular WAN protocols, Frame Relay. You will examine several configuration examples and learn the properties and parameters needed to use this WAN protocol.
- Hour 17: Understanding RIP—The first routing protocol covered in the book is RIP. You will learn how RIP works, and how to configure RIP in different environments.
- Hour 18: Routing with IGRP—IGRP is an important routing protocol. This lesson focuses on the configuration and use of IGRP.
- Hour 19: Learning EIGRP—EIGRP, the enhanced version of IGRP, is covered in Hour 19.
- Hour 20: Exploring OSPF—An extremely popular protocol, OSPF is used in many routing environments.
- Hour 21: Exploring PNNI—Discussed as a more advanced networking subject, PNNI is the focus of Hour 21. You will learn how the protocol works, and where it can be used effectively.
- Hour 22: Using IS-IS—This hour will introduce you to IS-IS, a protocol that grew from the DECnet networking standards. You will learn about DECnet and how IS-IS relates to both DECnet and today's routing networks.
- Hour 23: Understanding BGP—The final protocol covered in this book is BGP. This lesson will teach you the properties and functionality of BGP.
- Hour 24: Basic Router Security—To close the book, you will learn some basic router security lessons. These simple tips and tools will help you become more aware of security on your networks.

Who Should Read This Book

Sams Teach Yourself Routing in 24 Hours is helpful for anyone who wants to learn about routing. You will need no prior experience with routers to use and understand the lessons within this book. Designed for the reader who has not had much exposure to routing, it is the perfect primer for the novice tech. You will find that the lessons relate to real-life situations, and they will give you an added boost whether your goal is to become a routing engineer, or simply to learn the basics of the technology.

PART I
Routing Basics

Hour

1 Introduction to Routing

2 Routers, Protocols, and the OSI Model

3 Routing Algorithms

4 Understanding Routed Protocols

5 Understanding WAN Protocols

6 Understanding Routing Protocols

7 Understanding How Routers Move Data

Hour 1

Introduction to Routing

The importance of information routing is paramount in a society that runs and survives on the reliable delivery of electronic information. Routing is the main process by which information travels from location to location.

Imagine all the technological advances of the last decade. Many of them have revolved around the Internet (or some other form of "anytime, anywhere" technology). Now imagine these same advances without the capability to route information. Many of the things we take for granted, such as e-mail, e-shopping, and even the latest in computer telephony become nearly impossible. Many people do not realize just how important routing is to a technological society. The global economy is dependent on the capability to route information from system to system.

Networks today have become large masses of routers. The routers take data in the form of e-mail, Web-browsing requests, and file transfers, and deliver them to their appropriate destinations. The e-mail will be sent to the correct server, the Web requests will be forwarded to the Internet, and the file transfers will be delivered to their intended recipient. All these functions rely on properly set up and maintained routers.

Routers perform their duties by reading the contents of data packets and determining the correct source and destination for the packet. The router can then discover the best way to get the packet to its destination.

The definition of "best way" is open to interpretation. There are as many ways to interpret this phrase as there are networks in the world. The sum of the router's configuration, the protocols used on the networks, and the physical layout of the environment create the basis for the router's determination of the best way to move data between two networks.

In this hour's lesson, you will learn about

- Routing and the Internet
- Routing in everyday life

By covering the basics of routing and where it can be used, we will build a base of knowledge that will carry through the remaining lessons.

Routing and the Internet

Data and information routing can be found in most aspects of today's technological societies. Most people today communicate with some form of routed information. Whether we use e-mail, digital cell phones, or personal chatting services (such as instant messaging), we all rely on routers to stay in touch. However, the process of moving data from device to device is most prevalent on the Internet.

At its core, the Internet is a large web of interconnected routers. The routers that form the Internet take requests from a local user and forward those requests to the appropriate server. The server then sends back the Web pages to the local user. From end-to-end the process is reliant on the functionality of routers.

One of the most important technological innovations of the past few decades (if not the century) has been the Internet. What started as a form of communication between United States military installations has become a multi-billion dollar a year industry. The Internet now provides everything from news, shopping, and gaming, to television and telephone service. Without a doubt, the Internet is an integral part of today's society.

A Brief History of the Internet

The first incarnation of the Internet was not comparable to the cyber-world of today. As the first personal computers began flooding stores in the early 80s, small networks of bulletin board servers began cropping up around the country. Although the servers were generally on the campuses of larger universities (the only entities that could afford the technology), users could dial into them from the comfort of their own home.

A *BBS (bulletin board system)* is a collection of messages that users can dial-in via modem to read. A modern version of the original BBS is the Yahoo! message boards.

These small (by today's standards) clusters of users, all connected via modem to large dial-in BBSes, formed the first loose meshing of what would become the Internet. These conglomerations of BBS users could dial into specific hosts and access information, news, chat, and messaging services (an early form of e-mail). However, the e-mail wonders that were the beginning of mass computer communication were by no means perfect.

The major flaw of the BBS systems was the lack of inter-connectivity between them. For more then five years (a virtual lifetime in the world of technology), users around the world knew nothing but the joys of dialing into their local university's BBS and "talking" to a stranger in the next county. People were communicating with each other in ways they didn't before. However, unless you knew who to call and how to log in, you had to stay within your specific community. The BBS systems were, at this time, very centralized.

By the late 1980s the University of Minnesota had begun work on Gopher. Expanding upon technologies such as Lynx and Trumpet, Gopher would enable BBS users to view graphics on once text-dominated computers. For all intents and purposes, the Internet as we know it today was born.

There are many purists that will trace the history of the Internet back to the government networks of the 1960s. While these networks were truly the first "Internet," the average person on the street could not partake of the technology. The BBS and Gopher systems formed the first real communities of "common" users.

People signed up by the thousands for a chance to surf the Web with online services like Genie, Prodigy, and CompuServe. However, no one saw (or cared) how the information of the Internet was delivered to their screens. People were already beginning to take for granted the power of the routers that made this new technical wonder possible.

In the early days of the Internet, the function of a router was clear and well-defined; routers needed to move data from system to system in an efficient manner. When a user requested information in the form of a Web page, the router would fulfill the request and return the desired data.

These early routers functioned in much the same way as routers do today. Technically, they examine packets, calculate paths, and make intelligent routing decisions. These processes enable a router to determine where data originated from, where it is going, and how to get it there. The functionality of routing devices has actually changed very little over the cumulative life span of the Internet. What has changed in the world of routing is the amount of data being routed, and the number of networks that need routing.

It is fair to say that without routers and their capabilities, the Internet as we know it today would not exist. Without routers, every computer on the Internet would need to be connected to every other computer. Internet users would need to know the computer address of every Web site you wanted to visit (and what computers you need to pass through to get there). These are all functions provided by routers.

This explanation of how the Internet works should offer a view into some of the many uses of routers. While the subject of routing might seem a bit removed from the average person, there are instances in everyday life where normal people encounter routing.

Routing in Everyday Life

There are many places (some unexpected) where engineers and designers utilize routers. From telephone and cable television service, to the Internet, e-mail, and paging, routers are used in many situations. However, nowhere are routers more prevalent (or have more of an impact on daily life) than on the Internet.

In keeping with the theme of using the Internet as an example, let's discuss where routers can be used to facilitate the movement of data from device to device. Data such as search results, file transfers, and user authentication information must be moved from one PC to another. Regardless of how the user connects to the Internet, routers are used to achieve a desirable end result—the seamless flow of data between two places.

To better understand how routers are used on the Internet, we will use a scenario that should be familiar to you. Let's examine how routers are used during the process of viewing Web pages.

| The following explanation of how routers work on the Internet has been simplified. However, by the end of the book you will understand the whole picture. |

In this scenario, you want to visit the Web site www.marzdesign.com. To access the Web site, you enter the address into your Web browser. The browser then sends a message to the Internet service provider's (ISP) routers. The message notifies the ISP's routers that you want to see the information stored at the address www.marzdesign.com. The routers translate the natural language address www.marzdesign.com to the computer language address 207.217.96.36, and send the request to the routers that service this address.

> Routers, like computers, work solely in numbers. That is, the entire language of all computing devices is binary digits. To a router, all of the information in the world can be represented by ones and zeros. Therefore, when you enter the address www.marzdesign.com into your Web browser, it is translated into its binary address format. This number looks like this:
>
> 11001111.11011001.01100000.00100100
>
> This number is easier for people to remember when translated into base 10 notation as
>
> 207.217.96.36

The request travels through the ISP's routers. Each router examines the request, determines which IP address is being requested and which address is the requester, and matches this information against its own *routing table*. The router's routing table tells it where to find the IP address being requested, or if the routing table does not know where to find the address, it will know the address of another router to forward the request to.

This process continues until the request finally reaches www.marzdesign.com. At this point, because the routing tables have been keeping track of who made the request, they send the requested information back to the user. This scenario is repeated millions of times a day.

The use of routers is not confined to the Internet. Within the work place, routers are used in many different situations. One use that is becoming more popular is in the facilitation of telecommuters and users who work from home. Until recently, *wide area network (WAN)* technologies, whose primary purpose is connecting multiple networks, were used to connect home users and office users.

> Many routers can handle multiple types of interfaces. From WAN interfaces such as ISDN, DSL, and T-lines, to *local area network (LAN)* links like Ethernet, a single router can handle multiple connections on multiple media. It's likely that the first point of contact on an ISP's network is a router with some type of *firewall* enabled.
>
> The firewall's purpose is to protect the ISP from unwanted attacks. This makes routers both functional and practical security devices as well.

Although using WAN technologies such as ISDN and frame relay are common forms of
remote (home) networking technology, there is a more popular choice. Because WAN
technologies were originally designed to connect networks of people (rather than one
person to another), they can be very costly for businesses with great numbers of employees working from home. Therefore, more companies are choosing to implement *virtual
private network (VPN)* technologies.

Figure 1.1 illustrates a home-to-business network that implements a VPN. The network is
designed to enable users at a home-based office to connect to the company's network as
if they were onsite.

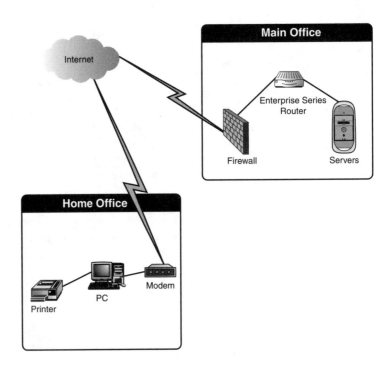

FIGURE 1.1

A home office-to-business VPN.

Taking a closer look at Figure 1.1, you will notice the lack of a router on the user's side
of the connection. A device such as a home router is not needed in the user's home to
implement a VPN. If we were working with other WAN options, a router would be
required on both sides of the connection. As long as the user has a sustained Internet
connection, she can exchange information with the main office.

On the business side of the connection, the same router that can be used to create a WAN
link with another network can also be used to implement the VPN. In fact, the same router
can run the VPN and the company's routing needs simultaneously. Therefore, a single
router can handle the remote networking needs of almost any business.

1

It is nearly impossible to design, implement, or work on a corporate network and not utilize the services of a router. The art of moving information from network to network is about more than just routers and hardware, however. To fully comprehend the routing process, one must understand the multiple concepts that make routing possible. Routers rely on the functionality of routed protocols, routing protocols, WAN protocols, routing tables, and algorithms to successfully carry data. All these topics will be covered within this text.

Routers cannot perform all of the functions described in this lesson alone. Routers require the assistance of protocols, tables, and updates to work smoothly and efficiently.

Summary

Modern conveniences such as e-mail, cell phones, and the Internet work because of the routers used to transport the data from device to device.

Businesses choose routers for many reasons, including LAN connectivity, WAN connectivity, remote networking, and network protection.

Q&A

Q If networking has been around since the early 1960s, why were routers only introduced in the mid-1980s?

A Before routers were introduced, computers were in charge of moving data from place to place. The computers on a particular network would run the routing protocols needed to connect networks together.

Q What is the main function of routers?

A To move information from network to network.

Q True or False: Routers can provide a basic form of network protection?

A True. Routers can use firewalls to protect devices.

Q True or False: Routers use protocols to facilitate the movement of data from network to network.

A True. Protocols are the software that routers use to carry data.

HOUR 2

Routers, Protocols, and the OSI Model

During this hour we'll explain the concepts behind protocols. Many people do not fully understand the most basic building block of routing—the protocols. All data movement, whether routing, switching, or simple data transference needs the assistance of a protocol. Protocols assist in the routing process in several ways. They encapsulate information and help transport data from source to destination. By the end of this lesson you will have a fuller understanding of how protocols are derived, and how they aid in the routing process.

In discussing protocols and their relationship with the OSI model, we will be examining the following topics:

- The OSI model
- Router Interaction with Protocols and the OSI model

Most protocols in use today, including TCP/IP, RIP, OSPF, and IPX, were designed around a common framework. This framework is known as the *OSI model*. By basing a protocol on a common architecture, designers can be assured that their product will be compatible with any other product based on the same architecture. This common thread makes some protocols more popular than others.

> Because protocol developers base their products on the OSI model, router developers using the same standards have no problems implementing their products.

Before we look at the specific relationship characteristics between protocols and the OSI model, you need to develop an understanding of what the OSI model is and where it came from. The next section will explain the sources of the OSI model and the reasons why it became popular among designers.

The OSI Model

In the early 1980s the International Organization for Standardization (ISO) developed the *Open Systems Inter-connection model,* or *OSI model*. Partially derived from the Department of Defense protocol model, the OSI model divides the functions of all protocols into seven distinct layers.

The seven layers of the OSI model are numbered from the bottom up. For information to get from one PC to another, the data must traverse these layers on both the sending and receiving devices. For example, if PC A wants to send a file to PC B, the path of the information would be as follows: First, the file would travel from Layer 7 through Layer 1 on PC A. Then after traversing the network, the file arrives at Layer 1 on PC B. The file is then passed from Layer 1 through Layer 7 on PC B. Figure 2.1 illustrates this process.

> Do not try to imagine the seven layers of the OSI model as physical entities. For all intents and purposes, the seven layers of the OSI model do not physically exist; they are logical concepts. Each layer of the OSI model represents a framework within which certain actions can be performed in preparation for network transmission.

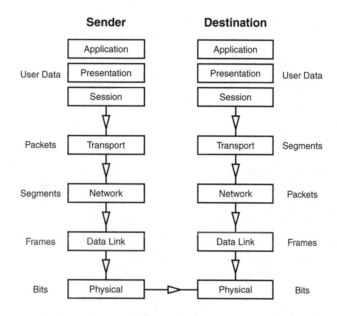

FIGURE 2.1

Information traversing the seven layers of the OSI model.

Each layer of the OSI model has a very specific function. Information traveling from one layer to another is altered slightly to make it readable by the next layer before being transmitted across the network. When this data reaches the receiving device, it travels through the layers in reverse order to undo the alterations made by the sending computer.

Routers function on Layer 3 of the OSI model. However, even though a router may only be concerned with the data after it has reached Layer 3, if Layers 7 through 4 are not functioning correctly, the router's capability will be affected.

The following sections look at each of the layers and their function to give you a better understanding of the role protocols play in routing.

The Application Layer

The application layer (Layer 7) is concerned with coordinating communication between applications. This layer of the OSI model synchronizes the data flowing between servers and clients by handling functions such as file transfers, network management, and process services. Within the application layer, consideration is also made for the identification of communication partners and cross-partner security authentication. Other duties of the application layer include handling the following:

- The World Wide Web (WWW)
- E-mail gateways
- Electronic Data Interchange (EDI)
- Chat services
- Internet navigation utilities

The application layer can be viewed as the first step data takes when leaving a PC to be routed. The application layer is routed information's direct access to the program it is bound for. That is, most if not all routed information either emanates from or is bound for an application residing on a device. The application layer of the OSI model creates the rules that govern how this data is treated. Figure 2.2 illustrates a computer's interaction with the application layer of the OSI model.

Figure 2.2

Functions of the application layer.

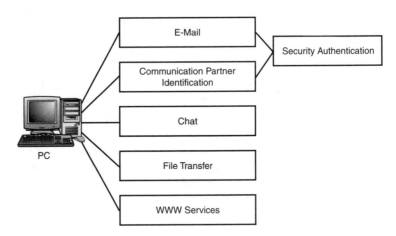

For example, when you view a Web page, you are viewing data at the application layer. The information that makes up the Web page traveled through the seven layers of the OSI model on a remote server. After traversing the Internet, the data climbed up the OSI layers of your PC. Finally, the information is made readable at the application level.

The Presentation Layer

The function of the presentation layer (Layer 6) is to translate the information from the application layer into a format that is readable by the other layers. All data encryption, decryption, and compression take place at the sixth layer of the OSI model. The presentation layer also controls all audio and video presentation functions. Services provided by the presentation layer include the following:

- MP3
- Real audio
- Real video
- JPEG
- GIF

Notice that all the services mentioned for Layer 6 require some form of compression or encryption. MP3s need extraordinary audio compression, whereas GIFs utilize image compression. Without this compression, the data that reaches the router would be too much to handle without error. The more data that is routed in one session, the higher the likelihood that it will not reach its intended recipient intact. Therefore, data compression (along with encryption and decryption) plays a large role in helping data get routed.

When preparing to send data onto a network, the application layer will pass unformatted, raw, information to the presentation layer. The presentation layer will then format this information using encryption, compression, or both. The end product is a chunk of data that is prepared for transmission. Figure 2.3 illustrates the functions of the presentation layer.

FIGURE 2.3

The functions of the presentation layer.

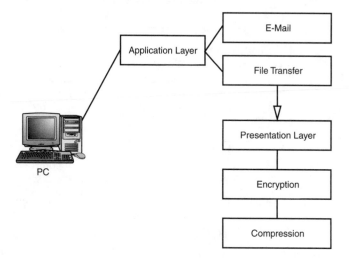

The Session Layer

The session layer (Layer 5) coordinates communications between network devices. The session layer, working with the session layer of another device, establishes a session between two applications. The two session layers monitor the "conversation" and, when appropriate, terminate communication. Other session layer responsibilities include control of the following:

- SQL (Structured Query Language)
- X Window System
- NFS (Network File System)

The information sent or received from the top three layers (Layers 5, 6, and 7) is known as *user data*. This user data is converted into other forms by the layers below. As you will see, the user data is converted into other forms of data suitable for the remaining layers to understand.

The Transport Layer

The function of the transport layer (Layer 4) is to take user data from the upper layers and break it (or reassemble, as the case may be) into chunks of data that can be easily transmitted. The chunks of data formed by the transport layer are known as *segments*. Segments are then passed to the lower layers for further processing.

Whether working with segments, frames, datagrams, or cells, knowing the terminology behind the layers of the OSI model will help you tremendously. Because each layer only deals with a specific data format, you can identify a particular layer (and usually a protocol) by the format of its data. For example, because TCP operates on Layer 4, all data from TCP is going to be in segment form.

The transport layer also provides services for data flow control. Flow control helps this layer ensure the reliable (connection-oriented) transmission of data from one device to another. It does this by taking user data from the upper layers and segmenting it. These segments are then transmitted one at a time to the intended recipient. The recipient, after receiving a segment, sends back an acknowledgment. If the sender does not receive an acknowledgment, it retransmits the segment. After several retries, the sending device attempts to re-initiate a connection with the recipient. If the recipient proves to be unresponsive (the receiving device is no longer on the network), an error is generated and the remaining segments are not transmitted.

The Network Layer

Layer 3 of the OSI model is one of the most important when dealing with routers. In the routing world, Layer 3 is the king of all layers. Although each layer serves a very important purpose, Layer 3 is the layer over which most routing takes place. Most connectivity devices (routers, Layer 3 switches, and bridges) work on the network layer of the OSI model.

For routing to function correctly, the network layer pieces together a logical network map. This map serves as a guide to route data across the network. Many devices, not just routers, use the services provided by the network layer to identify objects and devices within a certain environment. After all, what good is having a router on your network if none of the PCs can find it?

Converting transport layer segments into packets is the first step in constructing a network map. These packets are then passed to the data link layer, where addressing information is added.

When a device receives a packet, the sender's information is stripped from the packet and stored in a table. As this table grows, the network layer builds a clearer picture of the network environment. Other protocols and devices can use this information to route data in a more efficient manner. Figure 2.4 illustrates how routing table information is extracted from network layer data.

FIGURE 2.4
Network layer data extraction.

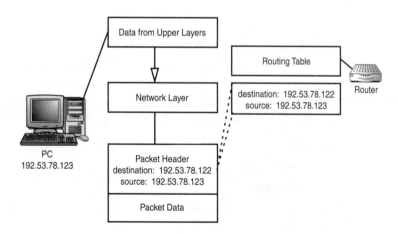

The data used by the network layer is also stored locally in a router's routing table. The specific information contained within the routing table depends on the routing protocol being used. Routing tables will be covered more comprehensively in later lessons dealing with routing protocols, such as Hour 17, "Understanding RIP."

For example, if a device on Network A wanted to send data to a device on Network B, it would send a broadcast across its local network (Network A). This broadcast would act as a scout, searching for the address of the recipient. Because the receiving device is not on Network A, no reply would be sent to the broadcast. The device on Network A would then assume the intended recipient is on Network B and send the data there.

Before reaching Network B, the packet travels through Router 1. This router searches through its own routing table (comprised of network layer data) and determines that the intended recipient is truly on Network B. Router 1 then forwards the packet to the appropriate networks. The router spanning the two networks will note the scenario in its routing table, and route all further packets for this device to Network B.

Keep in mind, the network layer is responsible for the logical addressing of clients. These are addresses that are software-based, and can usually be changed with ease. Physical computer addressing is a *hard-coded* address that cannot be manipulated. This form of addressing is handled by the data link layer.

The key element of this scenario is knowing the address of the device that you are trying to share information with. Compiling and tracking these addresses is the job of the data link layer.

The Data Link Layer

Whereas the network layer holds the map of the network, the data link layer (Layer 2) ensures that the information on the map is correct through addressing. The data link layer accepts packets from the network layer and frames them, thus converting them into data frames. These frames contain the following information:

- Preamble (The preamble signals the start of the frame)
- Destination address
- Source address
- Length field (in a standard Ethernet Frame, this indicates the size of the data contained in the frame)
- Type field (in Ethernet II frames, this indicates which protocol will receive the data)
- Data
- Frame check sequence (A verification number corresponding to the checksum of the frame)

For routing purposes, the data link layer has been broken into two sub-layers—the MAC and the LLC, discussed in the next sections. The data link layer itself provides a lot of functionality, most of which would be wasted on some devices. Therefore, Layer 2 has been split in two specialized sub-layers. Each sub-layer has its own rules and attributes.

The MAC Sub-Layer

The Media Access Control (MAC) sub-layer is in charge of framing the packets from the network layer. In framing the packets, the MAC sub-layer attaches the addressing information to the packet. This addressing information includes the MAC address.

> You should be familiar with the MAC sub-layer through the MAC address. Every networkable device has a factory-determined address, known as the *MAC address*, that uniquely identifies that component on a network.

The process of framing packets requires the MAC layer to dissect large amounts of data and break it into smaller, more manageable pieces. These smaller pieces are called *frames*. Frames can be viewed as pieces of a puzzle. When you reassemble all of the frames in a group, they form a larger packet of data.

Framed packets are sequenced in such a way as to determine whether any information was lost during a transmission. The MAC layer on the transmitting device will sequentially number each packet. The receiving device will reassemble the packets from the numbered frames in order. This will lessen the chance of data corruption, and allow for some basic error checking.

Another function of the MAC sub-layer is to provide connectionless services to the upper layers. Connectionless service takes place when data is sent to a device without a session being open. In other words, the sending device ships the data through the network without alerting the recipient beforehand.

TABLE 2.1 Pros and Cons of Connectionless Service

Pros	Cons
Faster than connection-oriented service	The delivery of frames is not ensured. There is no time spent opening sessions and waiting for responses.
Less network overhead	Recipient is not informed before data is sent. The machine you are sending may not even be functioning at the time data is sent.

As you will learn in later hours, the MAC sub-layer plays a big part in routing. Because MAC addresses are unique and are recognized by almost every protocol, they are found in many aspects of routing.

The LLC Sub-Layer

The LLC (Logical Link Control) layer provides three different services to the upper layers of the OSI model. Layers such as the MAC utilize the services of the LLC to make up for functionality they cannot perform on their own. The three services provided by the LLC are

- Unacknowledged connectionless (UCL)
- Acknowledged connectionless (ACL)
- Connection-oriented (CO)

Unacknowledged connectionless service is described in the previous section. Acknowledged connectionless service follows the same basic principles as UCL. No sessions are established between clients before data is sent over the network. However, ACL does provide a mechanism to allow receiving devices to send ACK (acknowledgement) packets back to a transmitting device. The ACK states that all of the frames within a transmission were received. If an ACK is not received by the transmitting device, it assumes that the frames were not received correctly and re-transmits them.

A device can tell if it has received all of the frames that were sent to it through the frame sequencing numbers. If a frame is out of order, the receiving device assumes that one or more frames have been lost.

Connection-oriented service provides for the establishment of sessions prior to the delivery of frames. By opening a session first, the sender is guaranteed delivery of frames. Like ACL, CO sessions utilize ACK packets for the confirmation of data delivery.

The Physical Layer

The first layer of the OSI model defines the physical connection between devices. The physical layer accepts frames from the upper layers and transmits them as bits over the media. This becomes more and more evident when dealing with Cisco router interfaces. The physical ports and interfaces that make up the Cisco routing hardware all operate on the physical layer of the OSI model.

After discussing the inner workings of the OSI model, let's take a look at how this information is used by routers to move data from system to system. Designing protocols to adhere to the OSI model is only part of the picture; devices need to function on the same layers as protocols to be effective.

Router Interaction with Protocols and the OSI Model

2

Because the OSI model covers a wide range of data specifications, it would be counter-productive for any one protocol to cover all of them. The OSI model has been divided into seven separate layers so protocols can be specialized by purpose, rather than generalized. Many protocols will only work on specific layers of the OSI model. These protocols are then combined to provide a full range of OSI capabilities. For example, IP works on the network layer of the OSI model, TCP is a transport layer protocol, and Telnet is a protocol that functions on the application layer. These are just three of the protocols that form the TCP/IP protocol suite. When combined, these protocols provide all the functionality allotted by the OSI model.

> *Specialized protocols*, or protocols that serve one main purpose (usually on one layer of the OSI model), can be smaller in size and quicker than protocols that try to handle main functions.

Protocols use the information and specifications provided by the OSI model as a road map to access the data they need and deliver data to the correct destination. Let's examine how routers obtain the information needed to perform their daily tasks from the OSI model. Because we have not fully examined how routers actually work or what they do, we will use general terms and scenarios to illustrate how routers and protocols work in correlation with the OSI model.

Using general terms, the functional purpose of routers is to move data from one location to another. Though this definition may seem straightforward enough, many intricacies and complications are associated with the routing process. Given this description of a router's job, let's do some visualization. Imagine yourself as a router: What information do you need to perform your job duties? The following list shows a sampling of the information needed by routers to move data between systems:

- Knowledge of the networking environment's layout—A router needs to know the location of every device on the network to successfully move data between them.

- A form of device addressing—Knowing where a computer is on a network does not help if you cannot target a specific (unique) device by address.
- A physical connection to the devices being targeted—Routers, like all devices on a network, need to have a physical connection to other devices for inter-computer communication.
- A mechanism to transport the data from source to destination—Data cannot be blindly transmitted onto a network. Careful thought has been put into packaging data in a way that makes network transmission reliable.

Each of the required pieces of information listed here can be derived (either directly or indirectly) from the OSI model. Each layer of the OSI model is responsible for one or more of these pieces of information, and the protocols designed to work on those layers will also carry that information. Let's discuss each of these points as they relate to routers, protocols, and the OSI model. The next section will examine how routers gain knowledge of networking environments from protocols, and how protocols in turn gather that information from the OSI model.

Network Maps, Protocols, and Protocol Addresses

To move anything from one area to another, whether it's people, cars, or digital information, you must know the location of any possible origins and destinations. For example, if you were to go on a hike through the forest, a map would help you keep track of your location. Using the map, you can easily find your destination. Marking your starting point enables you to return when you are finished. Maps are always important in finding places you have never been (or forgotten the way to).

Routers also need a map to find locations within a network. When a router needs to move data from one network to another, it refers to an internal map of the networking environment known as the *routing table*. The routing table contains within it a list of the addresses of (hopefully) every device in the environment. The router can look up the destination of any piece of data in this table to find out where the data needs to be sent.

The information in the routing table actually specifies the location of a device relative to the other devices on the network. This means that a routing table may indicate that data can be sent to Device A through Router B. Therefore any other device knows that if it wants to send data to Device A, it needs to forward that data to Router B. Thus, the location of Device A is somewhere behind Router B.

The information contained within the routing table is gathered from the third layer of the OSI model. The network layer is responsible for network mapping. This is the key reason why all routers function on Layer 3 of the OSI model. All network maps, including routing tables, are created with the assistance of protocols designed to work on the network layer of the OSI model. Routers use the mapping capabilities of Layer 3 protocols to maintain running lists of the locations of every device on a network. Examples of Layer 3 protocols are IP (Internet Protocol) and IPX (Internetwork Packet Exchange).

As discussed in the section on the network layer of the OSI model, the routing table is formed when the network layer extracts the source and destination data form the packet header.

As you progress through the hours in this book, you will gain a better understanding of how protocols participate in the creation of routing tables and network maps. For now, let's examine how routers determine the address of devices on the network.

Having a map of the networking environment helps routers determine the location of a specific destination (through that device's address); however, the router then needs to send information to that destination. To do this, the router needs to apply the address of the destination to the information being sent. For example, if you want to mail a postcard to a friend, knowing where she lives is one thing, but if you do not put that address on the postcard, it will never arrive. In the same way, routers look up the locations of devices in their routing tables, then attach the address of the device to the information being sent. This allows the information to arrive at the correct address regardless of how many devices it must pass through to get there.

The data link layer (Layer 2) of the OSI model is responsible for the addressing of devices on a network. Both protocols and routers use these addresses to identify specific locations within an environment. Whereas some protocols (such as IP) derive their own addresses from those used by the OSI model, others (such as IPX) use the data link layer's own MAC address as their form of identification.

Now that the router has used information from the OSI model to both identify and locate the devices on the network, the data can be sent off to its destination. Protocols are used to carry the data from location to location. For example, binary data is simply a collection of ones and zeroes that computers interpret as information. When a router sends data, the router needs to address that data with the address of the computer it is being sent to, like a postcard. However, how can a device determine the ones and zeroes that represent the address from those that represent the data? Making that distinction is also the job of protocols. Figure 2.5 illustrates a packet of binary data.

FIGURE 2.5

Binary data.

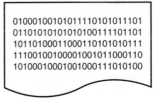

Protocols, acting as envelopes, *encapsulate* data, providing a standard form by which addressing information can be added to transmissible data. The protocols mark the beginning of the destination address, the beginning of the data, and the end of the data so that other devices can easily determine what is addressing information and what is not. The process of protocol encapsulation can be rather involved, and is covered in depth later in the book. Figure 2.6 illustrates the protocol address being extracted from a binary packet. The binary digits used in Figure 2.6 are arbitrary. The actual bits used for encapsulation and for addressing depend on the protocol being used. The figure is only meant to illustrate how the data is extracted.

FIGURE 2.6

Address extraction from a binary packet.

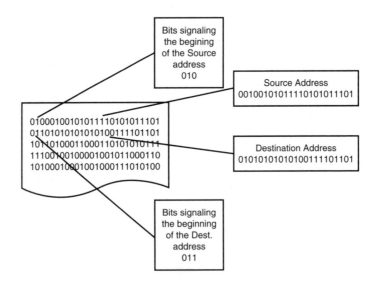

Finally, the data is prepared for transmission. The router needs a cable or link connecting it to other devices on the network. This connection, although seemingly elementary, is defined by the physical layer of the OSI model. Layer 1 contains the definitions of how different types of media (network cables) are used. Routers refer to these guidelines to determine how to transmit the data they are sending from the specific link they are using (that is, fiber optic, RJ-45, or 802.11 Wireless).

At this point, you should understand how the OSI model layers work and what information they provide for the routers.

Summary

The OSI model is comprised of seven layers of responsibility. Each layer defines a different area of functionality within a networking environment. Routers function on Layer 3, known as the network layer because of its capability to provide network-mapping.

Using the OSI model as a reference, protocols can be developed to focus on one area of responsibility. This allows protocols to be specialized, making them quicker and smaller.

2

Q&A

Q Why is there a need for the OSI model?

A The OSI model acts as a standard template, ensuring that any protocol or device designed to work within a specific layer is compatible with every other protocol and device designed for that same layer.

Q Why do protocols only cover one (sometimes two) layer of the OSI model? Why not create a "super protocol" that covers all of them?

A For a protocol to cover the full range of capabilities provided by the OSI model, it would need to be extremely large. The larger a protocol is, the more memory and time it takes to run. For these reasons, many developers choose to write smaller, quicker protocols that specialize in one or two layers of functionality.

Quiz

1. What are the seven layers of the OSI model?
2. Which layer of the OSI model is responsible for establishing sessions between devices?
3. What is the purpose of Layer 2 (the data link layer)?
4. What layer of the OSI model do routers operate on?

Answers

1. Physical

   Data link

   Network

   Transport

   Session

   Presentation

   Application

2. The transport layer (Layer 4)

3. Device addressing. The second layer of the OSI is responsible for addressing devices on a network.

4. The network layer (Layer 3)

Hour **3**

Routing Algorithms

Hour 3 will focus primarily on routing algorithms. The routing algorithm is a formula that is stored in the router's memory. The routing algorithm your protocol uses is a major factor in the performance of your routing environment. The purpose of the routing algorithm is to make decisions for the router concerning the best paths for data.

Think of the routing algorithm as the traffic officer of the router. In the same way that traffic officers guide and shape the way cars drive through busy intersections, routing algorithms make decisions concerning the path data will take from one network to another.

The router uses the routing algorithm to compute the path that would best serve to transport the data from the source to the destination. However, you cannot directly choose the algorithm that your router uses. Rather, the routing protocol you choose for your network determines which algorithm you will use. For example, whereas the routing protocol RIP may use one type of routing algorithm to help the router move data, the routing protocol OSPF uses another.

You are learning about routing algorithms in this lesson as a prerequisite to future lessons on routing protocols. Knowing how routing algorithms work will give you a better understanding of routing protocols and the concepts behind why some protocols work better in certain situations. Many of the differences between particular routing protocols are directly related to differences in their routing algorithms.

> The routing algorithm a protocol uses cannot be changed or altered. If the algorithm a particular protocol uses does not favor your networking environment, the only way to change it is to change routing protocols.
>
> Because the routing algorithm has so much impact on the overall performance of your network, you should research the algorithms each protocol uses before deciding which to implement on your network.

There are two major categories of routing algorithms that can be used by routing protocols—distance vector or link-state. When we begin to discuss routing protocols, you will find that the protocols are either distance vector or link-state. This convention is a direct result of the type of routing algorithm used by the protocol. Therefore, every routing protocol labeled "distance vector" uses the distance vector algorithm; conversely, every link-state protocol uses the link-state algorithm.

 The particulars of your network, such as the number of computers, the number of routers, and the existence (or lack) of a WAN will determine which type of algorithm you choose for your environment.

The next section will briefly discuss the relationship formed between routing protocols and their algorithms. Routing protocols provide information to routing algorithms in the form of variables or metrics. Routing algorithms, on the other hand, provide routing protocols with the best path for the router to send data.

Routing Algorithms Within Routing Protocols

Many properties separate routing protocols from each other. Characteristics such as the speed with which they operate, the way they conduct updates, and the information they gather to perform their job make routing protocols unique. However, one feature that routing protocols share with one another is their routing algorithm. While many different routing protocols are available for you to use on your network, they all utilize one of only two different algorithms.

The major job of the routing protocol is to provide the information needed by the routing algorithm to compute its decisions. This is where many protocols differ. The information provided to the algorithm (thereby affecting the calculation) can be different from protocol to protocol. A good way to illustrate this is to think of the routing algorithm as an Internet search engine, and you as the routing protocol. Let's say that you want the best place to get information about Cisco routers. You type the word "routers" into the search engine. The search engine processes your input and returns a myriad of results. Eventually you will reach the Cisco home page.

Using the same search engine, you could have entered the keywords "Cisco routers." This search would have produced a more direct result. Although the search engine (routing algorithm) did not change, the product of the formula was directly affected by the information that was given to it. Whereas some routing protocols will supply general information to an algorithm, others will be more specific. Knowing how the algorithm will react in these situations will help you choose the algorithm (and consequently, the protocol) that is best for you.

The routing protocol gathers certain information about networks and routers from the surrounding environment. This information is stored within a routing table in the router's memory. The routing algorithm is run against the information within this table to calculate the "best" path from one network to another.

The information contained within the table is plugged into the routing algorithm. Calculating the new values within the formula then generates a sum. The result of this calculation is used to determine where to send information in a particular scenario. For example, Table 3.1 illustrates a sample routing table for a fictitious routing environment.

The information being passed to the routing algorithm within the routing table is gathered by the routing protocol through a process known as a *routing update*. A network or routing engineer will assign this information to each router. Then, through a series of updates, each router will tell the other what information it has. Eventually, an entire routing table will be built. You will learn more about how routing updates work as we examine each routing protocol.

TABLE 3.1   A Fictitious Routing Table

Router Link	Metric
Router A to Router B	2
Router B to Router C	3
Router A to Router C	6
Router C to Router D	5

This scenario has been simplified to make a discussion of routing algorithms possible without focusing on one particular protocol.

Our sample routing algorithm states that the *best path* to any destination is the one that has the lowest *metric* value. When Router A is presented with a packet bound from Router C, the routing table immediately shows two possible paths to choose from. The first choice is to send the packet from Router A directly over the link to Router C. The second option is to send the packet from Router A to Router B and then on to Router C. The routing algorithm is used to determine which option is best. Figure 3.1 illustrates the network that Router A and Router C belong to. (Notice how the routers and metrics in the figure correspond to the routing table information in Table 3.1.)

FIGURE 3.1

A sample network.

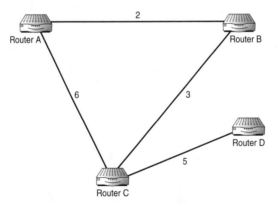

Whereas some routing protocols might only provide one metric to the routing algorithm, others might provide up to ten. As we cover each routing protocol, we will discuss what metrics they gather for the routing algorithm to use. On the other hand, whereas two protocols might both send only one metric to the algorithm, the origin of that metric might differ from protocol to protocol. One routing protocol might give an algorithm the single metric of cost, but that cost could represent something different than another protocol using the same metric.

The algorithm in our example states that the best path is the one with the lowest metric value. Therefore, by adding the metric numbers associated with each possible link, we see that the route from Router A to Router B to Router C has a metric value of 5, while the direct link to Router C has a value of 6. The algorithm selects the A-B-C path and sends the information along.

> A *metric* is a number used as a standard of measurement for the links of a network. Each link is assigned a metric to represent anything from monetary cost to use the line, to the amount of available bandwidth.

Although simplistic, this example demonstrates just how routing algorithms function as the true decision engine within the router. The specific information that is stored within the routing table, and how the algorithm uses it, depends on the protocol. Let's examine the differences between these two algorithmic types.

Distance Vector Algorithms

Distance vector algorithms are similar to the simple algorithm used in Table 3.1. A distance vector algorithm uses metrics known as *costs* to help determine the best path to a destination. The path with the lowest total cost is chosen as the *best path*.

When a router utilizes a distance vector algorithm, different costs are gathered by each router. These costs can be completely arbitrary, administrator-assigned numbers, such as five. Although the number five might not be of any significance to an outside observer, the administrator might have assigned it to a particular link to represent the reliability of that link.

Costs can also be dynamically gathered values, such as the amount of delay experienced by routers when sending packets over one link as opposed to another. All the costs (assigned and otherwise) are compiled and placed within the router's routing table. All the costs gathered are then used by the algorithm to calculate a best path for any given network scenario.

Although there are many resources that will offer complex mathematical representations of what distance vector algorithms are and how they compute their decisions, the core concept remains the same—by adding the metrics for every optional path on a network, you will come up with at least one best path. The formula for this is as follows:

```
M(i,k) = min [M(i,t) + M(t,k)]
```

This formula states that the best path between two networks (M(i,k)) can be found by finding the lowest (min) value of paths between all network points. Let's look again at the routing information in Table 3.1. Plugging this information into the formula, we see that the route from A to B to C is still the best path:

```
5(A,C) = min[2(A,B) + 3(B,C)]
```

Whereas the formula for the direct route A to C looks like this:

```
6(A,C) = min[6(A,C)]
```

This example illustrates how distance vector algorithms use the information passed to them to make informed routing decisions. Do not spend too much time memorizing the algorithm, as you will rarely see it in the real world. The algorithms used by routers and routing protocols are not configurable, nor can they be modified.

Another major difference between distance vector algorithms and link state protocols (covered in the next section) is that when distance vector routing protocols update each other, all or part of the routing table (depending on the type of update) is sent from one router to another. By this process, each router is exposed to the information contained within the other router's tables, thus giving each router a more complete view of the networking environment and enabling them to make better routing decisions. The process of router updates is described in more detail in the next section.

Examples of distance vector algorithms include RIP and BGP, two of the more popular protocols in use today. Other popular protocols such as OSPF are examples of protocols which use the link state routing algorithm.

Link-State Algorithms

Link-state algorithms work within the same basic framework that distance vector algorithms do in that they both favor the path with the lowest cost. However, link-state protocols work in a somewhat more localized manner. Whereas a router running a distance vector algorithm will compute the end-to-end path for any given packet, a link-state protocol will compute that path as it relates to the most immediate link. That is, where a distance vector algorithm will compute the lowest metric between Network A and Network C, a link-state protocol will compute it as two distinct paths, A to B and B to C.

This process is best for larger environments that might change fairly often. Link-state algorithms enable routers to focus on their own links and interfaces. Any one router on a network will only have direct knowledge of the routers and networks that are directly connected to it (or, the *state* of its own *links*). In larger environments, this means that the router will use less processing power to compute complicated paths.

The router simply needs to know which one of its direct interfaces will get the information where it needs to go the quickest. The next router in line will repeat the process until the information reaches its destination.

Another advantage to such localized routing processes is that protocols can maintain smaller routing tables. Because a link-state protocol only maintains routing information for its direct interfaces, the routing table contains much less information than that of a distance vector protocol that might have information for multiple routers.

Like distance vector protocols, link-state protocols require updates to share information with each other. These routing updates, known as *Link State Advertisements (LSAs)*, occur when the state of a router's links changes.

When a particular link becomes unavailable (changes state), the router sends an update through the environment alerting all the routers with which it is directly linked.

Link-state and distance vector protocols handle certain routing situations quite differently. As we discuss each protocol in the remaining lessons of this book, we'll look at how these protocols handle particular routing situations.

3

Summary

Every routing protocol uses a routing algorithm to facilitate the decision-making process for routers. A routing algorithm is a formula used to calculate the best path between two networks. The algorithm uses information gathered by the routing protocols, known as metrics, to compute the best path.

The two major types of routing algorithms are distance vector and link-state. Distance vector algorithms generally use one metric to calculate the lowest cost from source to destination. Link-state protocols use multiple metrics to calculate the shortest distance from a source to a destination one hop at a time.

Q&A

Q Why are there many routing protocols, but only two major routing algorithms?

A The algorithms that are in use today are very efficient. The protocols, however, might decide to implement those algorithms in slightly different ways. By this, one protocol might decide to pass the algorithm different metrics than another protocol. Thus, even though many protocols use the same algorithm, each one uses it in a different way.

Q **What are the two major types of routing algorithms?**

A Distance vector and link-state.

Q **What are metrics?**

A Values collected by routing protocols that are passed to algorithms. They are used to calculate the routing paths.

Q **Which type of routing algorithm maintains the smallest routing table?**

A Link-state.

Q **What will a link state protocol do when the state of one of its links changes?**

A Initiate a routing update.

Quiz

1. What are the two major types of routing algorithms?
2. What are metrics?
3. Which type of routing algorithm maintains the smallest routing table?
4. What will a link-state protocol do when the state of one of its links changes?

Answers

1. Distance vector and link-state
2. Values collected by routing protocols that are passed to algorithms. They are used to calculate the routing paths.
3. Link-state
4. Initiate a routing update

Hour 4

Understanding Routed Protocols

This hour will focus primarily on routed protocols. Protocols such as the familiar IP, IPX, and AppleTalk are all *routed protocols*. We will discuss the differences between the different classifications of routed protocols and explain how routed protocols prepare data from routing.

Routed protocols are responsible for the transportation of data from device to device. That is, a routed protocol is the sole element necessary to exchange data between devices—routed protocols do not need routers to move information. This may sound counterintuitive at first, but it is true.

You can have a solid networking environment without the use of routers. As long as every device on your network is using the same routed protocol (and the same addressing scheme), they will all be able to communicate freely. Figure 4.1 illustrates a simple network using only routed protocols.

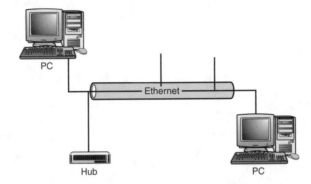

FIGURE 4.1

A simple network using routed protocols.

The first networks of the early 1960s did not have the luxury of self-contained routing devices (routers) to move data between devices. Software was developed to accomplish the task of preparing, transmitting, receiving, and reconstructing data between computers. This software was the first network protocol.

To this day, the job of routed protocols has changed very little. They're still responsible for preparing (a process that incorporates encapsulation and fragmentation), transmitting, receiving, and reconstructing network data. Without routed protocols, computer inter-communication would be impossible.

There are many different types of protocols that you might encounter in a networking environment. Routed, routing, and WAN protocols can all coexist within a single environment.

Routed protocols are protocols that are *routed* through a network. *Routing protocols* are protocols that *route* routed protocols. (Try saying that five times fast!) WAN protocols are protocols that carry data from a private network across a public interface. We will cover all three major types of protocols in the course of this book.

How Routed Protocols Work

All routers need one thing to successfully route data from one location to another—protocols. This hour will explain exactly how protocols work and how they relate to routers. The remainder of the book deals with (in one form or another) configuring the way a router works in relationship to the protocols that are already in use.

Keep in mind that not all protocols are routable. Some protocols, such as NetBEUI, are not routable, and thus incompatible with routing environments. Be careful to avoid such protocols when working with routers.

The main feature that makes a protocol "routable" is the capability for the protocol to distinguish between multiple networks. This means that the protocol must provide a mechanism to address or otherwise mark different networks. NetBEUI lacks this mechanism. For this reason, NetBEUI can only function on independent networking environments.

Routed protocols serve two important purposes in routing environments. First, they address networks, enabling routers to locate different networks and other routing devices in larger environments. The second job of protocols is to encapsulate the data and prepare it for transmission. Both of these concepts will be covered later in this chapter.

For now, let's jump right into discovering the major differences in routed protocols.

Routed Protocol Divisions and Classifications

There are multiple divisions into which protocols can be split. The major divisions within routed protocols are classless versus classful, connection-oriented versus connectionless, and routable versus non-routable.

Because the focus of the book is protocol routing, I do not feel that an in-depth discussion of nonroutable protocols is necessary. However, be aware that just because a protocol exists does not mean it is automatically routable.

Understanding how protocols work and how they transport data from system to system requires a knowledge of the inner working of the protocol—how is the protocol designed to work? What layers does it work on? What can you expect from it? Reviewing the different divisions within the protocols will help you understand how router protocols run and how routers handle them.

Connection-Oriented Versus Connectionless Protocols

Connection-oriented protocols are designed in a manner that facilitates the opening of sessions between systems. When two systems are using connection-oriented protocols, they establish a session between themselves before passing information.

Connection-oriented protocols such as TCP work on the transport layer of the OSI model. Because many routers work on the network layer, transport layer protocol data is passed to network layer data for transmission. The network layer of the OSI model can work with both connection-oriented and connectionless protocols.

> The network layer is connectionless by default, whereas the transport layer is connection-oriented. The network layer can use CONS (Connection-Oriented Network Services) to utilize connection-oriented data. However, to use CONS, the network layer must enlist the aid of other OSI model layers like the transport layer to establish and maintain sessions.

When one system wants to send information to a neighboring system, a session-open request is sent to the desired recipient. The sending system then waits for an acknowledgment to the request, indicating that the system is available to open a session. When the sending system receives back an acknowledgement, the session is opened and the two systems can freely exchange data. At the conclusion of the session, a *tear-down packet* is sent from the system that initiated the connection. This tear-down packet indicates that the session is over and the resources used to maintain it should be freed.

The act of initiating sessions before exchanging information does not pose many real issues; in fact, it is one of the more desirable aspects of this class of protocols. However, it is how the session is maintained that can be problematic for some environments.

When the requester sends out a session-open packet, the path over which it traverses is appended to the packet's protocol header. By doing this, the packet creates a route over which the two devices can communicate. The system that received the packet sends its acknowledgement over the same route the session-open packet took.

If a session is opened between the two systems, all packets sent between them will follow this same path. This ensures that there will be a guaranteed link between the devices.

However, the resources required for opening and maintaining a dedicated path will cause the router to set aside bandwidth that may not be utilized. Because connection-oriented sessions are normally associated with guaranteed throughput rates, the router will set aside a predetermined amount of bandwidth to meet the desired throughput. This bandwidth is blocked off whether it is used by the router or not. It is conceivable that a certain amount of bandwidth will be wasted (go unused) during a connection-oriented session. Connection-oriented protocols use more overhead than their connectionless counterparts.

Connection-oriented protocols do offer some advantages within a networking environment. Because every packet exchanged between two systems is acknowledged, data delivery is guaranteed. When two systems participating in a session exchange information, an acknowledgement packet is sent confirming the successful arrival of every bit of data.

Applications that deal with streaming video and audio rely on connection-oriented protocols for their success. The packets used to create a continuous video or audio signal must be sent, transported, and reassembled in precise order. A connectionless protocol would not be able to guarantee that the packets are delivered in the same order they were sent.

Connection-oriented protocol sessions also travel a set path. That is, every packet is sent over the same route as the previous one. This allows for easier troubleshooting of connection problems. Using tools such as packet analyzers or "LAN sniffers," an engineer can easily determine the path over which two devices are communicating and therefore diagnose potential problems.

Connectionless protocols utilize a "best effort" approach to data delivery. Because there is no dedicated connection between the two devices, each packet exchanged can follow a different path. Therefore, the possibility of packets arriving out of order, if at all, is much greater with connectionless protocols.

The major drawback of connectionless protocols is the inevitable loss of data because of undeliverable packets. In most cases, the losses are minimal and rarely noticed, but the risks are still there. While it is hard to put 100% of the blame for losing packets on a connectionless protocol, enough evidence exists to point to them as a leading cause.

Another disadvantage of not using a dedicated route between devices is that troubleshooting connection problems becomes exponentially greater the more routers you inject into the environment. Because each packet can use a different path to the same destination, it is extremely hard to predict where the problem is between any two devices.

Within a router, one way to control the delivery of data from one system to another is to use static routes wherever possible (static routes are generally required when working with connection-oriented protocols). Although static routes are certainly not practical in every situation—in fact, they almost defeat the purpose of routing to begin with—they can help with particularly troublesome systems. As we will discuss in Hour 13, "Dynamic Versus Static Routing," one situation in which static routes can be of benefit is when you anticipate few (if any) topological network changes.

Each brand of router has its own interface and method of defining elements such as static routes. Throughout this book, whenever we need to illustrate a router-specific configuration example, we will be using Cisco routers.

For more information on Cisco router-specific configurations try consulting *Sams Teach Yourself Cisco Routers in 21 Days* (Sams Publishing).

There are definite advantages to using connectionless protocols. They are typically faster and require less overhead than connection-oriented carriers. Connectionless protocols also use bandwidth more efficiently because they have no need for guaranteed throughput rates. Connectionless protocols are perfect for routing for these reasons. Given the polymorphic nature of routing, connectionless protocols offer a means to quickly move data from one system to another.

Because connectionless protocols do not require the establishment of a session to operate successfully, they can be designed to be fast. The time taken to build and tear down a session, along with the time needed to send and reply to acknowledgements, adds up when multiplied over a large network. Therefore, the speed of connectionless protocols is very conducive to today's routing environments.

Classful Versus Classless Protocols

The best way to contrast classful and classless protocols is with the example of IP. Understanding IP should be your highest priority with regard to protocols. The more scenarios we can make using IP as an example, the better off you will be.

The reason why IP is a good example of the differences between classful and classless protocols is that within recent years IP has become both—that is, IP can be configured in today's environments to be either classless or classful.

Classful IP

IP is, by nature, classful. When IP was developed with the first networking environments, it was designed to be a *classful* protocol. This means IP can be divided into different classes, with each class based on the needs of a particular network or client.

Classes are used to determine the ultimate size of an environment as a relationship of hosts to networks. Each class offers a different number of addressable hosts per addressable network. Although one class might offer 127 addressable networks and more than 16 million addressable host per network, another might supply 2 million networks and 254 hosts per network.

IP is divided into three commonly accepted classes. Each class was developed to meet the needs of various sizes of institutions.

Although it is generally accepted that IP is divided into three classes (A, B, and C), there are actually five IP classes. Classes D and E are rarely used, and it is unlikely that you will come across either. Class D is used solely for multi-casting and Class E has been reserved for future use.

When a protocol is classful, one address is used to specify both the host and network in a variable manner. That is, the portion of the address that is used to determine the network (as opposed to the host) can vary in size depending on the class in use. For example, a typical Class B IP license would appear as 136.54.220.95.

Dotted decimal is the most common format in which IP addresses are expressed. Some protocols, such as IPX, express their address in hexadecimal format.

Because this address is a Class B address, the first two *octets* (sets of decimal numbers) represent the network address, while the last two octets represent the host. Therefore, a PC assigned the IP address 136.54.220.95 would be computer 220.95 on network 136.54. Using this logic, you can assume that every device on the same network as this computer would also have an address that begins with 136.54. This process of addressing networks is essential for routers.

A router can determine which portion of the address is used for networks by applying a secondary or *mask address*. Mask addresses (unique to classful protocols) indicate to the routing device which bits of the protocol address represent the network. This determination is key to the functionality of routers. The Class B IP address in our previous example, 136.54.220.95, has a subnet mask of 255.255.0.0. This mask tells the router that the first two octets of the IP address represent the network.

The process used by routers to extract a network address from an IP address (with the subnet mask) is known as *ANDing*.

Classless IP

One problem with classful protocols such as IP is that they are finite. That is, there is definite limit to the number of addresses that can be assigned over the life of the protocol. Having such a definite lifespan means that at some point there will be no more addresses to assign to new networks and devices. When this happens to IP, no more networks will be able to access the Internet, utilize e-mail, and connect to other networks via WAN connections. For this reason, a classless way of utilizing IP has become popular.

The current version of IP is known as IPv4 (the fourth version of the protocol). Currently, development is underway on IPv6, which should replace the nearly depleted IPv4 in coming years.

Classless protocols such as IPX or AppleTalk, while having one address to represent both the network and the host, do so in a fixed manner. The host portion of the address is always a fixed length. Therefore, routing devices can easily and quickly determine the network bits of an address because they never change. For example, an IPX address would be expressed as 1423F3A.1234567ABC.

Because the address is always expressed as *network.host*, there is no need for a subnet mask to tell the router which bits of the address represent the network. The format of classless addresses never changes.

Classless Inter-Domain Routing (CIDR) has become very popular during the last few years. Developed to help ease the growing demand for Class B IP networks, CIDR is a classless form of IP.

Class B addresses were popular among ISPs because of their abundance of addressable hosts and equal balance of network addresses. ISPs could sell entire networks of addresses while retaining more than enough for their own clients.

When routers are configured to use CIDR, IP addresses are divided into *supernets*. During this process, entire networks can be grouped together based on (of all things) their class. In classful routing, each network is represented by a separate address, regardless of the address class. Therefore, the Class B networks 136.54 and 142.122 are two separate addresses. During CIDR supernetting, both of these networks would be represented by one supernet address. The supernet address knows that both are Class B networks, and as such the first two octets will be the network and the last two will be the host. As long as neither network changes its addressing scheme, the routers that supply information to these networks can now treat them as classless entities, knowing that their address structure will not change.

Protocol Encapsulation

Protocols facilitate the movement of data from one system to another through a process known as *encapsulation*. This means that the data being sent from one system to another is packaged in such a way that intermediary connectivity devices can determine where the data will be moved. Figure 4.2 illustrates the encapsulation process.

FIGURE 4.2

The encapsulation process.

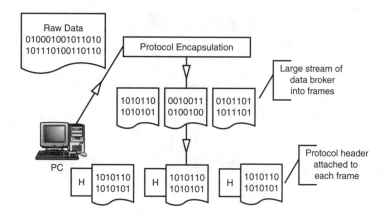

Devices use protocols to evenly divide data into small, easy-to-send packages. Encapsulation is a process whereby a large data stream is chopped into several small segments, all of uniform size. These small, uniform packages are easier to send and receive because of their size. Also, other devices on the network can easily predict the size of every packet they will receive. Therefore, the network can fine tune itself to work within the parameters of the particular size of the segmented data.

> The name given to each smaller package of data varies depending on the protocol being used and the layer of the OSI model it works on. Although some protocols work in packets, others use segments, frames, or cells. However, these are all different names for the same end-product—a post-encapsulation unit of data ready for routing.

The contents of the header can vary depending on the protocol being used. Specific header fields will be covered in the next hour. However, there are a few fields that will almost always appear in every protocol header. Figure 4.3 shows a packet with a generic (non–protocol-specific) header.

The first two fields represent the source and destination addresses. These two addresses are the indication to routers and other connectivity devices where the packet of data came from and where it should be delivered.

The next field is a sequence number. This field is very important to the encapsulation process. Because protocols take larger chunks of data and divide them into smaller, manageable pieces, a mechanism needs to be put in place to determine how to reassemble the data stream. Remember, routers work on the connectionless network layer, so packets will almost always arrive at their intended destination out of order. It is the job of routed protocols to ensure that those packets are reassembled in the correct order.

FIGURE 4.3
A packet of data with a protocol header.

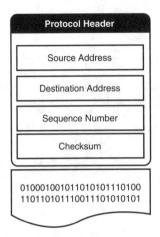

The final field we will cover here is the *checksum*. Basically, the checksum indicates the size of the packet being transmitted. After being received, but before being reassembled, the target device uses a checksum to determine whether the packet has been corrupted during the sending process. This function of routed protocols is essential to the proper operation of routers.

This short yet comprehensive look at routed protocols serves as a good introduction to the remainder of the book, which deals directly with more complicated protocols and routing concepts.

Summary

Routed protocols are used to encapsulate and carry routable data across a network. These protocols are responsible for the addressing of network devices and the preparation of data for routing.

Connectionless protocols such as IP work on the network layer of the OSI model. Unlike connection-oriented protocols that operate on the transport layer, they do not establish and maintain sessions during the data-movement process.

Classful protocols allow for the specification of different sizes of networks. That is, the protocol address of a device contains one distinct portion for the host, and one for the network. Classless protocols do not require the use of a subnet mask. Classless protocols have a fixed network and host address length. Routing devices can always determine the exact network and host address from a classless protocol because the size of those addresses will never change.

Q&A

Q Why are there so many different types of protocols (that is, routed, routing, and WAN)?

A Each protocol has a specific function. Not all of these protocols or their functions relate directly to routing. For example, WAN protocols and routed protocols can easily be used without the aid of a router. WAN protocols are primarily run on devices known as switches, while routed protocols can easily move data from PC to PC with any external aid.

Routing protocols are used specifically by routers to calculate paths (for sending data). They are also used for updating other routers about the current network conditions. Each type of protocol performs a function that the others do not; therefore, they are all necessary to create fully functional, harmonious networks.

Quiz

1. What layer of the OSI model do connection-oriented protocols work at?
2. What is CIDR?
3. What is the process protocols use to prepare data for routing?

Answers

1. transport
2. Classless Inter-Domain Routing, the classless form of IP
3. protocol encapsulation

4

HOUR 5

Understanding WAN Protocols

Wide area network (WAN) protocols mark the third and final type of protocol you will be introduced to in this book. *WAN protocols* are specialized protocols that carry data across WAN links. Physical links that connect two or more environments require special attention when it comes to information transportation. These links utilize protocols specifically developed for one purpose—providing WAN communications.

While WAN protocols do not actually run on routers (in the same context as routed or routing protocols do), they play an important role in the routing process. As you will discover in this hour, WAN protocols are specialized transport mechanisms that run on devices known as *switches*. Routers, though not required to run the WAN protocol, need to understand how these protocols work to effectively move data between switched networks and routed networks. Without WAN protocols and routers that can interface with them, information would never leave the confines of a single LAN environment.

The WAN protocols addressed in this hour provide a good cross-section of the technologies you are likely to see in real-world situations. From ISDN, the protocol with the smallest data capacity, to Frame Relay, which has the largest; each has a particular set of requirements when it comes to routing. However, before we can thoroughly examine the actual protocols, we must discuss what sets WAN protocols apart from other routing and routed protocols.

In this hour, we will examine the reasons why WAN protocols exist and their function in the routing process. In subsequent hours, we will tackle specific WAN protocol topics such as ISDN, Frame Relay, and X.25, and discuss what sets each apart from the other.

To recap what you have learned about the different types of protocols thus far, routed protocols are protocols such as IP or IPX. These protocols are used to carry data from device to device. Routed protocols, if needed, could function without the use of a router. However, routers cannot function without the aid of a routed protocol.

The purpose of routing protocols, on the other hand, is to provide a mechanism by which routers can update each other regarding the current topology of the environment. This information is critical in the facilitation of the router's job, to move data from network to network. Keeping the descriptions of the other protocols involved in the routing process in mind will help you better understand the remainder of this hour.

The Purpose of WAN Protocols

All WAN protocols that exist today were created with one specific purpose—to connect networks which span different geographic locations. Although other protocols focus on connecting networks that exist within one environment, WAN protocols connect networks that might utilize public area environments.

Figure 5.1 illustrates the context in which WAN protocols exist. The network in Figure 5.1 utilizes routed, routing, and WAN protocols.

Using Figure 5.1 as a guide, you can easily follow the path of information from device to device and protocol to protocol. Try to visualize the path used as information leaves the PC and is passed to a routed protocol. This scenario is the base on which networks are built. Networks function around the concept that information can leave one device and be safely delivered to another.

As the information leaves the PC, it is acted upon by the routed protocol. The routed protocol resides on the PC itself. Using the routed protocol as a guide, the information makes its way through the layers of the OSI model, eventually ending at Layer 1, the physical layer. The physical layer transmits the routed protocol-encapsulated data to the device directly connected to the PC. (In the scenario provided in Figure 5.1 that device is a hub.)

FIGURE 5.1

WAN protocols used in context.

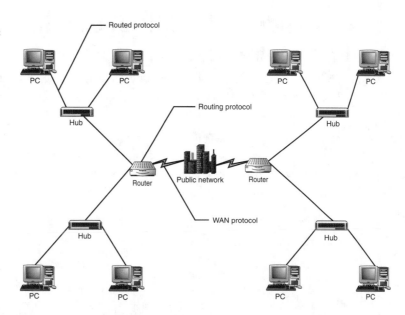

The hub broadcasts the data to every device connected to its multiple ports. One of those devices is a router. When the information reaches the router, it is passed to a routing protocol. The routing protocol examines and breaks down the encapsulated packets. The routing protocol then determines the intended destination of the information, and if necessary, the router passes the data to a WAN protocol for delivery across the WAN link.

Unlike routed protocols (which deliver data from PC to PC), and routing protocols (which deliver information from network to network within the same environment), WAN protocols deliver information from network device to network device in different geographic locations. In the previous scenario, the WAN protocol was used to deliver packets from one network, across a public switched network, to a network in a different location.

To perform their specialized duties, WAN protocols combine the functionality of both routing and routed protocols with the added capability to distinguish between different environments. WAN protocols carry data between devices, like routed protocols; however, they move data between networks like routing protocols.

The key feature in the operation of WAN protocols is that they can move information over public networks. Public networks, such as the telephone company's *public switched network (PSN)*, are the main transition path for WAN protocols. In fact, in Figure 5.1 you will notice that the WAN protocol does not move information on the private (corporate) networks—they move data between the networks. To be more accurate, the WAN protocols specifically move data between the routers that connect the geographically separated networks.

Understanding the Difference Between Public and Private Networks

For novices, deciphering all the terminology and concepts behindrouting for the first time can be confusing. One especially confusing aspect of learning routing is recognizing the different environments protocols operate in.

WAN protocols can be especially difficult to understand for two reasons. First, they operate on public networks, as opposed to the private networks we have been discussing. Second, the public networks that WAN protocols operate on are switched (not routed), providing an extra layer of confusion.

Routing Versus Switching

There are many differences between routing and switching. The most significant is in how they move data from place to place. Switches move data on a per-session basis between individual devices. Switches also form the opening of circuits between devices to provide a statically-defined path between two machines.

Routers, on the other hand, move information between networks based on metric data that can change for each individual packet.

Recognizing the difference between PSNs and private networks is easier than understanding the reason behind the difference. Simply put, a private network is one that resides fully in one geographic location and has restricted access to its resources. Any company or home network is considered a private network. Figure 5.2 illustrates a typical private network.

The network in Figure 5.2 is a small yet typical representation of a private network. PCs and other devices connect via network media (in this case, an Ethernet connection) to servers, printers, and hubs. Information flows freely through the network; however, access to its resources is restricted to those devices within the environment.

A private network configured like the one in Figure 5.2 has no access to or from any area outside the network. Conversely, PSNs are open to access from anyone.

PSNs began as the major infrastructure of the telephone network, and they still are. The network of devices that carries your telephone calls from home to home and business to business is the same network used by WAN protocols. Figure 5.3 shows the basic architecture of a PSN.

FIGURE 5.2

A typical private network.

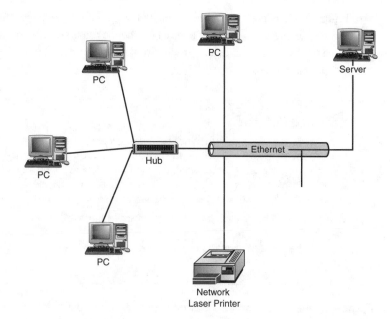

FIGURE 5.3

A basic public switched network.

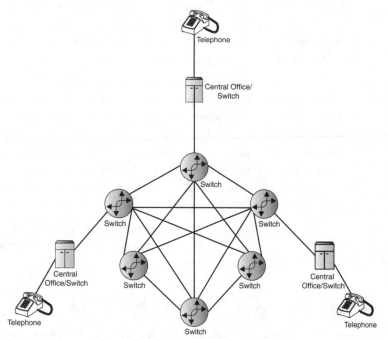

5

In Figure 5.3, a telephone call being placed at any of the telephones is sent onto the PSN. Based on the telephone number entered by the user, the switches all determine where the call needs to go and establish a virtual circuit between the telephone placing the call and the telephone receiving it.

Switched Circuits

Virtual circuits are termed virtual not because they are built up and torn down electronically, but because they exist only within the logic of the switches they connect. An actual circuit (as on the telephone network) would be the mess of wires that we generally envision early telephone operators sitting in front of. When a call comes in, the operator physically moves the circuit's cable to connect the two callers.

When discussing virtual circuits, do not confuse them with actual circuits. To compound the situation, virtual circuits are divided into two categories: permanent virtual circuits and switched virtual circuits. We will discuss the differences between these in future hours.

The virtual circuit between the two telephones allows an uninterrupted call to take place between the two parties. At the conclusion of the call, the virtual circuit is torn down, allowing more calls to use the lines. If the same two telephones were to again call each other, another virtual circuit will be established between them; however, it may not be the same circuit as the first.

The capability to build up and tear down circuits per-session is an advantage to the PSN architecture. Recalling the private network from Figure 5.2, which is a non-switched environment, the cable between two devices is only used when those devices are communicating. If two devices are currently not communicating, the line connecting them is idle—or as some may view it, being wasted. In a switched environment, the switches can utilize different lines to accommodate changes in network traffic. This means that a switch will almost always be able to create a connection between two parties, regardless of the current network congestion.

We have established the difference between the public switched network and private company networking environments. However, what do WAN protocols have to do with the PSN telephone network?

WAN Protocols and the PSN

WAN protocols are the mechanisms that allow computers to communicate over PSNs. Because the telephone companies have established a large infrastructure spanning the nation, and network technology has advanced to the point where connecting multiple geographically-separated networks was possible, the logical carriers for such data are the telephone companies. Several specialized line types were developed to provide connectivity from private networks to the PSNs.

Because computers do not communicate the same way people do, using the lines people use to communicate did not prove to be efficient in large networks. Specialized lines were created, each to serve a different purpose and handle a different amount of data.

ISDN and T-Lines

When a company wants to establish a connection between two geographically separated locations, a carrier will be used to supply a solution. The carrier will set up a specialized line based on the networks' needs connecting the two sites through the PSN. Figure 5.4 illustrates two networks (similar to those in Figure 5.2) connected through a PSN (pictured in Figure 5.3).

FIGURE 5.4

A completed WAN.

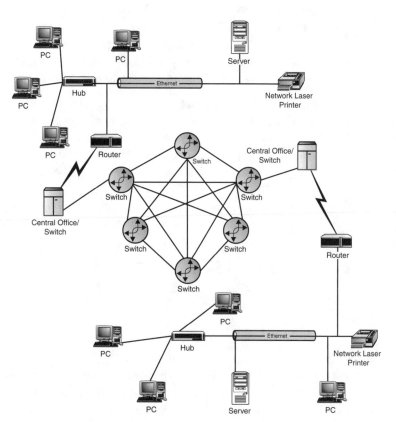

In Figure 5.4 we introduce two new pieces of hardware to complete the connection—routers. Routers are the connecting hardware between the private networks and the PSN. The *comm links* between the routers and the PSN are the specialized line types.

> In Hours 14,15,and 16, you will learn that depending on the WAN protocol being used, the router may need the assistance of additional hardware to complete a successful connection. Hardware such as a CSU/DSU can be added to a router to help it communicate with a WAN protocol.

Of the many WAN lines available, the two we will discuss here are ISDN and T-lines (more specifically, T1 lines).

Integrated services digital network (ISDN) lines are digital lines that offer multiple channels over which to transport data. Described further in Hour 15, "Understanding ISDN," ISDN BRI lines offer two channels of 64k throughput for transmitting data. (For larger environments, ISDN PRI offers 23 channels of 64k throughput.) ISDN BRI lines are more commonly used in small networks and in small office home office (SOHO) connections, while PRI lines are commonly used in WAN connections.

T1 connections offer more channels (24), allowing for a lot more throughput. T1 lines are used to connect slightly larger networks than ISDN lines. T-lines are available in larger sizes that offer more channels to accommodate larger networks. Many companies will establish connections using multiple T1 lines to one destination.

> Many WAN protocols can handle connections using multiple channels at once, this process is known as *trunking*.

In the upcoming hours we will discuss specific WAN protocols in more detail. These chapters will also include more scenarios and explanations of the line types each protocol prefers.

Summary

WAN protocols are a specialized type of protocol that facilitate the transportation of data across PSNs. WAN protocols carry data between network devices (where routed protocols move between devices, and routing protocols move between networks).

PSNs are the core of the public telephone network. Within PSNs, data is switched between network devices in sessions that utilize virtual circuits.

Routers, in relation to WAN protocols, are used as the connection device between the local area network (LAN) and the WAN link (usually the PSN). The WAN protocol does not run on the routers that form the WAN link. Instead, the protocol is contained completely within the WAN environment (the PSN); the routers serve as a translation device between the LAN and the WAN.

Q&A

Q Are WAN protocols required for connecting two geographically-separated locations?

A Yes. Any traffic that is carried over a PSN requires the assistance of a WAN protocol. The WAN protocol acts as the one link between the two networks involved in the connection.

Q Is it possible to connect multiple geographically separated networks without the aid of a PSN?

A Yes. While it is possible to connect networks without utilizing a PSN, it is rare. Solutions such as satellite service exist to connect networks in areas where security is an issue, or the PSN infrastructure does not exist. However, because they're expensive and difficult to use, such systems are rare.

Quiz

1. What do WAN protocols move data between?
2. What do switches establish to facilitate communication between devices?
3. How many channels are in a T1 line?

Answers

1. network devices
2. virtual circuits
3. 24

5

HOUR 6

Understanding Routing Protocols

The purpose of this hour is to introduce you to the concepts behind routing protocols. To this point in the book, we have covered two different types of protocols—WAN and routed—neither of which are specific to routers. Rather, they are the objects of the router's function. Routers simply move these protocols from location to location. Routing protocols are the tools that routers rely upon to perform this task.

You will be familiar with many routing protocols before the conclusion of this book. OSPF (Open Shortest Path First), RIP (Routing Information Protocol), IGRP (Interior Gateway Routing Protocol), and EIGRP (Enhanced Interior Gateway Routing Protocol) are just four of the protocols we will cover. The topics covered in this hour are common to all these protocols.

Routing protocols work by facilitating the movement of data between networks. However, unlike routed protocols and WAN protocols, routing protocols do not "carry" the data from source to destination. Instead, they provide the direction needed for the router to move the data.

Recapping from previous hours, both routed and WAN protocols use the process of data encapsulation. Through data encapsulation, the protocol creates a container for transporting data to and from various locations. One of the main responsibilities of both routed and WAN protocols is to provide this container for other mechanisms to act upon.

The goal of routing protocols is to act upon the already encapsulated data and facilitate the physical transportation of the data from source to destination. Because data needs to be encapsulated by a routed protocol before it leaves the PC, it is in a prepared state when it reaches the router. For routing protocols to also perform data encapsulation on previously encapsulated data would be redundant and time-consuming.

Routing protocols have two major responsibilities in relation to routers. The main responsibility of routing protocols is to calculate the best path for sending data. This means that when a router is given a packet of data to send from one network to another, the routing protocol decides how to send it. The router uses complex calculations to determine precisely how to move the data to the target network. The responsibility of performing this calculation is delegated to the routing algorithm.

The routing algorithm is the heart of any routing protocol. The routing algorithm is the key formula used by routing protocols to make routing decisions. In this hour, you will discover how routing protocols work in relationship to the OSI model and how they utilize their routing algorithms to ensure data is sent to the correct destination.

Because we have already covered routing algorithms in Hour 3, "Routing Algorithms," the primary focus of this hour will be the secondary responsibility of routing protocols—overseeing and facilitating routing updates.

The second responsibility of routing protocols is to ensure that every router within an environment is working from the same information. That is, each router sees the current environment the same way all other routers on the same network see it. For example, you have just completed a network with three routers, Router A, Router B, and Router C. After functioning on the network for a few weeks, Router C is taken down for maintenance. Router B quickly adjusts its view of the network, realizing that there are now only two routers. One of the responsibilities of a routing protocol is to ensure that Router A also knows that there are now just two routers on the network. This will ensure that both routers are working from the same "view" of the network, and no routing confusion occurs. This view of the network is the information that is fed into the routing algorithm.

Because each router uses a separate routing algorithm, yet must arrive at the same result as every other router, it is imperative that they all work from identical network information. The routing protocol distributes routing data contained within routing tables between routers. This update process ensures that all of the routers within the network have the same copy of the latest routing data.

The Big Picture

Routing protocols are designed for a slightly different purpose than other types of protocols. At no point in the workflow of a routing protocol does it change the data traveling across the network. However, because routing protocols do not directly manipulate data, it can be hard to follow the progress of that data as it moves from the source network to the destination.

This section will guide you through the flow of data as it moves from network to network and the role the routing protocols play in that process. You will learn to identify where routers pick up data, how the routing protocols enter the picture, and what effect routing protocols have on the overall routing process.

When a PC or other device has data to send to another device in another network, that data must pass through a router. However, before information can reach the router, it must be encapsulated by a routed protocol on the sending device. As the information traverses the OSI model on the sending device, the routed protocol being used (usual IP) encapsulates the data to prepare it for transmission across the network media (the physical layer). Figure 6.1 illustrates the encapsulation process.

FIGURE 6.1

Preparing data for network transmission.

Data to be transferred

6

The routed protocol within the PC accepts the raw data and encapsulates it in a packet, adding all the pertinent addressing information in the process. The packet is then passed to the physical layer of the OSI model and sent out onto the network.

On its journey through the network, the packet reaches the router. The router passes the packet to the routing protocol. The routing protocol strips off the routed protocol's header and reads through the header information to extract several key pieces of information. Figure 6.2 illustrates the process used by the routing protocol.

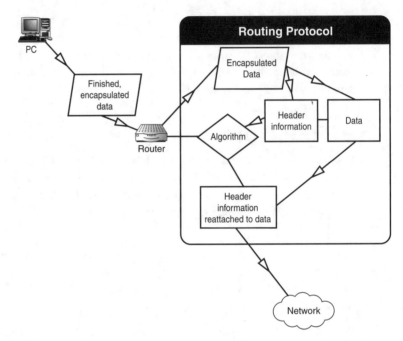

FIGURE 6.2
Stripping the protocol header.

The routing protocol determines the source, destination, and any pertinent metrics associated with the packet. *Metrics* are values associated with a packet that help determine the path over which the packet will be forwarded. Metrics will be covered in greater depth later in this hour.

The routing protocol sends the information gathered from the packet header to the routing algorithm. The information is then used by the algorithm to determine the best way to send the packet to its intended target. The protocol header is reattached to the packet and sent onto the network.

The routing protocol then summarizes the transaction that just occurred and places the information in a table. The *routing table*, maintained by the routing protocol and stored within the router's memory, contains a detailed list of possible destinations on a network and their relative path information.

For example, if a router has just sent a packet to Network 5 from Router A to Router B to Router C (Router C is attached to Network 5), that information would be recorded in the routing protocol's routing table. The routing table would then hold the information stating that "Router A is connected to Router B, which is connected to Router C, which in turn is connected to Network 5." In the future, if the router is searching for a way to send another packet to Network 5, it need only consult the routing table. The routing protocol then compiles the information found within the routing table and sends it to every other router in the network. The process by which these tables are sent from router to router is known as *dynamic route updating.*

Dynamic Route Updates

Dynamic route updates, also known as routing updates, serve an extremely important purpose in the routing world. Most routing protocols implement some form of dynamic updating. In other words, these protocols have some mechanism in place that allows them to share information pertaining to a select area or group with other routers. Although several parameters vary from protocol to protocol, such as the number of hops updates can traverse and what information can be included in the updates, there are some general rules that apply to routing updates.

The process of updating a router's table information is arguably one of the most important functions of a routing protocol. The following describes the process by which routers and routing protocols utilize dynamic route updates:

- Update routing table information. This allows the routing protocol's algorithm to make decisions based on the current network conditions.

- Ensure each router has an accurate view of the network. Without knowing the exact details of its surroundings, a router may forward packets to incorrect destinations.

- Speed up network transactions by allowing routers to collect smaller copies of tables.

Let's examine how routing updates achieve these objectives in a general manner. As we begin discussing individual protocols, we will look at these objectives more specifically. You should already have an understanding of the reasons why updates affect the overall routing process as they do.

Most routers only gather the information that pertains directly to their interfaces. In other words, a router will only have first-hand knowledge of the links that are directly connected to its interfaces. Figure 6.3 illustrates a linked routing environment.

The environment pictured in Figure 6.3 shows seven routers, each with arbitrarily assigned metrics. This is typical of what a network environment might look like. Tables 6.1–6.7 show the routing tables for each router in Figure 6.3, as they would appear before any routing updates.

6

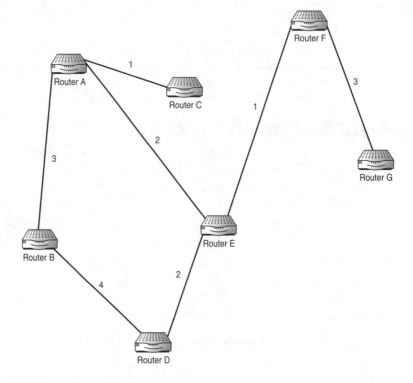

FIGURE 6.3
A linked routing environment.

TABLE 6.1 Routing Table for Router A

Link	Metric
A–C	1
A–B	3
A–E	2

TABLE 6.2 Routing Table for Router B

Link	Metric
B–A	3
B–D	4

TABLE 6.3 Routing Table for Router C

Link	Metric
C–A	1

TABLE 6.4   Routing Table for Router D

Link	Metric
D–B	4
D–E	2

TABLE 6.5   Routing Table for Router E

Link	Metric
E–A	2
E–D	2
E–F	1

TABLE 6.6   Routing Table for Router F

Link	Metric
F–E	1
F–G	3

TABLE 6.7   Routing Table for Router G

Link	Metric
G–F	3

Looking at each of the router's tables, it becomes obvious that not every router knows a path to every other router. In fact, every router only sees its most direct neighbor. If a packet destined for Router F were to be presented to Router A, it would have no way to determine which path is best. However, if Router A were using a distance vector protocol, it would know the complete path to Router F; and if it were running a link state protocol, it would have no way of knowing if any links beyond its own were still functional. Therefore, each router needs to update the others as to what their view of the network looks like.

After a large-scale update, in which every router tells its neighbor what information its routing table is holding, the new collective table would look like Table 6.8.

6

TABLE 6.8   Updated Table for Router A

Link	Metric
A–B	3
B–D	4
A–C	1
A–E	2
D–E	2
E–F	1
F–G	3

After the update is complete, it is much easier for Router A to send a packet to Router F. Examining its table, Router A can see that Router F lies beyond Router E, which can be reached either directly or through the path A–B–D–E.

Routing updates like those used in this scenario can occur one of two ways. They can be triggered by an event, or they can occur at a set interval. Some protocols will initiate the update process at a set time, for instance every 30 seconds. In this case, as soon as the interval expires, each router will send out an update containing the information from its table. This information might contain vital network changes, or no information at all.

Some protocols use a triggered event to initiate a routing update. For example, if the link between Router A and Router E were to go down, an update might be triggered to immediately notify the other routers not to rely on that link.

Either way, the product of routing updates remains the same—convergence. Network *convergence* occurs when all of the routers in a particular network arrive at a common (correct) view of the network's current topology. Speedy network convergence is highly desirable and a major selling point for any protocol. A fast convergence can eliminate problems such as routing loops and lost packets.

Convergence

When it comes to routing, convergence is the magic word. For example, if one link in a network becomes unavailable, a routing update begins. From the time the link fails until every router's table has been updated, the routers are out of convergence. Any packet sent over a network that is not in convergence risks being misrouted or lost.

Convergence is harder to achieve in larger environments with complicated paths. Therefore, the type of protocol chosen for certain environments is critical. In very large environments, link state protocols achieve convergence more quickly than distance vector protocols. However, in small networks, distance vector protocols can route information more quickly. Keep in mind, link-state protocols only send routing updates to their direct neighbors. Because there are fewer updates to process, the routers can converge much more quickly.

The goal of this brief lesson was to introduce you to some of the topics that will be covered throughout the remaining hours of this book. As we discuss each routing protocol, we will cover the topics of algorithms, updates, and convergence as they apply to a particular protocol in greater depth.

Summary

Routing protocols are the heart of a router's functionality. They use algorithms to calculate the best path from one network to another. All routers maintain a routing table, which enables other routers to view the entire network and their connections to each other. Convergence is the point at which all routers within an environment are working from the same picture of the surrounding environment.

Q&A

Q Why don't routing protocols encapsulate and carry data from network to network?

A Basically, that functionality would be redundant. The routed protocol already performs that function. However, because routed protocols have no inherent knowledge of networks, an external mechanism is needed to move the routed protocol data between networks. These external mechanisms are routers and routing protocols.

Q Why is convergence so important in routing?

A If a router is removed from a network, that router leaves a hole where no information can be moved. If the surrounding routers do not realize that there is a hole in the network, they will continue to forward data to the nonexistent device, expecting it to be routed. The sooner the routers agree that the missing router no longer exists, the less data that will be lost.

Quiz

1. What is the goal of all dynamic updates?
2. True or false: Routing protocols attach their own protocol header to all packets.
3. What is the term used to describe the value extracted from the protocol header and sent to the routing algorithm?
4. Which type of routing protocol can achieve convergence the quickest?
5. Where is information about the network's topology stored on a router?

6

Answers

1. convergence

2. False. Routing protocols reattach the routed protocol header.

3. metric

4. link-state

5. routing table

HOUR 7

Understanding How Routers Move Data

We have discussed how the three major types of protocols (routing, routed, and WAN) work together to help routers perform their duties. However, before we move forward and examine specific protocols, you must have a better understanding of the function routers provide within network environments. A major part of understanding how routers work is gaining a full understanding of routing itself. Knowing how your router is expected to work will help you determine future configurations and troubleshoot potential routing issues.

You will discover that only a small amount of time (when compared to the overall life of a network) is devoted to the setup of a routing environment. In fact, the majority of any router user's time is spent maintaining and diagnosing routes and processes.

This hour's lesson will serve as an introduction to the concepts behind routing and what it takes to move data across networks. We will discuss the roles protocols take in the routing process and how routers use them to pass data over a network.

By the end of this hour you will have a complete picture of the routing process on many levels. We will examine routing from the OSI model level, the protocol level, the packet level, and the hardware level. You will also learn about important routing concepts, such as convergence. This information will help you understand the following protocol-specific chapters. All the protocols we will cover in the remaining hours that have direct interaction with routers operate on the network layer of the OSI model.

Routers and the Network Layer

All protocols, whether routed, routing, or WAN, conform to one common specification. The protocols in use today have been designed to work within the specifications set forth in the OSI model. The OSI model is a common framework by which developers model their protocols to work with other developers' products. This common set of rules ensures that computers and other devices can all communicate with each other seamlessly, regardless of manufacturer, developer, or platform.

The theory behind basing your protocols on a common framework is twofold. First, by following a preset guideline for how your protocol should be written, you are assured that you will not leave out any critical functionality.

For example, if a protocol developer begins working on a new transport layer protocol, he/she needs to follow the rules of the transport layer of the OSI model. Therefore, the protocols must be connection-oriented and handle flow control (among other things).

According to the specifications of the OSI model, the transport layer is responsible for the establishment of connections between two devices (and subsequent destruction of those connections), error detection, error correction, flow control, and packet numbering. All protocols developed for this layer must conform to these functions.

Another advantage to using a common set of specifications such as the OSI model to develop protocols is that the protocol will work with everything else built to work on that layer. This creates a very harmonious environment within which to build a network.

Routers use this common framework to their advantage. The process of moving data from one location to another is strictly based on the principles of the OSI model and protocol encapsulation. Routers function on the network layer of the OSI model. This enables them to work with any protocol created to work within that specification.

All routers operate on the network layer for one simple reason—it's the layer responsible for protocol addressing. Therefore, any protocol written on the network layer must be able to address each system within an environment. These addresses are the key to routing.

> It is a common mistake to confuse *protocol addressing* with *system addressing*. The data link layer of the OSI model is responsible for system addressing. System addresses, like the MAC address of the data link layer, are normally hard-coded identifiers that are unique to the systems. Protocol addresses are assigned by a protocol, and can be changed as the network's topology dictates.
>
> Although the system address will not change, the protocol address can differ depending on the protocol being used. Some protocols, such as IPX, use the system address as a part of the protocol address. However, please do not confuse the two.

Routing information from one location to another is not unlike driving from one house to another. To get your car from one place to the next, you need to know where your destination is. That is, you need to know the address you are trying to drive to. After you know the address you are trying to reach, you look at a map to find the best way to get there. Finally, you get in your car and drive to the location. Once there, you exit the car and enter the building.

The address of the buildings within this fictional city can be analogous to the IP address of different devices. You, as the packet, get in your car to move from one address to another. The car in this case is the protocol (IP). However, the protocol alone cannot get you through the maze of streets that make up the city.

The streets in this case are the routing protocols. They carry your car from location to location. This is a good example of how routing works on a very broad level.

Picturing each building in our example as a router, you get a better understanding of how that process works. The packet needs to get from the router to a destination. Although the destination address is known (it is read from the protocol header information), the physical location might be unknown.

The router checks a routing table listing all the known addresses on the network and their physical locations. The router, knowing now where to send the packet, encapsulates it within a routing protocol (even though it has already been encapsulated within a routed protocol) and sends it off to the destination.

This is a rough summary of the routing process. The main process does not change from this description. However, if it were always this easy, there would not be a need for a book such as this one.

7

The complicated processes that people usually associate with routing occur when we start adding metrics and other policies to the basic routing process. The added rules are what give routing its bad rap for being hard to understand.

> A *metric* is a value that the router's routing algorithm uses to calculate the best path for a packet of data. The metric for each specific packet is stored in that packet's protocol header information.

As you might have noticed, the driving force behind routing is the use of protocols. One of the functions protocols play in aiding the routing process is to encapsulate the data being transported. This helps the routing process in many ways.

Protocol Routing

When an application on a device such as a PC needs to send data to another application on a different PC, the data is given to a protocol residing on the PC.

This protocol performs one major task that enables the transmission of this data anywhere— it encapsulates the data and prepares it for delivery.

This process of *data encapsulation* is the one key factor that makes information routing possible. Encapsulation serves two purposes when involved in the routing process. The first is to address the data and format it according to a standard template. The other is to break longer data streams into smaller, manageable pieces that can be transmitted quickly.

Protocol Headers

As discussed earlier, one of the duties of routed protocols is to encapsulate data. By encapsulating the data stream, the protocol can format the data in such a way that it can be easily understood by any other systems that might encounter it. However, the protocol does not want every other device to read the entire data stream. Instead, the information is formatted so that the other device only needs to read a small portion of the data to understand who the packets are meant for.

To do this the protocol adds *protocol headers* to the data stream. These headers contain information about the encapsulated data that every device using the same protocol can understand.

By encapsulating data from a device, the protocol does not alter its contents. Headers are prepended to the data without changing it in any way.

To illustrate the purpose of protocol headers, let's take a look at the header fields for the IP protocol. When a data stream is passed to IP to transmit over a network, one of the functions it performs is to add the header data seen in Figure 7.1 to the information. This data gives any device that comes into contact with the data stream (such as routers) several key pieces of information about the encapsulated data.

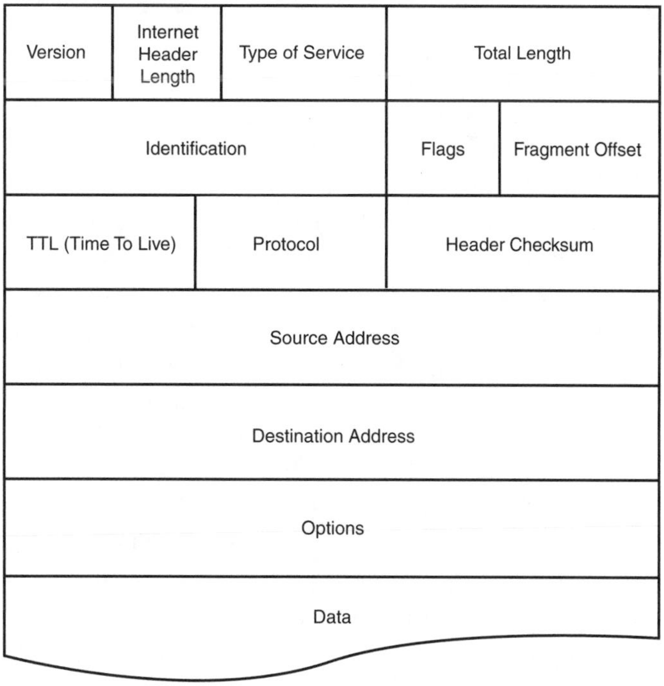

FIGURE 7.1
IP header fields.

Version	Internet Header Length	Type of Service	Total Length	
Identification			Flags	Fragment Offset
TTL (Time To Live)		Protocol	Header Checksum	
Source Address				
Destination Address				
Options				
Data				

The following list examines each of the header fields individually:

- Version—This field tells the router what version of IP was used to encapsulate the package. Although IPv4 is the most current version of IP in use today, IPv6 is quickly becoming a reality. Routers need a standard way of knowing what version of a protocol they are dealing with.

7

IP Versions

The current version of the IP protocols in wide use today is version 4 (IPv4). IPv4 gives us our familiar 4-octet IP addresses (10.15.76.1). These IP addresses are 32 bits long. Each of the four octets is comprised of 8 bits. Almost every IP address in use today is an IPv4, 32-bit, 4-octet address.

IP version 6 (IPv6) is the newest version of the IP protocol to gain popularity. Though it is still not nearly as widely used as IPv4, it is becoming more accepted in larger environments. Ipv6 uses a 128-bit address, giving it a much larger address space than IPv4.

Problems can occur when running the two protocols. Although IPv6 is backward compatible (it can understand and work with the older IPv4 addresses), IPv4 is not.

- Internet Header Length—As it states, this field indicates to the router the size of the protocol header. By determining the size of the header, the router knows where the header ends and the encapsulated data begins.

- Type of Service (TOS)—This field assigns a priority to the encapsulated packet. Although this is an advanced routing topic, many routers can utilize or participate in what is known as *type-of-service* routing. Type-of-service routing moves data based on this field. Therefore, although you might not have any need for the field now, the TOS field does affect the way information is moved from one place to another.

- Total Length—This field is the length of the entire encapsulated packet. From this, the router can derive the length of the data that follows the header by using the formula (Total length–header length = data length). In using this formula, the router can determine if the data portion of the packet has been corrupted. By knowing the length of the header and the length of the packet, the router will be able to predict the length of the data field. If the actual length turns out to be different from the predicted length, the packet is assumed to be corrupted and discarded.

- Identification—This field indicates the unique number assigned to each packet. This aids the target device in reassembling the packets when they are received.

- Flags—The Flags field is used to indicate whether the packet can be fragmented. If the packet can be fragmented, the Flags field will also indicate whether the current packet is the last in the fragment array.

- Fragment Offset—This field is closely related to the Flags field. It indicates the byte at which the fragmented packet ends. This enables the destination device to correctly reassemble the fragmented packets into full packets (for reassembly into a full data stream).

- Time To Live (TTL)—The TTL field specifies the maximum amount of time that a router can continue trying to deliver a packet before discarding it as undeliverable. When a router attempts to deliver a packet and the target system is not available, the router notes the time indicated by the TTL field and begins counting down from there. If the packet cannot be delivered to the target system before the TTL expires, it is discarded.

> A low TTL can cause problems on larger networks. For example, if a packet needs to pass through multiple router hops spanning multiple networks, the TTL timer might expire before the packet even reaches the destination. Therefore, target systems that otherwise appear functional might not be receiving information because of the low setting. A higher setting would give the packet more time to reach its destination.

- Protocol—This field is used by the target device (rather than a router). The Protocol field tells the target device which protocol to pass the information to after it has been delivered and reassembled.
- Header Checksum—A calculated field that computes the length of the header and safeguards against packet corruption. By checking the header, the router ensures that no corrupted packets are forwarded.
- Source Address—This field is one of the two most important pieces of information for the routing process. The Source Address field tells the router who sent the packet. This address can be used to apply filters and determine path integrity. For example, a router might be configured to forward packets from one location to a specific network. The router would use the Source Address field to determine whether the packet meets those criteria.
- Destination Address—Appears directly after the source address and is arguably the most important field in the routing process. The Destination Address field will show the address of the target device. Obviously, without the benefit of a destination address, routing would be next to impossible.
- Options—For IP-specific options.
- Data—This field contains the actual information being sent between the systems.

The protocol provides most of the information needed for routing through the use of the protocol headers. These headers pass all the necessary data for moving a packet from one location to another. Routers read through these protocol headers to determine the critical material needed to successfully route information.

7

Another important function of data encapsulation is to break a data stream into small, manageable pieces. These small pieces are easily read and processed by routers.

Data Packeting

Protocols also break data streams into manageable packets during the encapsulation process. By doing so, the routing hardware is spared the work of trying to route large bursts of data. Even in today's age of seemingly endless bandwidth, bursting data without the advantage of segmentation would cause far too many clog-ups.

However, traffic is not the only problem resolved by protocol encapsulation. By sending data in short, mostly uniform packets, there is a better chance that the target device will remain online during the entire transmission, thus increasing the chances that the information will be routed successfully.

During the encapsulation process, the data marked for transmission is cut into variable-length pieces by the protocol, then each piece or packet is identified and a header is attached. Because the header is attached to each individual packet, they can be released at different times.

 Every protocol has different specifications for the size of individual frames or packets. In the event of network problems, examining the sizes of the packets through a packet viewer can identify certain protocols.

When the packets reach their destination, the target system can read each header to determine the sequence of packets and in what order to reassemble the packets. The device can then strip the header off the packets and reassemble them into one continuous data stream.

At this point, you have enough information to understand how protocols aid in the routing process. However, the functions provided by routed protocols are only one-third of the entire picture. The router hardware still has a lot of work to do before the data can reach its target.

The Mechanics of Routing

Contrary to popular belief, routing itself is fairly simple to understand. All routing is based on logical rules and policies. Routing becomes complicated when layers of security, secondary and tertiary protocols, and complex network divisions are added.

As networks grow in size, importance, and corporate value, certain measures are exercised that would not necessarily concern a smaller network. Issues such as security become paramount in larger business structures. The process of adding security policies to a router can add to the numbers of internal steps taken by the router before a single packet can be routed.

Larger networks also tend to outgrow their use of a single protocol. Whether through rapid expansion or the acquisition of an existing environment, many networks utilize more than one routed, routing, or WAN protocol. Using multiple protocols complicates the routing process by adding to the number of protocol conversions that must take place before information can reach a particular destination. All these functions and aspects of routing are integral parts of the routing process.

The remainder of this hour is geared toward presenting you with the information required to understand how routing works and how routers in general move data from network to network.

Whereas simple network routing is moving data from one network to another, complex routing entails moving data across several routers and spanning multiple networks. Multiple metrics and complicated algorithms are much more prevalent in complex routing environments.

Therefore, let's examine the physical routing process separately as it applies to both simple and complex routing environments.

Simple Network Routing

Simple routing (for the purposes of this scenario) takes place when information needs to be moved between two networks. Figure 7.2 illustrates a simple two-network environment.

Notice that the environment is divided into two separate networks (Network A and Network B), each with its own IP address. Because these networks are separated physically and they're using different IP addressing schemes, data cannot freely flow between them. The solution here is to create a simple routing environment, thus establishing a segmented network.

The scenario and solution provided here is extremely simplistic. However, all routing environments (no matter how simple or complex) are based on the same principles.

7

FIGURE 7.2

A simple two-network environment.

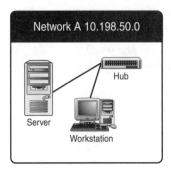

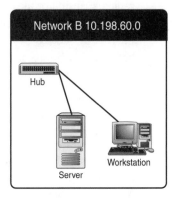

Let's examine how a router will function if placed between the two networks.

The PCs and other addressed systems (servers and such) should be configured with the address of the new router. Usually labeled as the *default gateway*, the parameter for the location of the router can vary depending on the operating system in use. However, no matter the label, each system needs to know the address of the router. Figure 7.3 illustrates these same two networks with a router between them.

Notice that the router is actually linked to a hub on each network. Keep in mind, routers cannot route to individual systems; rather, the job of routers is to move information between networks. Therefore, another connectivity device must be employed to connect the devices of each network with the router.

Placing the router correctly between the two networks might be the hardest part of the process for one reason: You must assign a valid address on each router interface for the network to which it will be connected. In other words, the interface connected to Network A (10.198.50.0) needs an address in the 10.198.50.x range, whereas the interface connected to Network B (10.198.60.0) needs an address in the 10.198.60.x range.

In most networking environments, the first five to ten addresses in a network are reserved for routers. Although this is not a written rule by any means, it is a convention that most engineers seem to abide by.

FIGURE 7.3

Two networks joined by a router.

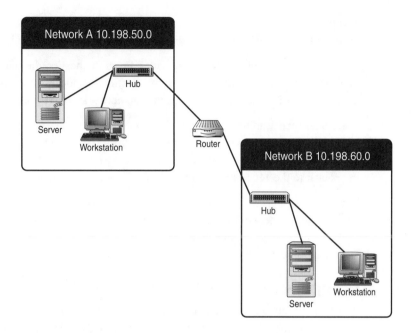

Now that the router is in place and each PC has been configured with its address, we can see how data will move from Network A through the router to Network B.

PCs on Network A (10.198.50.0) normally send messages to each other through the hub. That is, a packet from 10.198.50.5 meant for 10.198.50.8 is sent from the PC. From the PC the packet has only one place to go—the hub. The hub, being an unintelligent device, simply relays that message to every other device physically connected to it. One of those devices is 10.198.50.8. When this device receives the message, it processes it and sends the appropriate response.

The other devices attached to the hub determine whether the packet is for them by reading the protocol header. The header of the protocols indicates the addresses of the device that sent the packet and the device to which it should be sent. If a device reads a header and determines that the packet is not meant for it, it simply discards it and waits for more.

With the router in place, the PCs in Network A can send packets to the PCs in Network B. When the packet leaves a PC in Network A and reaches the hub, the hub will broadcast that packet to every device attached to it. Every device that receives the packet (from the hub on Network A) will check whether the packet is addressed to them; if it is not, it will be discarded.

7

The packet will then reach the router. At this point, the router will begin examining the protocol header to determine whether it knows the location of the intended recipient.

First, the router opens and read the header. From the header, the router ascertains the destination address of the packet. Taking this destination address (10.198.60.17), it applies the subnet mask to determine the destination network (10.198.60.0).

The router then searches through its internal configuration to determine whether any configured interfaces match this network address. The router should find that interface 10.198.60.1 is on the 10.198.60.0 network. The 10.198.50.1 interface now passes the packet to the 10.198.60.1 interface for forwarding to the hub on Network B.

This rather simplistic view of how routers move protocols and how protocols help to carry data from network to network is actually very accurate. However, the chances of finding a routing environment configured like this are pretty slim. Most networks today fall under the category of complex routing environments.

Complex Network Routing

A complex routing environment consists of multiple routers and multiple networks, producing multiple paths between each network. Figure 7.4 illustrates a complex routing environment.

FIGURE 7.4

A complex routing environment.

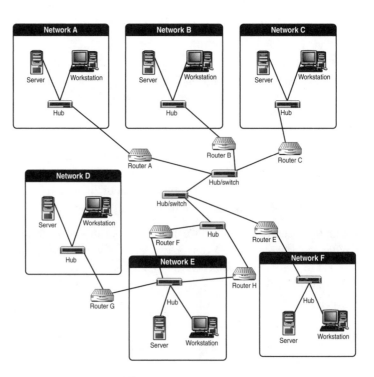

Let's say that a device from Network A wants to send information to a device in Network D. In logical order, the steps taken by the routing equipment are as follows:

1. The packet, having been encapsulated by a routed protocol, reaches Router A.

2. Router A searches through its routing table for an entry indicating the location of Network D. Using the routing table, Router A finds that there are two paths to reach Network D. The first path is through Router F to Router G, and the other is through Router H to Router G.

3. Router A runs its routing algorithm against the stored metrics for both paths, and finds that of the two, the route from Router F to Router G is the best. The routing algorithm is based on the routing protocol in use; in this case OSPF.

4. Router A encapsulates the packet (which was already encapsulated by IP) in OSPF. It then sets the destination field of the OSPF header to the address for Network D.

5. Router A now sends the OSPF-encapsulated packet to Router F.

6. Router F reads the OSPF headers and sees that the packet is targeted for Router G.

7. Router F searches its routing table to find that it has a physical link to Router G and forwards the packet.

8. Router G receives the packet, strips off the OSPF header and forwards the IP-encapsulated packet to Network D.

Even this scenario could be more complex. In most environments, there are access lists and multiple metrics to deal with (both of which will be covered later in this book).

Access lists are rules that can be configured on routers. The router applies these rules to each packet it handles, testing for whatever criteria are defined in the access list. Packets are then either accepted or denied by the router based on the results of the access lists.

Regardless, this should give you a good overview of the routing process. Knowing this process will help you understand what parameters need to be set to configure your Cisco router in different situations.

In all the scenarios we have seen thus far, one routing element that remains constant is the routing table. The *routing table* is a database that resides within the router's physical memory. This database contains all the information needed by the router to find the location of a destination network.

7

Routing Tables

Every router, regardless of make or model, stores a routing table. The routing table can be likened to a small database. However, the problem with trying to explain the contents of the routing table is that the format of the table can change, depending on the routing protocol in use.

Therefore, this discussion will contain general information about the contents of routing tables. If there is more specific information to be added, we will discuss it in the lesson concerning that particular routing protocol.

One important piece of information stored with the routing table is a one-to-one relationship of router to network address. For example, an excerpt of the routing table for Router A (in the scenario illustrated in Figure 7.4) might look like this:

Network A—ME

Network B—Router B

Network C—Router C

Network D—Router F

Network D—Router H

Network E—Router F

Network E—Router H

Network F—Router E

Examining this list closely, you should notice a discrepancy with the routing table and the environment in Figure 7.4. Router G is actually the gateway router for Network D, but Router A sees Routers F and H as the routers to Network D. The reason for this is that most routing protocols do not enable a router to see more than what is currently physically connected to it. In other words, because Router F is the next router connected to Router A, Router A will only recognize Router F (or Router H) as the path to Network D.

Router A will know about the existence of Network D; however, it will not care about how to get there. Rather, it will only concern itself with knowing who it needs to send packets to for Network D. In this case, Router A could send the packets to either Router F or Router H. Within the routing tables on both Router F and Router H is the entry:

Network D—Router G

By organizing routing tables in this way, specific routers do not need to be responsible for the entire environment. Rather, each router watches over its own little (physically connected) portion of the network. If every router had a full copy of the routing table for the entire environment, several problems would emerge.

The first problem is just the sheer size of the table itself. The routing table would become so large that looking through it for entries would take longer each time, thus increasing the amount of time needed to route data. Also, the larger a routing table gets, the more memory is required to store it. This would take away from the memory used by the routing algorithms and the configuration files.

The second problem that would surface as a result of owning a full copy of the database is known as convergence. The goal in routing is to reach convergence as quickly as possible. This means that every router on the network has an updated routing table (that agrees with the routing tables on all other routers) as quickly as possible. If every router had a full table, a change made on one end of the network would take longer to reflect within the routing table of a router on the other end. Therefore, convergence would be very hard to achieve. This would create routing holes and loops where information would simply be lost.

Another important function of routing tables is to track and store routing metrics. Routing metrics are the deciding factor when one route needs to be chosen over another. That is, the metrics within the routing table that are assigned to each route are used to calculate whether a packet will be forwarded over one route, as opposed to another route to the same destination. Metrics are values that represent many different environmental factors. For example, depending on the configuration of the network, a metric can represent the amount of bandwidth over a particular link, or the amount of money charged to the company for using a leased line. Metrics can be defined by the network/router administrator to stand in for any meaningful value.

In the scenario featured in Figure 7.4, Router A had two routes to choose from when sending packets to Network D. The data could be forwarded to Router F or Router H, both of which eventually lead to Network D. Router A used the metrics assigned to each path to decide which router to use.

The specific metrics used by a router to determine what route to use vary from protocol to protocol. Whatever the protocol, one factor of metrics remains the same—99% of them are arbitrary numbers assigned by the network administrator or router engineer.

Metrics like cost are values assigned by engineers that indicate the relative value of using one path over another to a specific destination. There are any number of factors that would cause an administrator to assign a lower value to one link and a higher value to

7

another. Factors such as traffic flow, equipment reliability, and line cost (in dollars) can all be influential in causing one value to be assigned over another. However, the metrics themselves are ultimately at the discretion of the engineer.

In this scenario, the route to Router H could have been assigned a metric of 200, where the route to Router F was assigned a metric of 100. When Router A's routing protocol is run against all the metrics (some protocols can use up to 10), a final figure is produced. The route with the lowest figure is chosen as the best path.

Now let's examine the ever-important topic of convergence in greater detail.

Achieving Convergence

Convergence is just as integral to router functionality as any of the other factors we have discussed thus far. Put simply, if each router is operating from a routing table with a different conclusion of the network's topology, each router is going to move data differently. This will result in many problems, and most likely the environment will cease to operate.

Therefore, a system needs to be implemented to ensure that every router within a given environment will be working from the same table. The product of this system is known as convergence.

The responsibility of achieving convergence belongs to the routing protocol. There are as many ways to achieve convergence as there are routing protocols. However, the basic concept behind the process remains the same.

To arrive at a state of router convergence, each router on the network passes a piece of its routing table to every other router within the same environment. After the target routers receive their updates, they apply the changes to their own tables, then send out more updates pertaining to the information they just received. This continues until every router agrees on the topology of the network.

As we cover different routing protocols in this book, we will discuss their particular ways of achieving convergence.

Summary

Routers function mainly on the network layer of the OSI model. The network layer provides the mapping capability needed for routers to locate networks within an environment and keep track of routing lists.

A routing table is a small database that is located within the router's memory. This database contains all the information necessary to keep track of all possible routers to and from specific networks.

All routers within a given environment share their routing tables with each other. When all routers have been updated with the latest tables, they are said to have achieved convergence.

Q&A

Q **Can routers only work with network layer protocols? If so, why are there protocols written for other OSI layers?**

A Yes, routers can only work with protocols written specifically to work on the network layer of the OSI model. Devices such as switches work with protocols on other layers (switches work with the data link layer to take advantage of the MAC address).

Quiz

1. What layer of the OSI model is responsible for the internal mapping of a network?
2. Where is the protocol's specific information stored (and therefore passed to the router)?
3. What is the product of the routing update process?

Answers

1. The network layer
2. The protocol header
3. convergence

7

PART II
Basic Protocols

Hour

8   Introducing IP

9   Discovering IP Router Configurations

10 Understanding Segmented Networks

11 Using CIDR

12 Understanding IPX Basics

13 Dynamic Versus Static Routing

14 Understanding ISDN

15 Learning X.25

16 Learning Frame Relay

17 Understanding RIP

18 Routing with IGRP

HOUR 8

Introducing IP

The last seven lessons have brought you straight through the theories associated with routing as a logical and physical process. You have been exposed to all the core information necessary to understand how routers work. The majority of the remaining hours (including this one) are devoted to specific protocols.

TCP/IP is by far the most popular protocol suite in use today. Therefore, it is the protocol you are most likely to come across in any routed environment. TCP/IP actually isn't a single protocol; it is a suite of protocols. TCP is a transport layer protocol, and IP is its network layer counterpart. Therefore, when dealing with routing, we are more concerned with IP than TCP. For this reason, we'll focus primarily on IP. However, to fully understand IP, you'll need to expose the TCP/IP stack as a whole.

TCP (Transmission Control Protocol)

Transmission Control Protocol (TCP) is the transport layer protocol in the TCP/IP protocol stack. All the functionality of TCP is governed by the standards outlined in the fourth layer of the OSI model. To fully understand IP and how it works, you must understand the full complement of IP-related protocols.

The transport layer of the OSI model is responsible for the conversion of user data into segments and the reliable delivery of those segments to their intended recipient. TCP, like any protocol that resides on the fourth layer of the OSI model, must be able to perform these duties. How does TCP comply with the functions outlined by the transport layer?

TCP takes user data from the upper layers of the OSI model and breaks it into segments. These segments are numbered by TCP before delivery across the network. The segments are numbered as a form of checks and balances to ensure that all segments for a particular session are delivered.

When all the segments are ready for delivery, TCP requests a session with the transport layer of the destination device. (Knowing the destination is the function of IP, which is covered in the next section.) TCP is considered a connection-oriented protocol because it opens a session or connection with the destination device before sending segments. By doing this, the sender can be assured that the destination is active and ready to receive segments. When the connection is established, TCP sends off the segments.

After TCP numbers segments for delivery, they are placed into a queue for transmission across the network. TCP then builds a virtual circuit to the destination device. This ensures that the segments arrive in the correct order.

The destination device's TCP reassembles the segments by number and requests that the sender resend any missing packets. If you were using a connectionless protocol in this example, any missing segments would be lost. This could result in lost or corrupt data.

TCP seems like a very good, reliable protocol on its own. However, TCP is just half of a dynamic protocol stack. How does TCP know where to send those segments? The second half of the TCP/IP protocol stack addresses this issue.

IP (Internet Protocol)

It is almost impossible to work in the computer industry today and not know what IP is. However, do you really understand how it works, or why it is so popular? This section covers how IP works, and addresses some common issues such as addressing and subnetting.

IP facilitates the network layer's role of mapping the network environment. Through IP's addressing scheme, the network layer can produce a detailed map of the network around the host. IP operates purely on the network layer.

8

A standard IP address looks like this: `128.95.95.178`—four sections containing four bytes each. An IP address is comprised of 32 bits, or four bytes. Because the bits are in binary, the largest achievable value for one set of four bytes is 255 (actually 254, because 255 is set for broadcasts). This means that the achievable range of IP addresses is `0.0.0.0` through `255.255.255.255`. (These numbers are achievable, but are not all valid.) Therefore, be careful not to use any of the reserved address in your routers.

Table 8.1 is a list of IP addresses that are considered reserved.

TABLE 8.1 Reserved IP Addresses

Address Reserved	Binary	Reason Address Is
`0.0.0.0`	`00000000.00000000.00000000.00000000`	An address cannot contain only 0s. Used by RIP (Routing Information Protocol) for routing.
`255.255`	`255.255.11111111.11111111.11111111.11111111`	An address cannot contain only 1s. Used for broadcasts.
`127.0.0.1`	`01111111.00000000.00000000.00000001`	Reserved for internal loopback testing.

Depending on the class of the address, anywhere from one to three bytes are used to identify the host, and anywhere from one to three bytes are used to identify the network. The first part of an address is used to identify the network, whereas the second part is used to identify the host. Being able to discern the host from the network is very important in routing.

 The host address can also be referred to as the *node address*.

IP addresses are divided into three classes. These classes were created to keep track of the number of addresses being allotted to certain size institutions. The classes for IP addresses are Class A, Class B, and Class C. There is also a lesser known (and even lesser used) Class D, which we will not be discussing. (Class D is primarily used for multi-casting.) Knowing the class of an address will help you correctly identify the proper subnet mask when configuring an interface.

Class A Addresses

For Class A addresses, the first byte of the address represents the network, and the last three bytes represent the hosts. Figure 8.1 shows a Class A address divided into its network and host portions.

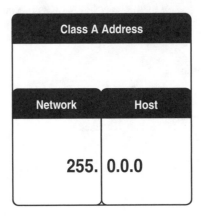

Class A addresses have a network range between 1 and 127. Therefore, an IP address starting with a number between 1 and 127 will be a Class A address.

Class B Addresses

In Class B addresses, the first two bytes represent the network and the remaining two bytes represent the host. A valid Class B network range is 128–191. Figure 8.2 shows a Class B IP address divided into its network and host portions.

Class C Addresses

In Class C addresses, the first three bytes represent the network and the last byte represents the host. A valid Class C range is 192–223. Figure 8.3 shows a Class C IP address divided into its network and host portions.

FIGURE 8.3

The host and net-work portions of a Class C address.

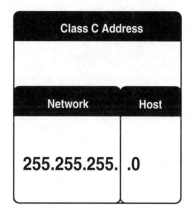

Class C Address

Network	Host
255.255.255.	.0

You might have noticed that the valid range of addresses for Class C only goes up to 223, but IP addresses can reach 256. This leaves room for Class D (224–239) and Class E (240–255). Don't spend too much time worrying about these addresses; they are not used very often.

However, for troubleshooting purposes it's good to know that these ranges exist. For example, if you are configuring a router's interface for a Class C network and assign it an address of 230.230.230.0 with a subnet mask of 255.255.255.0 (the valid subnet mask for a Class C network), you might run into problems.

In this particular example, the device would not be able to communicate with any other devices in the 255.255.255.0 subnet. However, on the surface, the address 230.230.230.0 appears to be valid, even though it is actually Class D.

The Subnet Mask

The *subnet mask* is used by IP to distinguish the host address from the network address. To understand how the subnet mask works, convert an IP address to binary. The following is the Class C address 198.68.85.114 in binary:

```
11000110.01000100.01010101.01110010
```

The subnet mask for a Class C IP address is `255.255.255.0`. In binary, the subnet mask looks like this:

`11111111.11111111.11111111.00000000`

How does this help IP distinguish the network address from the host? As you can see from the binary representation of the address and the mask, the binary 1s mark the network portion. Conversely, the 0s mark the host portion of the address. This might seem obvious now, but it becomes harder to see when you start subnetting your networks.

> The class of IP addresses you are using will determine the subnet mask you need. The following are the default subnet masks for the three classes of addresses:
>
> Class A—`255.0.0.0`
>
> Class B—`255.255.0.0`
>
> Class C—`255.255.255.0`
>
> Although subnetting is easier to understand the more you do it, it can be a complicated and at times mentally trying task. I can only suggest that you plan out on paper any subnetting schemes before trying to implement them.

A technique you should become familiar with is network subnetting. Network subnetting allows you to logically and functionally divide your network along borders created by IP.

Network Subnetting

When a network is subnetted, bits are passed from the host portion of an address to the network portion. This allows for the addressing of more networks (or sub-networks) from one IP license. Figure 8.4 shows a network that would benefit from subnetting.

We need to subnet the license `10.0.0.0` to fit three subnets. Where do we start? You should start by looking at the subnet mask. Even though you are creating three networks, they need to share one subnet mask. By converting the subnet mask into binary, you can easily see how subnetting is accomplished.

The subnet mask for `10.0.0.0` is `255.0.0.0`. `255.0.0.0` in binary is

`11111111.00000000.00000000.00000000`

FIGURE 8.4

A non-subnetted network.

8

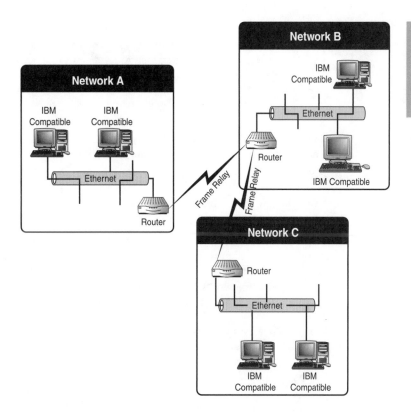

You then need to determine the number of bits that should be given to the network address to allow for three more networks. For example, if you were to pass two bits from the host portion of the mask to the network, you would create two networks, with a possible 4,194,302 hosts on each one. Looking at the mask in binary form you can now see the result:

`11111111.11000000.00000000.00000000`

As you can see, we passed two bits from the host to the network. This gives us a new subnet mask of `255.192.0.0`. Our new networks would have the addresses of `10.64.x.x` and `10.128.x.x`.

The following equation can be used when factoring the number of bits necessary to supply the required number of networks:

2^x-2 = `Number of addresses`

where *x* equals the number of bits in the address. Therefore, in the third octet of our example address, we used two bits for the network ($2^2-2 = 2$), giving us two networks.

That left a total of 22 bits for the hosts ($2^{22}-2 = 4,194,302$).

Why do you subtract 2 from the total number of addresses? You cannot use all 0s or all 1s as an address; therefore you must subtract those two possibilities. Referring back to Table 8.1, the addresses 000.000.000.000 and 111.111.111.111 are reserved. When calculating the subnet, you must account for the lack of these two possibilities.

A second equation is used to figure out the network addresses:

256-x = y limit x

where x is the new subnet mask; y will equal the interval between networks until y reaches x. This is how we arrived at the answer from our example (10.0.0.0 with a subnet mask of 255.192.0.0 yields the networks 10.64.0.0 and 10.128.0.0).

256-192 = 64

Therefore, the valid networks are 10.64.0.0 and 10.128.0.0 (64+64). If you were to add 64 again, you would get 192, which is the subnet mask.

You need three networks to successfully subnet the example in Figure 8.4. Therefore, you should use a subnet mask of 255.224.0.0. This would give you six networks, with 2,097,150 hosts each. You would obviously never need that many hosts, but it is the number of networks we're concerned about.

By subnetting the networks, you can better direct the traffic around the networks. Had you not subnetted the networks, the traffic (produced by broadcasts and CSMA/CD packets) would start to degrade the performance of the network. Now that the networks are subnetted, the traffic stays on its particular subnet, creating a less hectic network environment.

Subnetting is discussed further in Hour 10, "Understanding Segmented Networks."

While subnetting works by moving bits to the network portion of the IP address, *supernetting* works by doing the exact opposite.

Supernetting is used to define an upper-level "super network" to which all your other networks belong. Supernetting is used most notably during Classless Inter-Domain Routing (CIDR). CIDR will be covered in Hour 11, "Using CIDR."

Supernetting an IP Network

With the growing popularity of CIDR, it became necessary to supernet a group of networks. Because the addressing authorities were running painfully low on large classes of IP address, it became necessary to devise a method to extend the life of the remaining addresses. The result was supernetting.

Using CIDR also reduces the size of routing tables. In environments where routing tables can become very large (ISPs), CIDR is utilized to keep the tables a manageable size. Through CIDR, there are less network IP addresses to track, so there is less space consumed on the table.

When a group of addresses are supernetted, a mask is created to indicate that the individual networks involved belong to one larger supergroup. For example, if an environment is assigned the two network addresses 215.50.25.0 and 215.50.26.0, a supernet can be created to combine and relate the two networks for use within the same physical environment.

The binary form of the subnet mask 255.255.255.0 (the Class C mask for both of the assigned network addresses) is 11111111.11111111.11111111.00000000. Whereas subnetting passes bits from the host portion of the address to add more networks, supernetting passes bits from the network portion to add fewer.

If two bits are passed from the network portion to the host portion, the mask will become 11111111.11111111.11111100.00000000, or 255.255.252.0. When combined with the network address 215.50.25.0, this mask will tell the router that two network addresses are included in the supernet. If you start counting your networks with 215.50.25.0, the two network addresses covered by the new mask are 215.50.25.0 and 215.50.26.0.

Using the same calculations that were introduced in the last section, passing two bits from the host to the network (2^2–2) will include two networks in your supernet.

> If you're wondering how the router knows that the new mask of 255.255.252.0 is not a Class B subnet instead of a Class C supernet, the answer is actually quite easy. The first octet of the network address is 215.x.x.x. Only a Class C network can begin with 215, so the new mask has to be for a Class C supernet.

Supernetting is easier to understand when looked at in relation to subnetting. Therefore, you should practice both supernetting and subnetting on paper to get the hang of it.

Summary

TCP/IP is a protocol stack that contains two major protocols, TCP and IP. TCP is the transport layer protocol, and IP is the routable network layer protocol.

IP addresses are divided into five classes (A through E). Each IP class can serve a different number of networks and hosts.

Subnetting is used to create more network addresses than what is supplied in your particular IP license. This allows you to utilize your IP license in the most efficient manner.

During the subnetting process, bits are passed from the host portions of the address to the network portion.

Q&A

Q Why is IP so popular in routed environments?

A IP gained popularity early in the history of networking. As one of the first universally portable protocols, IP quickly gained a larger installed base as networking technologies expanded. When the Internet began gaining popularity, the majority of systems involved already used IP as their primary protocol.

Q Why is subnetting so important on IP networks?

A Subnetting lets you divide a network into more defined areas. By separating a network, you can better control the utilization of its resources. Subnetting also allows you to make the most of your IP license by creating many networks with one environment.

Quiz

1. What protocols within the TCP/IP protocol stack are used for the establishment and destruction of sessions?

2. What IP class has a subnet mask of `255.255.0.0`?

3. True or false: During subnetting, bits are passed from the host to the network portion of an IP address.

Answers

1. TCP operates on the transport layer of the OSI model, which is responsible for session management.

2. Class B

3. True

HOUR 9

Discovering IP Router Configurations

To best understand how routers work with certain protocols, it is necessary to examine those protocols in a context that exposes the configuration information required by routers. This hour will use some examples from a Cisco router to demonstrate how routers are configured to use IP.

You will also learn about one other protocol within the TCP/IP stack that is very important to router and network maintenance—*ICMP (Internet Control Message Protocol)*. ICMP is a protocol that is closely linked to IP. Used for diagnostic purposes, ICMP is a strong tool in the world of routing. Mastering ICMP and its tool set will help you diagnose many of the issues that can occur with routers. Issues such as end-to-end connectivity problems can be effectively handled using ICMP. A portion of this chapter will deal directly with ICMP.

Router Interfaces

IP is normally configured to operate within a specific router interface. Although all routers will have at least two addressable interfaces, many will have more. Each interface should be configured for the network to which it attaches. For example, if your router spans two networks (128.56.40.0 and 128.57.40.0), the interfaces would be configured with a legal address for its respective network.

> The term *legal address* is often used when referring to IP addresses. A legal address is one that fits correctly within the overall IP addressing scheme of a particular network.

The following command example illustrates how an IP address is configured on a Cisco router. You will need to give a router several key pieces of information to establish an address on that interface. The following command sample (as with the majority of code samples in the lesson) has been abbreviated to supply only the pertinent information:

```
Router(configure-interface)#ip address 10.156.4.16 255.255.0.0
```

On this particular interface, you have told the router that you want to configure it with an IP address of 10.156.4.16 and a subnet mask of 255.255.0.0. (Repeat this command on all the physical interfaces you need IP functionality on.) You have configured this particular interface to work on a Class B IP network with a network address of 10.156.0.0. Therefore, you must confirm that the network to which this interface is attached is in fact a Class B IP network with an address of 10.156.0.0.

After IP addresses have been assigned to all the interfaces involved in a particular routing environment, routes can be established. Although we will cover the concepts of dynamic and static protocol routing in Hour 13, "Dynamic Versus Static Routing," we will explore some basic subjects related to the establishment of routes here.

> A *route* is a path used by a router to send information from a specific source to a specific destination.

Dynamic routes are routes that a router "learns" through updates with neighboring routers. That is, when a router receives an update from its neighbor, it might discover that the neighbor is connected to a particular network. Based on the update information alone, the router could then formulate that any data bound for that particular network should be sent to the neighboring router. Dynamic routes are the most common type of route within networking environments.

Static routes, on the other hand, are paths that you specify to a router. These routes tell a router that any information needing to be moved form Network A to Network B must travel through Router C. Static routes are coded into the router and stored manually within the router's memory (These manual route entries cannot be changed by the router like their dynamic counterparts). Let's examine how a static route is defined on a Cisco router:

```
Router(configuration)#ip route 198.52.2.0 255.0.0.0 Ethernet 0
```

This command (in essence) tells the router that any information destined for the network address 198.52.2.0 should be passed to the interface Ethernet 0. By defining static routes, you can control the flow of data out of your router.

Now, let's walk though some IP routing scenarios. For example, how would the router in the following network diagram be configured to run and route IP from Network A to Network B? Figure 9.1 shows a sample routing network.

FIGURE 9.1

A sample IP network.

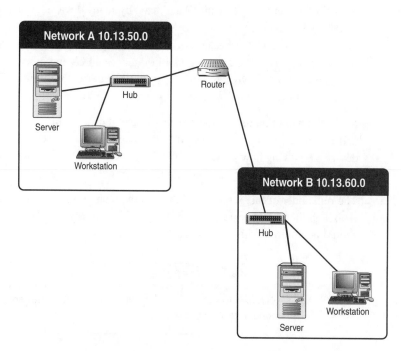

In this example, the router interface Ethernet 0 should be configured with a legal address on the 10.13.50.0 network:

```
Router(configure-interface)#ip address 10.13.50.1 255.255.0.0
```

The router interface `Ethernet 1` needs to be set up with a address for the `10.13.60.0` network:

```
Router(configure-interface)#ip address 10.13.60.1 255.255.0.0
```

Two routes should then be established to inform the router where the information needs to be sent.

```
Router(configure)#ip route 10.13.50.0 255.255.0.0 ethernet 0
Router(configure)#ip route 10.13.60.0 255.255.0.0 ethernet 1
```

Although this scenario might seem simple on an engineering level, all networks are essentially a scaled-up version of this basic functional operation.

After configuring IP functionality on a router, other protocols within the TCP/IP protocol stack will also be available to you. One such protocol is ICMP.

ICMP (Internet Control Message Protocol)

ICMP is tied very closely with IP and used by many devices to monitor connections and report on environmental factors. Being so closely related to IP has its upsides and downsides. The upside is that because of the popularity of IP, many devices are capable of running ICMP. However, there are still quite a few PCs and other devices that do not use IP. Therefore, one downside to ICMP is that any device not running IP cannot be detected with ICMP for diagnostic purposes.

Most PCs and other networkable devices have the capability to use tools such as `ping` and `traceroute`. These tools use ICMP packets to test connectivity factors among devices. Knowing how these tools work and being able to use them to your advantage will help you keep your network and router in good maintenance.

The remainder of this section will discuss the technology and concepts behind ICMP. Although there is no extra configuration required to install ICMP on a Cisco router, you should be familiar with how to use it.

 There should not be any extra configuration required to install ICMP or ICMP services on a router; however, the router does need at least one functional interface using IP.

Using ICMP and ICMP Tools

ICMP is a protocol that is used almost exclusively for testing and diagnosing network connectivity issues. Because of the complex nature of routing, diagnosing even the simplest of problems can be difficult without the correct tools. To better understand how difficult it can be to diagnose network problems in a routed environment, let's look at a sample network.

Networking environments today are larger and more complex than ever before. It is not uncommon to have five to ten separate routers within one network. However, most networks do not stop at the office walls. Having connections to the Internet adds hundreds, if not thousands, of routers to a company's routed environment. Figure 9.2 illustrates a typical routed environment.

FIGURE 9.2

A typical routed environment.

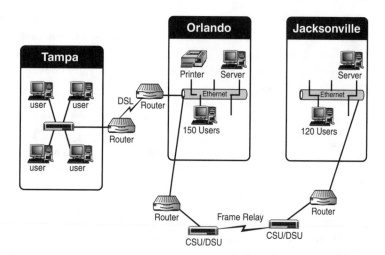

When the number of routers that are added to a network grows, the level of complexity within the networked environment grows as well. One common complexity that arises from adding routers to a network affects tracking packets within the environment. Using ICMP, an administrator can track the router of packets from end to end. This can help engineers and designers not only determine whether there are connectivity problems on the network, but also whether the routers are actually using the correct paths.

There are two ICMP tools that routers can use to determine the overall health of a route. These tools are ping and traceroute. Both tools offer powerful diagnostic capabilities, so we'll take a look at each one separately.

The `ping` Utility

The `ping` utility is used to test for the existence of the host system. `ping`, using ICMP echo packets, works like a submarine's sonar (hence the name *ping*). By pinging the host's IP address, you can tell whether the machine is running and whether the protocol is functioning properly. This will enable you to scale down the scope of possible problems.

> `ping` works by sending ICMP echo packets to an IP address you select. When the specified address receives the ICMP packets, it echoes them back to the sender.

However, the only thing you can be assured of when using `ping` is that a device is on and functioning properly. `ping` tells you little else. For example, if you ping a server's IP address and receive no replies, there might be many different problems. The server might be powered off, the server might not be configured to run IP, or the router you are pinging from might be configured incorrectly. There is really no way to tell, but at least you have a starting point.

> Keep in mind that when using any of the ICMP tools, your router needs at least one configured interface that is running IP. If you do not have at least one line up, you will see an error on your router.

The standard version of `ping` is activated on most platforms by entering `ping` at a command prompt, followed by an address to test. To assemble a fully functional `ping` command, you need to specify the IP address of the device you want to ping:

```
Router>ping 10.16.4.152
```

A standard ping will produce an output similar to the following. At first glance, the output message might seem cryptic and somewhat hard to follow; however, if you take it section by section, it really is easy to understand:

```
Router> ping 10.16.4.152
Sending 5, 100-byte ICMP Echos to 10.16.4.152, timeout is 2 seconds:
!!!!!
Success rate is 100 percent, round-trip min/avg/max = 1/3/4 ms
```

The first line is a status message generated by, in this case, the Cisco IOS. This line reiterates the intent of the ping command. In this example, the ping command is going to send five 100-byte packets to the IP address 10.16.4.152. The timeout is set to two seconds.

> The Cisco IOS (Internal Operating System) is the operating system that powers most Cisco routers. Every brand of router uses a different type of operating system. The examples I've used in this book are from Cisco routers, therefore any messages generated are from the Cisco IOS.

The *timeout* (also referred to as *TTL*, or time-to-live) is a clock used by the devices involved to determine whether a packet can be discarded. When a packet's TTL expires, it is discarded by the device holding it. Therefore, the sending device can infer that if no responses are received within two seconds, the destination address is unreachable. Otherwise, the sending device would be waiting indefinitely for a response that may never come.

The next line in the output message is actually a representation of the ping execution. Each icon displayed, in this case an exclamation point, represents one packet sent by the router to the destination address. The fact that the icon in the example is an ! illustrates that the ICMP packets were successfully echoed back to the router. Had the icons been ., the packets would have been lost, meaning the destination address did not echo the ping.

There are eight icons that Cisco routers use to express the results of the ping command. These icons include the following:

- !   Success
- .   Failure
- U   End node unreachable
- Q   Source quench
- M   Packet was too big to be routed (it could not be fragmented)
- ?   Unknown packet type

The final line of the output message is a summation, alerting you as to whether the ping was successful and how long the packets took to be echoed back (if the echoes were received).

Routers on a network are commonly referred to as *hops* (describing the number of routers a piece of information must traverse before reaching its final destination). For example, a packet that must go through three routers to reach its destination has covered three hops.

ping will only test a maximum of nine hops. Therefore, any address you are testing that is more than nine router hops away (even if it is fully functional) will produce a Destination Unreachable response.

We will discuss hops further as they relate to routing protocols in later chapters.

Another powerful troubleshooting weapon in the IP arsenal is traceroute. traceroute works similarly to ping, even though traceroute supplies more information to the user.

traceroute

Whereas ping can only test for the existence of end nodes, traceroute can be used to further diagnose any connectivity problems between them. As you discovered, ping can successfully determine whether an end system responds to ICMP echoes. However, it does little to explain why a particular node does not respond.

traceroute is another IP-related tool that uses ICMP packets to test for end node connectivity. traceroute not only sends echo packets from the target address; it sends echoes from every device that it traverses to reach the destination address.

```
Router>trace 10.16.4.153

Type escape sequence to abort.
Tracing the route to 10.16.4.153
1 Router.testnode.com (10.16.4.199) 62 msec 82 msec 78 msec
2 RouterB.testnode.com (10.16.4.189) 80 msec 99 msec 117 msec
3 RouterC.testnode.com (10.16.4.177)100 msec 110 msec 124 msec
```

Notice that at the end of each reply are the times it took to receive the echo from the particular device. As you can see, the default number of packets traceroute sends is three (as opposed to the five sent by ping).

If you have a PC and a connection to the Internet, you most likely have access to both ping and traceroute. For example, if you are working from a Microsoft Windows environment and are connected to the Internet, try running ping www.marzdesign.com from the command prompt. Next try using tracert www.marzdesign.com and compare the outputs.

ICMP tools help you on a daily basis, even if you do not work with routers. These tools are especially useful when working with larger routing environments.

Troubleshooting larger networks can be very difficult given the number of paths and hops data can traverse at any one point. Tools such as `ping` let you quickly evaluate potential routing problems and locate areas in your networks where issues might occur.

Summary

In routing environments, IP is configured on each interface of a router. Each interface must have an address corresponding to the network on which it resides.

`ping` and `traceroute` are two popular ICMP tools used to diagnose networks. Each one sends echo packet statistics to and from specific destinations. These echo packets are used to pinpoint "dark" areas in your networks where information may be lost. The `ping` utility helps identify hosts that are not communicating, while `traceroute` returns the path used to reach specific destinations.

Q&A

Q In the IP configuration examples, IP addresses were assigned to a specific interface. However, the static routes related to those addresses were not. Why?

A The interfaces were assigned specific addresses to identify them on the networks within which they reside. The static routes were not assigned a specific interface because they affect the router as a whole.

Q Using `traceroute`, why would you want to know the path information used to get to a specific destination?

A In dynamic routing environments it can be nearly impossible to predict which path a particular packet will take. In a situation where problems occur in large dynamic environments, knowing the probable path of a packet of data can make a big difference in solving the issue.

Quiz

1. What protocol (in the TCP/IP stack) supplies `ping` and `traceroute` with their functionality?

2. Which tool offers a glimpse at the specific route a piece of data traveled to reach a destination?

3. What are the two different types of routes that can exist on a router?

Answers

1. ICMP
2. `traceroute`
3. static and dynamic

HOUR 10

Understanding Segmented Networks

This lesson takes you into the realm of network design. Working with routers entails not only configuring the routers and ensuring that they are maintained correctly, but also placing the routers in the most effective places on the network.

This chapter deals with routing IP data between segmented networks. However, it does not discuss routing protocols. Understanding routing requires knowledge of both routed and routing protocols. This lesson introduces IP routing, and later lessons cover routing protocols such as Routing Information Protocol (RIP).

The remainder of this book jumps right into some of the most prevalent topics and technologies that router users face. This lesson focuses on segmented networks, which are often a thorn in the side of many networking and routing professionals. Segmented networks have complexities and intricacies that make them truly difficult to work with.

Mastering segmented networks requires you to expand your understanding of IP and IP routing. To this point, we have only discussed such topics in a *flat* environment—that is, an environment that is fairly static and consists of one path spanning two networks. If you have worked with computer networks before, you know that the majority of companies that use routers do not use flat environments.

The most common type of LAN configuration today is the IP segmented environment. In segmented environments, IP networks are subnetted to create dozens of smaller IP networks. Each of these subnets is linked back to the main network and to the other subnets. This can create a confusing array of paths and addressing schemes that can be daunting to even the most seasoned professional.

Hour 8, "Introducing IP," quickly covers the binary process to creating an IP subnet and deriving a subnet mask from it. This lesson expands on those concepts and shows the physical side of network subnetting, as well as more concepts to help you segment your own environments.

Learning the Basics of Subnetting

So far in this book, all we have discussed about subnetting is the fact that bits of the IP address are borrowed from the host portion and given to the network portion. You have learned that although this increases the number of networks you can address, it decreases the number of hosts that are possible. There are many valid reasons for subnetting an IP network. One of the biggest reasons is to make better use of the ever-dwindling supply of IP addresses.

The current IPv4 (IP version 4) addressing scheme is finite and usable addresses are becoming more scarce. Since the advent of the dot-com age, the static pool of IP addresses has been running out quickly. Network administrators, routing engineers, and ISPs need to conserve the few addresses they have.

IPv4 is the most widely used version of IP today, but IPv6 (IP version 6) is still on the horizon. IPv6 offers a greater range of addresses and should carry us further into the future of computing.

A Word on IPv6

Many of the major operating system developers, including Microsoft, Novell, and various UNIX and Linux developers have software available to adapt current systems to the IPv6 standard. However, full implementation may still be years off. A lot of work is necessary to convert legacy systems to the new standard, and the technology, time, and money to make such upgrades possible is beyond the operational scope of many corporations.

To understand how subnetting is used in a networking environment, let's look at a sample network.

Subnetting IP Networks

When a network is designed and created, the administrator must formulate a functional IP addressing scheme. The network administrator needs to weigh several factors when trying to establish an adequate number of IP addresses to meet the needs of the environment. Every device that will communicate on the network needs an address, from the PCs to the servers to the routers. Therefore, a great deal of planning and foresight are required to ensure that the environment is properly addressed.

Designers devote a lot of time to devising a functional and feasible IP addressing scheme for their networks. You should take some time out to work on a sample IP network. This short exercise will give you an idea of the time, preparation, and effort needed to plan a functional IP network. Try to draw out a network that

- Uses the network IP address 10.0.0.0 and subnet mask 255.0.0.0.
- Uses two servers and at least 13 clients.
- Features connectivity devices, such as hubs, that are placed where necessary to preserve the flow of data.

A *hub* is a piece of equipment that connects multiple networked devices. Hubs are used to interconnect computers in simple networks; they do not require IP addresses to function.

An *IP addressing scheme* is a group of IP addresses (both network and host addresses) that are assigned to and used within a single operating environment. An IP addressing scheme can consist of one class of addresses or several addresses from multiple classes. Either way, the term *IP addressing scheme* describes the relationship between the IP protocol and a networked environment as a whole.

For example, one network may use the IP addressing scheme of 10.0.0.0 subnet 255.0.0.0. Another equally valid IP addressing scheme could subnet the address 10.0.0.0 to create multiple networks within the environment.

Figure 10.1 illustrates a proposed network environment for the fictitious company FooCorp. This environment defines the geographic locations and estimated staffing requirements of the network. Our imaginary administrator Dave can use this information to roughly estimate the number of IP addresses needed to meet the proposed requirements.

FIGURE **10.1**

FooCorp's network environment.

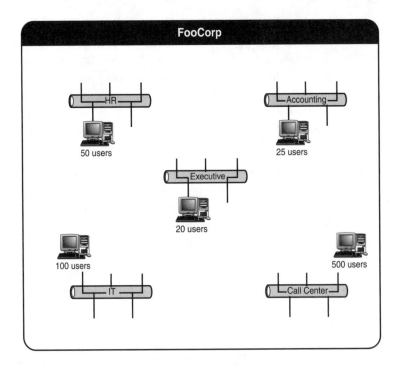

Using the numbers in Figure 10.1, Dave sees a requirement of 695 IP addresses. In addition to this number of addresses, the business needs to add addresses that can be reserved for future expansion (that is, for new employees or equipment). Dave and the business unit agree that FooCorp's IP addressing scheme should include at least 750 host addresses and one network address.

To meet this requirement, a Class B IP license is required. Class B IP licenses are capable of accommodating 65,534 hosts. That might seem like overkill on a network that requires only 750 addresses, but remember that a Class C license supports only 254 hosts. Therefore, the business unit purchases a Class B license and prepares to build the new network.

The demand for IP licenses has been growing over the past few years. Because of this overwhelming demand, it is unlikely today that an entity of 750 people would be assigned an entire Class B license. In all likelihood, the business in this example would be assigned a subnet of an ISP's Class B license. However, to fully illustrate the process of subnetting, we need to assume FooCorp has been granted the entire license.

The Class B license that is assigned to the business is 135.55.0.0, with a subnet mask of 255.255.0.0. Keep in mind that this license allows for one network (135.55) and 65,534 hosts (1.1 through 254.254). Dave applies the new addresses to the proposed network by assigning each device an IP address from the Class B license. Figure 10.2 illustrates this new networking environment.

FIGURE 10.2

FooCorp's network environment IP addressing scheme.

10

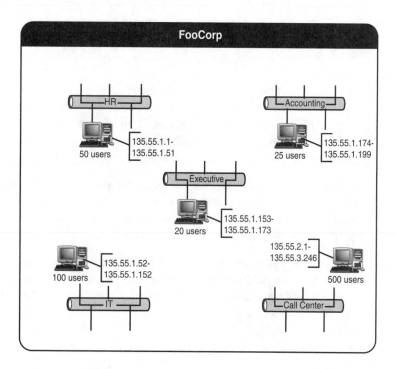

When creating the IP addressing scheme, Dave treated the entire environment as a single entity (which it technically is) and assigned different host addresses based on PC location. The PCs in the HR department were assigned the host addresses 1.1 through 1.51; the IT department PCs were assigned the addresses 1.52 through 1.152, and so on. However, this may not have been the most efficient way to distribute the addresses. While the solution presented in Figure 10.2 is functional, this network might be better served by subnetting.

For example, if FooCorp were to add a new office or acquire a smaller entity, there would be no network addresses left to assign because the only network address, 135.55, is in use. Because any new networks added to the environment would need to be addressed before they can participate in the environment, no new expansion is allowed under the current IP addressing scheme. Therefore, Dave needs a way to create more network addresses while still having enough host addresses to assign throughout the environment. The Class B license needs to be subnetted.

Subnetting a Class B license results in the creation of multiple networks. By dividing the single network address 135.55 into multiple network addresses (for example, 135.55.4, 135.55.8, and 135.55.12), you can use one address for the current network and keep the others for future use. This will keep the environment as scalable as possible.

> The term *scalable* is used to define a network that can expand (or shrink) and still be as functional as the original environment.

However, subnetting an IP network address does have a downside. When you create more network addresses for an environment, you decrease the number of hosts that can be assigned to each of the networks. For many entities, the need for networks outweighs the minimal loss in the number of hosts. Let's examine how FooCorp's network (Figure 10.1 and Figure 10.2) can be subnetted to maximize its use of IP addresses.

Because subnetting increases the number of network addresses available to the IP addressing scheme, you need to forecast how many networks the company could need in the future, while still maintaining an adequate number of hosts. Dave already knows that FooCorp needs at least 1 network and 695 hosts.

Next, you need to figure out how many bits of the IP address need to be passed from the host to the network. You need to assign the correct number of bits to the network portion of the IP address in order to provide an adequate number of networks. Table 10.1 illustrates how many networks and hosts are available for each bit that is passed.

TABLE 10.1   The Number of Networks Available via Subnetting

Number of Bits	Binary Address	Number of Networks	Number of Hosts per Network
2	11000000.00000000	2	16,382
3	11100000.00000000	6	8,190
4	11110000.00000000	14	4,094

Table 10.1 Continued

Number of Bits	Binary Address	Number of Networks	Number of Hosts per Network
5	11111000.00000000	30	2,046
6	11111100.00000000	62	1,022
7	11111110.00000000	126	510

Dave chooses to pass 6 bits from the hosts to the network, so FooCorp can possibly use 62 network addresses, with 1,022 hosts for each. That would be more than enough to keep the environment addressed and working properly.

Now that Dave has determined how many bits to use for the correct number of network and host addresses, he needs to assign those addresses to the network. The first step to assigning the new addresses is to figure out what the usable network addresses are and what their related subnet masks are. There is a formula for determining the network addresses of subnetted networks:

```
256-subnet mask[es]first network address
```

For example, if you wanted to know the first network address for the subnetted IP address 10.135.0.0 with a subnet mask of 255.255.128.0, the equation would look like this:

```
256-128[es]128
```

Therefore, your first network address is 10.135.128.0, with a subnet mask of 255.255.128.0.

All subsequent addresses are determined by adding the first address to itself, until you reach the subnet mask. This might sound complicated, but it will make sense after you see it in action. The first variable in the equation is the subnet mask. Therefore, you must determine what the mask for the new IP addressing scheme is going to be.

The subnet mask remains constant throughout the IP addressing scheme. That is, even though we have subnetted an IP address into multiple networks, all those networks will share a common subnet mask. This will be the thread that ties these networks together. This rule holds true for any IP addressing scheme you are subnetting.

To figure out the subnet mask, you simply convert your IP address to binary format. Then, change the digits representing the network portion of your address to all 1s (the host portion should be represented by 0s). This provides you with a common subnet mask to use across the environment. Table 10.2 illustrates various subnet masks that are available for Class B addresses.

TABLE 10.2   Examples of Class B Subnet Masks

Number of Bits	Binary Mask	Subnet Mask
1	11111111.11111111.10000000.00000000	255.255.128.0
2	11111111.11111111.11000000.00000000	255.255.192.0
3	11111111.11111111.11100000.00000000	255.255.224.0
4	11111111.11111111.11110000.00000000	255.255.240.0
5	11111111.11111111.11111000.00000000	255.255.248.0
6	11111111.11111111.11111100.00000000	255.255.252.0
7	11111111.11111111.11111110.00000000	255.255.254.0

According to Table 10.2, the subnet mask that Dave chooses for FooCorp (the example from Figure 10.1) should be 255.255.252.0. This is the mask for a Class B network where 6 bits have been passed from the host to the network.

Now that Dave has determined the subnet mask, he can plug that value into the formula presented earlier and find out what the network addresses are.

Dave can plug the subnet mask value 255.255.252.0 into the equation for determining the first network address in his new subnet:

```
256-252 = 4
```

By using this formula, Dave determines that the first addressable network will be 135.55.4.0, with a subnet mask of 255.255.252.0. Using this network address, Dave can begin to readdress the FooCorp's network (Figure 10.2). The first 1,022 addresses of the 135.55.4.0 network are 135.55.1.1 through 135.55.7.254. Figure 10.3 shows the sample network with the assigned subnet addresses.

Compare the network in Figure 10.2 with the one in Figure 10.3. Whereas the design in Figure 10.2 uses only one network address and wastes roughly 64,000 host addresses, the new design uses 1 of 63 networks and has only roughly 300 spare hosts. This is a much more efficient design, and it is much more router-friendly.

After the network is complete, the business expands to a second office. The new network needs to be addressed by using the same IP addressing scheme as the first. Finally, a router should be placed between the two networks to establish connectivity. Figure 10.4 illustrates this new network setup.

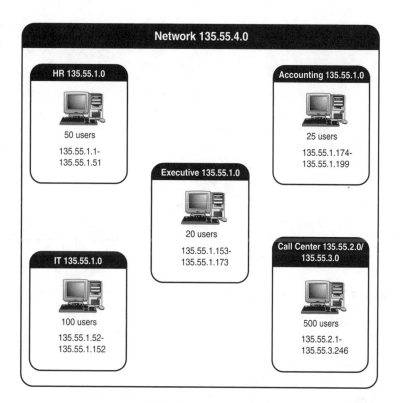

FIGURE 10.3

A sample network with subnetted address information.

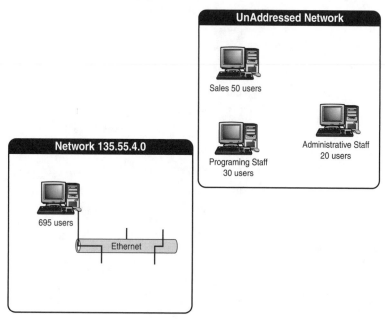

FIGURE 10.4

A second network to be subnetted.

10

Remember that this is the formula the administrator used to determine the first subnetwork address (135.55.4.0):

256-252 = 4

To get the remaining network addresses that can be used under the subnet mask of 255.255.252.0, add the first network address to itself. Therefore, taking the difference of the equation and adding it to itself (that is, 4 + 4 = 8) yields the second network address (135.55.8.0). This second network has all the same characteristics of the first. That is, the second network allows for 1,022 hosts and uses the subnet mask 255.255.252.0.

You can repeat this process of adding the first network address to itself (to produce the second address) until you assign all the subnet mask addresses. All the available networks can be determined this way. Table 10.3 shows the available remaining networks for the Class B subnet in this example.

TABLE 10.3   Remaining Subnet Network Addresses for 255.255.252.0

Subnet Mask	Subnet Networks	Start host range	End host range
255.255.252.0	135.55.4.0	135.55.4.1	135.55.7.254
	135.55.8.0	135.55.8.1	135.55.11.254
	135.55.12.0	135.55.12.1	135.55.15.254
	135.55.16.0	135.55.16.1	135.55.19.254
	135.55.20.0	135.55.20.1	135.55.23.254
	135.55.24.0	135.55.24.1	135.55.27.254
	135.55.28.0	135.55.28.1	135.55.31.254
	135.55.32.0	135.55.32.1	135.55.35.254
	135.55.36.0	135.55.36.1	135.55.39.254
	135.55.40.0	135.55.40.1	135.55.43.254
	135.55.44.0	135.55.44.1	135.55.47.254
	135.55.48.0	135.55.48.1	135.55.51.254
	135.55.52.0	135.55.52.1	135.55.55.254
	135.55.56.0	135.55.56.1	135.55.59.254
	135.55.60.0	135.55.60.1	135.55.63.254
	135.55.64.0	135.55.64.1	135.55.67.254
	135.55.68.0	135.55.68.1	135.55.71.254
	135.55.72.0	135.55.72.1	135.55.75.254

TABLE 10.3 Continued

Subnet Mask	Subnet Networks	Start host range	End host range
	135.55.76.0	135.55.76.1	135.55.79.254
	135.55.80.0	135.55.80.1	135.55.83.254
	135.55.84.0	135.55.84.1	135.55.87.254
	135.55.88.0	135.55.88.1	135.55.91.254
	135.55.92.0	135.55.92.1	135.55.95.254
	135.55.96.0	135.55.96.1	135.55.99.254
	135.55.100.0	135.55.100.1	135.55.103.254
	135.55.104.0	135.55.104.1	135.55.107.254
	135.55.108.0	135.55.108.1	135.55.111.254
	135.55.112.0	135.55.112.1	135.55.115.254
	135.55.116.0	135.55.116.1	135.55.119.254
	135.55.120.0	135.55.120.1	135.55.123.254
	135.55.124.0	135.55.124.1	135.55.127.254
	135.55.128.0	135.55.128.1	135.55.131.254
	135.55.132.0	135.55.132.1	135.55.135.254
	135.55.136.0	135.55.136.1	135.55.139.254
	135.55.140.0	135.55.140.1	135.55.143.254
	135.55.144.0	135.55.144.1	135.55.147.254
	135.55.148.0	135.55.148.1	135.55.151.254
	135.55.152.0	135.55.152.1	135.55.155.254
	135.55.156.0	135.55.156.1	135.55.159.254
	135.55.160.0	135.55.160.1	135.55.163.254
	135.55.164.0	135.55.164.1	135.55.167.254
	135.55.168.0	135.55.168.1	135.55.171.254
	135.55.172.0	135.55.172.1	135.55.175.254
	135.55.176.0	135.55.176.1	135.55.179.254
	135.55.180.0	135.55.180.1	135.55.183.254
	135.55.184.0	135.55.184.1	135.55.187.254
	135.55.188.0	135.55.188.1	135.55.191.254
	135.55.192.0	135.55.192.1	135.55.195.254
	135.55.196.0	135.55.196.1	135.55.199.254
	135.55.200.0	135.55.200.1	135.55.203.254

10

TABLE 10.3 Continued

Subnet Mask	Subnet Networks	Start host range	End host range
	135.55.204.0	135.55.204.1	135.55.207.254
	135.55.208.0	135.55.208.1	135.55.211.254
	135.55.212.0	135.55.212.1	135.55.215.254
	135.55.216.0	135.55.216.1	135.55.219.254
	135.55.220.0	135.55.220.1	135.55.223.254
	135.55.224.0	135.55.224.1	135.55.227.254
	135.55.228.0	135.55.228.1	135.55.231.254
	135.55.232.0	135.55.232.1	135.55.235.254
	135.55.236.0	135.55.236.1	135.55.239.254
	135.55.240.0	135.55.240.1	135.55.243.254
	135.55.244.0	135.55.244.1	135.55.247.254
	135.55.248.0	135.55.248.1	135.55.251.254
	135.55.252.0	135.55.252.1	135.55.255.254

Although any network address from Table 10.3 can be assigned to the new network in the sample environment, Dave chooses 135.55.8.0. The new addresses from the 8.0 network can then be assigned to the environment. Following the same process used for the first network, the new addresses are assigned by corporate function. For example, Sales is assigned addresses 135.55.5.1 through 135.55.5.51. Figure 10.5 illustrates the fully addressed environment.

The two networks in the environment lack one important feature—the ability to communicate. Because they are addressed as two separate networks, the two networks cannot exchange data with one another. To facilitate the movement of data, the administrator needs to place a router in a position where it can serve both portions of the environment.

Placing Routers Within Segmented Environments

When you place a router between segmented networks, you need to consider several factors. A router that has just been placed in an environment, without regard for the surrounding architecture, will not function efficiently. You need to pay careful attention to elements such as network traffic and the number of available interfaces. Here are some of the factors you need to consider when placing a router:

FIGURE 10.5

A fully addressed two-network subnetted environment.

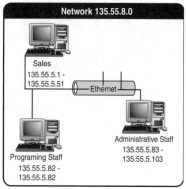

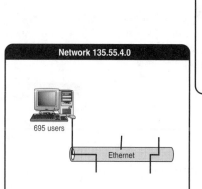

- You need to keep track of the available interfaces on the router. Most routers have two LAN interfaces. Whereas one router can span two networks, three networks might require up to three routers to configure the paths you need.

- You should place the router where the busiest parts of the network will be served the best. For example, you might want to have a separate router for the busiest part of a network, even if you are routing between only two networks.

- If you are connecting critical network segments, you should place the routers in such a way that you can build redundant links.

- You should physically locate routers in common areas, close to the other communications devices. This helps during expansions, especially where the Internet is involved.

- You should keep in mind your routing protocol as you place routers. Certain routing protocols require that you place routers in certain locations or not exceed specific limitations. For example, if you use RIP, you cannot reach networks beyond 16 router hops. RIP is covered in Hour 17.

Although you should always consider the routing protocol to be used in your environment, we have not covered any routing protocols to this point in the book. Therefore, in this lesson, we'll consider only the other factors when placing routers.

With these factors in mind, the administrator needs to find the best area to place the router. The obvious location is between the two networks, in a geographic location that is close to both. Figure 10.6 illustrates the logical placement of the router in the sample environment.

FIGURE 10.6

A router placed between two networks.

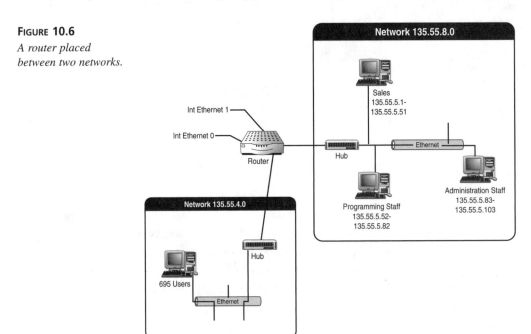

When you're working with only two networks, it might seem obvious that the correct placement of a router would be between the two networks. However, working with routers can be difficult, especially when you are working within environments that contain more than two or three networks. Because the current scenario includes only two networks, Dave can easily place the router between them.

Configuring Static Routes Between Subnets

Static routes (which will be covered in more detail in Hour 13, "Dynamic Versus Static Routing") are a good tool in certain situations. Static routers are rules that dictate how the router should move data from one particular source to a specific target. Three main network situations warrant the use of static IP route definitions:

- The routers in the environment do not use a routing protocol.
- Security elements dictate that only certain traffic may pass through certain routers.
- The routing environment does not change.

> Dynamic routes, which are supported only by routing protocols, are also covered in Hour 13.

10

Configuring static routes between subnets is quite easy. We'll use the Cisco router command interface for the following examples. You can examine the information required by Cisco's `ip route` command to establish these routes. There are several optional parameters that you can enter to perform different tasks. However, the process is fairly straightforward. The command string format for `ip route` is as follows:

```
ip route <Destination Network> <Destination Subnet> <Next Hop | Interface
➡| Null> <Next Hop | perm>
```

Table 10.4 describes the function of each of the `ip route` parameters.

TABLE 10.4   `ip route` Parameters

Parameter	Description
`<Destination Network>`	The IP address of the destination network. That is, the path to which data should be sent.
`<Destination Subnet>`	The subnet mask of the destination network.
`<Next Hop	Interface	Null>`	The next hop, interface, or null parameter can be used here.
	`Next Hop` is the IP address of the router to which packets for the destination network should be forwarded.
	`Interface` is the internal interface to which packets for the destination network should be forwarded.
	`Null` designates that the static route is going to be used with another command. This option is mainly used with routing protocols such as BGP.

TABLE 10.4 Continued

Parameter	Description
`<Next Hop | perm>`	The Next Hop or the perm parameter can be used here.
	Next Hop is optionally used in this position if the interface parameter was used as the previous parameter. It indicates the router to which packets should be sent, as related to the specific interface.
	perm tells the router to write the route to the startup-config file, thus making it a permanent route.

Using Table 10.4 as a guide, let's configure the static routes for a sample network segment. Figure 10.7 illustrates a portion of a large subnetted network.

FIGURE 10.7

A network segment.

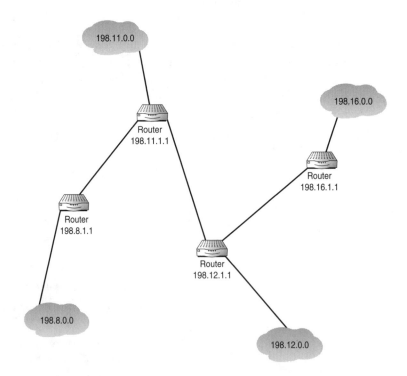

This scenario shows four interconnected routers, each serving a small segment of a large subnetted network. To move data from Network 198.8.0.0 to Network 198.16.0.0, the following route should be configured for Router 198.8.1.1:

```
RouterA(configure)#ip route 198.16.0.0 255.248.0.0 ethernet 1 198.11.1.1 perm
```

The following route should be configured for Router 198.11.1.1:

```
RouterB(configure)#ip route 198.16.0.0 255.248.0.0 ethernet 1 198.12.1.1 perm
```

The following route should be configured for Router 198.12.1.1:

```
RouterC(configure)#ip route 198.16.0.0. 255.248.0.0 ethernet 1 198.13.1.1 perm
```

The following route should be configured for Router 198.16.1.1:

```
RouterD(configure)#ip route 198.16.0.0 255.248.0.0 ethernet 1 perm
```

When you configure these four routes, information is carried from one router to the next, until it reaches its destination. The basic language of the ip route command states that information for Network 198.13.0.0 should exit the router through a specific interface and (in three cases) be passed to another router.

Keep this exercise in mind when you learn about routing protocols such as RIP and OSPF. In Hour 17, "Understanding RIP," and Hour 20, "Exploring OSPF," we will combine routing and routed protocols to create a fully functional environment. It is possible to combine both dynamic routes (through routing protocols) and a static IP router within the same router. Therefore, what you have learned in this lesson will be particularly useful in larger dynamic environments.

You should now have a fairly comprehensive knowledge of IP routing and IP subnetting. Both of these tools will be used in later lessons.

Summary

One of the biggest reasons to subnet a group of networks is to conserve the dwindling supply of IP addresses available. Subnetting is achieved by passing bits from the host portion of an IP address to the network portion. The process of passing bits from the host to the network is performed after converting the IP address into binary form. The binary form of the IP address (after the host bits have been moved) also provides the subnet mask. Every network within a subnetted environment shares the same subnet mask.

You should always place routers in areas that are complementary to the routing protocol you plan to use. Static routing definitions should be used only in areas where the routing protocols are not used, where security dictates that certain data should be sent certain places, or where the routing environment does not change.

Q&A

Q **If the IP address I subnetted was originally a Class B address, why can't I use the subnet mask 255.255.0.0?**

A The subnet mask 255.255.0.0 accommodates only one Class B network. To see this better, you can look at the mask in its binary format. The mask 11111111.11111111.00000000.00000000 has two octets reserved for the host addresses on the network. After an address is subnetted, some of these bits are no longer available. Therefore, the original mask can no longer be used.

Quiz

1. How many networks are available in a Class B address with a subnet mask of 255.255.224.0?

2. How many bits need to be passed to a network in order to accommodate 2,000 hosts?

Answers

1. 14

2. 5

HOUR 11

Using CIDR

The protocol that kick-started the Internet, IP, has also been the greatest hurdle for the Internet. As discussed in Hour 8, "Introduction to IP," IP has a classful, finite addressing system. Over the years, as the Internet has grown in popularity, the number of available IP addresses has dwindled. This disappearing supply of IP addresses fueled the creation of a classless form of IP, known as CIDR (Classless Inter-Domain Routing).

 Classful protocols function by dividing a single address into two distinct parts: one to represent the host and one to represent the network.

In this lesson you will learn how CIDR helps overcome the addressing problems that are common in routed networks in today's classful IP architecture. Learning how CIDR works will greatly improve the proficiency with which you handle IP routed networks. You will commonly find CIDR implemented on IP-based routed environments, and being able to understand how it works will help you recognize the problems that may occur during processes.

Before we can properly discuss how CIDR provides a timely solution to the problems presented by the misuse of classful IP addresses, we must identify the problem presented by the classful form of IP.

The Problem: Classful IP

When the first IP networks were conceived, no one could have imagined their future popularity. Class A IP licenses were issued to enterprises that could have functioned just as well with Class B licenses. Over time, the number of Class A, then Class B, licenses began to reach their limits.

 Recall that IP is divided into five major classes: Class A, Class B, Class C, Class D, and Class E. The most popular of the five are A, B, and C.

A Class B license in essence provides 16,620 network addresses and 1,069,547,520 host addresses (that is, 65,536 host addresses for each of the 1,069,547,520 networks). Even today there are very few entities that could fully utilize a Class B license, but when the original IP licenses were issued, the thought of running out of available numbers was so absurd that no one ever envisioned the possibility. Class B licenses were therefore granted rather liberally, and today we are nearing the end of the available Class B licenses.

As a result of this early inability to recognize the potential problem with classful IP and the arbitrary issuance of licenses, today it is very hard (if not impossible) to obtain a full Class B license. It is as rare now as it was in the early days of networking to find enterprises that need the number of addressable hosts a full public Class B license has to offer. Most typical companies do not require full public addressing on their internal networks.

 Public IP addresses are addresses that have been designated routable on the Internet. *Private IP addresses* are reserved for internal network use and are considered invisible on the Internet.

Many companies follow a basic network blueprint. Masses of workstations are connected to a handful of servers. The entire network is then filtered through one (or maybe two) Internet gateways for providing e-mail and Internet services. Figure 11.1 illustrates this type of network.

FIGURE 11.1

*A basic network blue-
print with an Internet
gateway.*

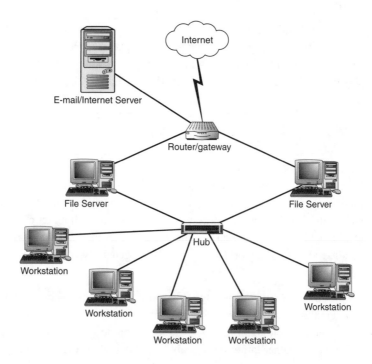

Given such a network blueprint, an average environment would possibly need only two
public IP addresses, which would be assigned to the Internet gateways. The remaining
computers could be assigned private addresses that could be translated via Network
Address Translation (NAT) at the gateway. Although this scenario might seem foreign,
until recently it was the popular solution to dealing with the shortage of IP addresses. It
basically means that only the computers that have direct contact with the Internet are
granted public IP addresses. Table 11.1 lists the available private IP addresses.

TABLE 11.1 Private IP Addresses

IP Class	Private Address Range
Class A	10.0.0.0–10.255.255.255
Class B	172.16.0.0–172.31.255.255
Class C	192.168.0.0–192.168.255.255

The Class B address space of 169.254.0.0–169.254.255.255 has also been reserved for us by Microsoft's Automatic Private IP Addressing (APIPA). APIPA is implemented on many Windows PCs to automatically assign an IP address to PCs configured for DHCP (Dynamic Host Configuration Protocol) when no DHCP server is present.

 NAT is covered in detail in Appendix A, "Using NAT."

However, the use (or misuse) of the current IP situation is only half of the problem. A more pressing issue is that every network that connects to the Internet requires a routing table entry. As the number of networks attached to the Internet continues to grow, the routing tables of the Internet backbone expand to uncontrollable sizes. The routers that handle traffic for the world's major ISPs are generally considered to form the backbone of the Internet.

As the size of a router's routing table grows, two problems occur. The first is an obvious problem that occurs every day in computing. As file sizes (of any type) grow, the memory needed to hold them must grow, too. If you do not expand a router's memory to safely hold a rather large routing table, the table clogs the remaining table and seizes the router.

Normally, the size of a routing table is not as great a concern to administrators as other router maintenance issues. However, some sources indicate that as many as 1,200 new networks are added to the Internet every day. This means that 1,200 new entries are added to every backbone router's routing table. At this rate, it is easy to see how the size of routing tables can get out of hand.

Constantly adding memory to a router for the purpose of holding the routing table can be expensive both in dollars and in revenue lost while the router is offline. Eventually, if a routing table grows beyond a specific size, you hit the limit to the memory a router can accommodate. At that point, you cannot expand any further and must simply purchase a new router.

The second problem routers can experience as a result of expanding routing tables is that the time needed to effectively route information grows with each new table entry. In routers with relatively small routing tables, you should never detect any kind of table-related routing delay. However, when you are dealing with tables the size of those on the Internet's backbone routers, delay becomes an almost crippling factor.

As the routing delay grows, so does the risk of reaching the TTL of all your routable packets. When the router begins to drop packets, the network slowly grinds to a halt. This can cause major disruptions in an environment.

> The TTL of a packet indicates the amount of time a router has to move the packet to its final destination. If the TTL expires, the router assumes that the final destination does not exist, and the packet is dropped.

To control the problems associated with classful IP routing, a solution needed to be developed. Therefore, a classless form of IP routing, known as CIDR, was developed.

The Solution: CIDR

Because the addressing authorities have been running painfully low on large classes of IP addresses and Internet-related routing tables have been growing dangerously large, a way to extend the life of the remaining addresses (and reduce the size of routing tables) has become necessary. The solution is CIDR, with which groups of networks can be super-netted.

11

IP Addressing Authorities

Addressing authorities are organizations that have been charged with the rights to over-see how IP addresses are distributed. While most individuals and private corporations will obtain their IP addresses from their local ISP, the ISPs obtain addresses from the address-ing authorities. These authorities are IANA (Internet Assigned Numbers Authority), ARIN (American Registry for Internet Numbers), APNIC (Asia-Pacific Network Information Center), and RIPE (Réseaux IP Européens).

CIDR allows for the classless routing of IP. This means that many unrelated addresses can be supernetted (thus grouping addresses into one *class* that refers to all the addresses rather than to a small portion of them). When a group of addresses is supernetted, a mask is created to indicate that the individual networks involved belong to one larger super group. For example, if an environment is assigned the two network addresses `215.50.25.0` and `215.50.26.0`, a supernet can be created to combine and relate the two networks for use within the same physical environment.

The binary form of the subnet mask `255.255.255.0` (the Class C mask for both of the assigned network addresses) is `11111111.11111111.11111111.00000000`. Whereas subnetting passes bits from the host portion of the address to add more networks, supernetting passes bits from the network portion to create fewer networks.

If two bits are passed from the network portion to the host portion of the address, the mask will become `11111111.11111111.11111100.00000000`, or `255.255.252.0`. Figure 11.2 illustrates this concept.

FIGURE 11.2
Passing binary bits.

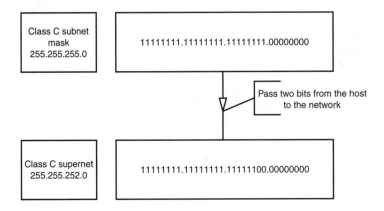

When combined with the network address `215.50.25.0`, this mask tells a router that the two network addresses are included in the supernet. Figure 11.3 illustrates this relationship.

FIGURE 11.3
Two network addresses included in a supernet.

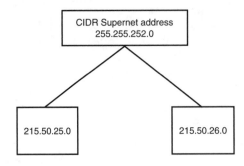

You might be wondering how a router knows that the mask
255.255.252.0 is not a Class B subnet but a Class C supernet. The answer is
actually quite easy. The first octet of the network address is 215. Only Class
C network can begin with 215; therefore, the new mask has to be for a
Class C supernet.

When CIDR is implemented within a large routing environment, only the supernet
address needs to be referenced within the routing table. This dramatically cuts down on
the number of entries within a routing table. For example, rather then having 400 entries
for all the addresses leading to a particular ISP, a routing table might only require two or
three supernet addresses to move all related information to the correct destination.

Supernetting is easier to understand when you look at it in relationship to subnetting.
Therefore, you should practice—on paper—both supernetting and subnetting to get the
hang of it. Figure 11.4 shows a sample network that could benefit from CIDR.

FIGURE 11.4

*A sample network in
need of CIDR.*

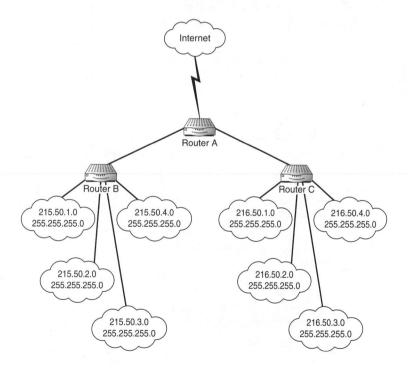

11

Currently the routing table for Router A in Figure 11.4 contains entries for all the networks attached to its child routers. This routing table would look similar to Table 11.2.

TABLE 11.2   Router A's Routing Table

Destination	Next Hop
215.50.1.0 255.255.255.0	Router B
215.50.2.0 255.255.255.0	Router B
215.50.3.0 255.255.255.0	Router B
215.50.4.0 255.255.255.0	Router B
216.50.1.0 255.255.255.0	Router C
216.50.2.0 255.255.255.0	Router C
216.50.3.0 255.255.255.0	Router C
216.50.4.0 255.255.255.0	Router C

Even for this small sample network, the routing table is quite large (most ISPs will have routing tables thousands of times this size). The administrator can implement CIDR to simplify the routing situation. By passing two bits from the host to the network (on the networks attached to both Router B and Router C), you can produce a supernet address that can be used to address all of the networks. Figure 11.5 shows this environment after CIDR.

After moving two binary bits from the host portion of the IP addresses to the network portion, we create the supernet mask address of 255.255.252.0. In Figure 11.5, the address 215.50.0.0 255.255.252.0 can now be used to represent all of the networks attached to Router B, while 216.50.0.0 255.255.252.0 can be used for Router C.

With CIDR implemented, the routing table for Router A would be much shorter. Table 11.3 represents Router A's new routing table.

TABLE 11.3   Router A's Routing Table After CIDR

Destination	Next Hop
215.50.0.0 255.255.252.0	Router B
216.50.0.0 255.255.252.0	Router C

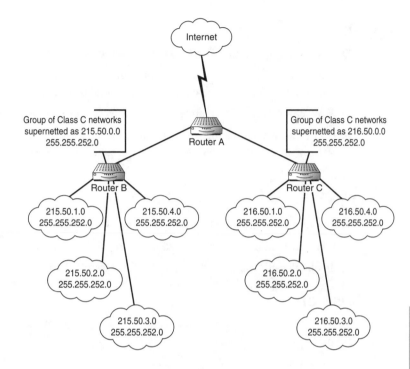

FIGURE 11.5

Sample environment after CIDR.

CIDR is not meant for every network. That is, most networks, large or small, will never require the services of CIDR. You will find that the networks that do require CIDR will be very large environments with multiple networks connected to each other. CIDR can be implemented with great success in situations where all of the child networks are addressed using different IP addressing schemes, and one main network location serves as the Internet gateway for all of the child networks.

Summary

IP is a classful protocol. As such, its addresses are divided into a network and a host portion. This configuration causes problems because the address scheme is finite, and the number of routing table entries required to represent one entity can grow uncontrollably if it's not carefully monitored.

CIDR offers a solution to these problems: With it you can supernet addresses. You can group together under one supernet many of the addresses used by one environment. You can then reference these addresses with a single routing table entry.

Q&A

Q **Should I implement CIDR on every routed network?**

A Not necessarily. CIDR is effective only in a network that connects to the Internet and utilizes an IP scheme comprised of several different address fragments.

Q **How can I determine a supernetted address from a subnetted address?**

A You need to examine the first octet of the IP address. For example, the address `215.50.0.0 255.255.252.0` is a Class C supernet address because `215` is within the Class C IP address space.

Quiz

1. If a router's routing table grows too large, what problems can occur?

2. Classful IP addresses are divided into two parts. What are they?

3. In classless IP routing, which part of the classful IP address is consolidated?

Answers

1. The router can seize, the router can take too long to process packets, or the packet's TTL can expire.

2. Network and host

3. The network address

HOUR 12

Understanding IPX Basics

This lessons introduces a routed protocol that is not as popular as IP, but just as important. Used mainly by networks running Novell NetWare, *Internetwork Packet Exchange (IPX)* is a crucial technology for anyone working with the Novell operating system. This lesson both introduces you to IPX and demonstrates some sample router code that illustrates how IPX is configured on routers.

> The sample configuration code from this hour is taken from a Cisco router. However, if you are working with other brands of routers, you will notice that they all require much of the same information.

Because you should have a basic understanding of IP at this point, this lesson compares IPX to IP. We will discuss topics and concepts that help you learn IPX in a way that will also enhance your knowledge of IP.

This lesson will give you an understanding of the IPX routed protocol, thus expanding your routing knowledge to the two most popular routed protocols in use today.

Introducing IPX

Until the release of Novell NetWare version 5, IPX was the default protocol run on Novell networks. IPX is a routed protocol that's similar in design to IP: Both IP and IPX operate on the network layer of the OSI model and are connectionless.

Because IPX is a Layer 3 connectionless protocol, routers have no trouble working with it in a routed environment. Most routers can freely and easily route IP, IPX, or both in the same network (even the same router).

There are a few differences between IP and IPX. The first, and most obvious, has to do with the formats of the IPX addresses and IP addresses. IPX addresses, which are hexadecimal rather than dotted decimal, might appear foreign to anyone who has never worked with IPX before.

Although IPX is not the most common routed protocol, it is used in a number of production environments. The most common routed environment which you will find is when you are connecting IPX networks and IP networks. For example, if an IPX environment needed a connection to the Internet, the IPX packets would need to be converted to IP. Most routers can easily handle this type of project.

Let's begin this lesson by taking a look at the IPX address format and how IPX addresses are assigned.

IPX Addressing

IP addresses are similar to IPX addresses in that one address is used to identify both the network and the host. Whereas IP addresses have a variable-length network designator (that is, the network portion of the address can be represented by one, two, or three octets, depending on class), IPX addresses are a set length. An IPX address always follows the convention *network.host* (with the host portion of the address represented as six dotted values; for example, `1234ABCD.12.34.56.78.9A.BC`).

Hexadecimal Digits

Before exploring IPX addressing any further, you should be familiar with the hexadecimal number format. The number format we commonly use is known as base 10. Base 10 uses 10 digits to represent all the numeric values (0–9). Hexadecimal numbering consists of 16 digits (0, 1, 2, 3, 4, 5, 6, 7, 8, 9, A, B, C, D, E, and F). Therefore, the letter D in hexadecimal numbering represents the number 13.

In base 10 each "place" for a digit is a factor of 10 (for example, 10 is 1 in the tenths place, and 100 is 1 in the 10×10 or hundredths place). Each numeric place in hexadecimal numbering is a factor of 16. For example, the hexadecimal number

---

> 0x1A4
>
> is a 4 in the 0s place, a 10 in the 16ths place, and a 1 in the 256ths place. (The notation 0x is always placed before a hexadecimal value to distinguish it from other values). Translated into base 10, 0x1A4 is 420, or 4+(10×16)+(1×256).

An IPX address is a 32-bit network address followed by a 48-bit host address. This makes IPX addresses a total of 80 bits (that is, 10 bytes) long, which is substantially larger than 4-byte IP addresses. Having a larger address size gives IPX addresses an advantage; many more IPX addresses than IP addresses are available for device addressing. Figure 12.1 illustrates a typical IPX address.

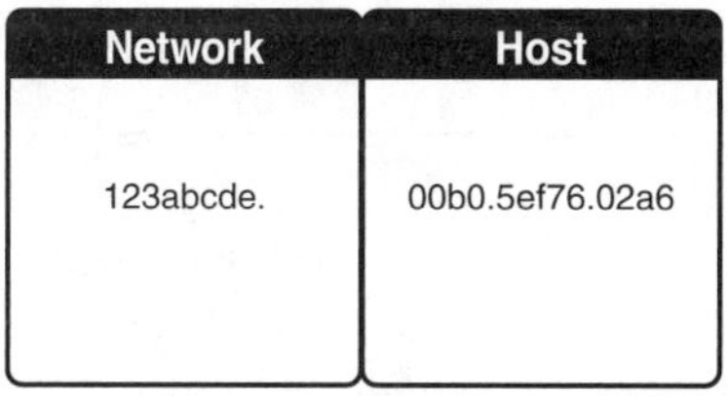

FIGURE 12.1
An IPX address.

Network	Host
123abcde.	00b0.5ef76.02a6

The network portion of an IPX address is an administrator-assigned value: The network administrator assigns a unique number as an IPX network address for the entire environment. The number assigned as the network address must be four bytes, or eight hexadecimal digits. It should remain constant throughout the routing environment, to eliminate router confusion.

If you have never worked in hexadecimal, it might take some getting use to. Hexadecimal digits represent a base of 16; remember that decimal is base 10 and binary is base 2. The hexadecimal digits, along with their binary and decimal equivalents, are shown in Table 12.1.

TABLE 12.1 Hexadecimal Digits

Hexadecimal	Binary	Decimal
0	0	0
1	1	1
2	10	2
3	11	3
4	100	4

12

TABLE 12.1 Continued

Hexadecimal	Binary	Decimal
5	101	5
6	110	6
7	111	7
8	1000	8
9	1001	9
A	1010	10
B	1011	11
C	1100	12
D	1101	13
E	1110	14
F	1111	15

If an administrator assigns a network address that is shorter than eight hexadecimal digits in length, the router automatically prepends the digit 0 to the address, until it is eight digits long. For example, if an administrator assigns the network address 76b8 to an IPX environment, within its internal memory, the router converts that address to 0x000076b8.

The host portion of an IPX address, on the other hand, is not as arbitrary as the network address. One feature of IPX that sets it apart from protocols such as IP is that the host address is set dynamically. That is, unless otherwise specified by an administrator, IPX dynamically assigns the host portion of the address for the specific device it is residing on. IPX will obtain the host address from the data link layer of the OSI model.

 Referring back to Hour 2 "Examining the Relationship Between Protocols and the OSI model," The Media Access Control (MAC) sub-layer of the data link layer in the OSI model is responsible for the physical addressing of all devices.

The host address for an IPX device is generally composed of the device's MAC (Media Access Control) address. Because MAC addresses are globally unique by design, there is always an IPX address available for any given host. As long as the protocol has access to read the device's network interface card, the MAC address becomes the host address.

A device's MAC address is a number assigned to every network device (including NICs) at the time the device is manufactured. Every network device manufacturer is assigned a group of numbers (from a central control agency) that it can give to the products it manufactures. This address is a permanent number that corresponds to the data link layer of the OSI model.

> Although some manufacturers allow you to change the MAC addresses of their devices, most MAC addresses are permanent.

Its uniqueness and global availability makes a MAC address particularly attractive as a protocol address. Every device has one, and every device's MAC address should be unique. Thus, because IPX uses the MAC address as the host address, there are theoretically an endless number of IPX addresses to be used.

Let's examine how IPX, IPX routing, and IPX addresses are configured on a Cisco router.

Sample IPX Router Configuration

In Hour 9, "Discovering IP Router Configurations," we discussed how IP is configured on a Cisco router. You learned that as a routed protocol, IP is installed on a particular interface. IPX follows the same approach. IPX is installed and configured per interface rather than per router. This allows routers to run different protocols on different interfaces. You should find that configuring IPX is not much different than configuring IP.

Most IPX routers require three key pieces of information for a router to utilize it as a protocol: the host and the network addresses (which together comprise the IPX address) and the IPX encapsulation type. Using the `ipx network` command on a Cisco router allows you to specify the network address, the host address, and the encapsulation type for the interface. The syntax of the `ipx network` is as follows:

```
#ipx network <network number> encapsulation <encapsulation type>
```

> Notice that the `ipx network` command lacks parameters for specifying the interface's host address. Because IPX dynamically assigns the host address based on the MAC address, you do not need to initiate it. However, the host address is not assigned until you complete the `ipx network` command. Therefore, using the `ipx network` command indicates to the Cisco router that it can assign a host address to the device.

12

> There are more commands for configuring IPX on Cisco routers than are listed here. For a more in-depth look at configuring Cisco routers, try *Sams Teach Yourself Cisco Routers in 21 Days.*

The first parameter for the `ipx network` command is the network address. This number should be configured on all IPX devices that are in the same environment. The network address indicates to the router where it should (or should not) route packets.

As you know, the network address can be no longer than eight hexadecimal digits, and if you specify an address that is shorter than eight digits, the router adds 0s to the front of it until it is eight digits long. In the example in this chapter, we will be using the network address 1234, which the Cisco router will store internally as 0x00001234.

Immediately following the network address is the `encapsulation` keyword. The `encapsulation` keyword is used to indicate the particular encapsulation method to be used by the router for IPX packets.

The encapsulation type is a very important part of IPX configuration. As you have learned in previous lessons, when a piece of data is passed to a protocol, the protocol encapsulates it. When the protocol encapsulates the data, it adds fields to indicate key pieces of information about that data. However, depending on the type of network in use, the encapsulation may need some changes in order to be routed correctly. The next section explains IPX encapsulation in detail.

IPX Encapsulation

One very important element in the configuration of IPX on a router is the selection of an IPX encapsulation method. The encapsulation method specifies the types of fields and their order in the protocol's header. However, you need to keep in mind some important factors when choosing the encapsulation method for IPX. First, the same encapsulation method must be shared across an environment. That is, every device that comes in contact with the IPX packets must use the same type of encapsulation. Second, the encapsulation must correspond with the type of network that is in place (for example, Ethernet encapsulation for Ethernet networks).

Table 12.2 illustrates the options for IPX encapsulation that are available on Cisco routers. The encapsulation methods are grouped together by network type. You should first select the correct network type for your network, then choose a corresponding encapsulation type.

TABLE 12.2   IPX Encapsulation Types

Network Type	Encapsulation Type
Ethernet	Ethernet II, Ethernet 802.3, Ethernet 802.2, Ethernet 802.2 SNAP
FDDI	FDDI 802.2 LLC, FDDI 802.2 LLC SNAP, FDDI raw
Token Ring	Token Ring, Token Ring SNAP

> The model of router that you use on your network must match the network type. In other words, if you have a Cisco 1605R (an Ethernet router), you must choose the Ethernet network type and one of its encapsulation methods.

The type of network you run is the main factor in determining which IPX encapsulation type to use. Each of the four encapsulation types for Ethernet represents a different version of the network. The type of encapsulation you choose determines what fields are attached to the IPX packet because different fields are readable by different network types. The following section examines the fields that are associated with the Ethernet encapsulation methods.

Ethernet Encapsulation Fields

As discussed in the preceding section, during the process of configuring IPX routing, you must select an encapsulation method that corresponds to the type of network in use. You can understand the process of encapsulation by examining the fields associated with the four different versions of Ethernet: Ethernet II, Ethernet 802.3, Ethernet 802.2, and Ethernet 802.2 SNAP.

12

> Although encapsulation types are available for Token Ring and FDDI network types, we will not discuss them in detail. For more information about these encapsulation types, you can search the Cisco Connection Online Web site at www.cisco.com.

The most popular type of Ethernet encapsulation for IPX is Ethernet version II, known as Ethernet II. Ethernet II is the latest incarnation of the widely used network standard. Therefore, if you configure IPX for an Ethernet environment, you will most likely use Ethernet II encapsulation.

The following output shows the Cisco keywords associated with the different methods of Ethernet encapsulation:

```
Router(config)#int e0
Router(config-if)#ipx network 1234 encap ?
  arpa         IPX Ethernet_II
  hdlc         HDLC on serial links
  novell-ether IPX Ethernet_802.3
  novell-fddi  IPX FDDI RAW
  sap          IEEE 802.2 on Ethernet, FDDI, Token Ring
  snap         IEEE 802.2 SNAP on Ethernet, Token Ring, and FDDI
```

Notice that the Cisco keyword for Ethernet II encapsulation is arpa. Therefore, to configure the interface e0 for Ethernet II encapsulation, you should use the following command:

```
Router(config-if)#ipx network 1234 encapsulation arpa
Router(config-if)#^Z
```

This command configures the current Cisco interface for IPX network 0x00001234 and an encapsulation of Ethernet II. Choosing the Ethernet II encapsulation method adds certain fields to the IPX packet that are required for packet routing across the specified network type. Figure 12.2 shows an IPX header with Ethernet II encapsulation.

FIGURE 12.2
Ethernet II field headers.

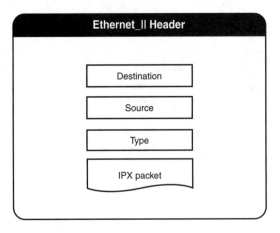

For comparison, the field headers added to an IPX packet during Ethernet SNAP encapsulation are shown in Figure 12.3.

FIGURE 12.3

Ethernet SNAP field headers.

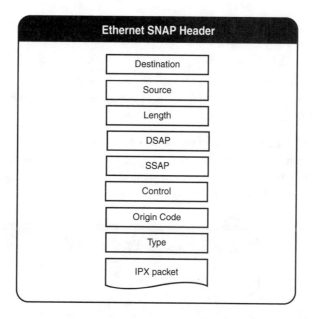

There are two important things to keep in mind when dealing with IPX encapsulation types. First, the encapsulation type chosen does not change the structure of the IPX packet itself. Rather, it adds fields to the header of the packet. When a device receives the encapsulated IPX packet, it simply strips off the encapsulation fields and leaves the IPX packet intact. For example, Figure 12.4 illustrates a typical IPX packet header. Included in this figure are the fields of the IPX packet header as they would appear prior to any encapsulation.

12

When an IPX packet is sent from a device, it is encapsulated for the particular type of network being used. Figure 12.5 shows the same packet as in Figure 12.4, after encapsulation.

Notice that the original IPX fields are still intact. When the target device receives the packet, it strips off the fields that were added during encapsulation. What is left is the original IPX packet.

The second thing to keep in mind when dealing with IPX encapsulation is that different encapsulation methods can be defined on the same interface. Therefore, if one router is connected to multiple networks (each using a different network type), you can assign the correct encapsulation as needed.

FIGURE **12.4**

An typical IPX packet header.

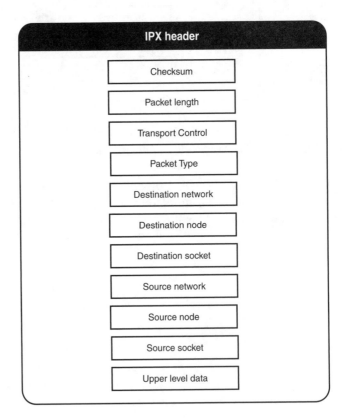

FIGURE 12.5

An typical IPX packet after encapsulation.

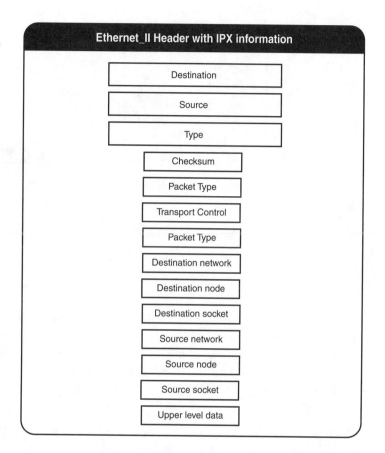

Ethernet_II Header with IPX information

- Destination
- Source
- Type
- Checksum
- Packet Type
- Transport Control
- Packet Type
- Destination network
- Destination node
- Destination socket
- Source network
- Source node
- Source socket
- Upper level data

12

IPX Routing

IPX routing can be more complicated than IP routing. One factor that affects this is the multiple encapsulation types that can be found within IPX networks. Although one encapsulation type must be shared throughout a network, one router can span multiple networks—and those different networks can use different encapsulation types. Therefore, to successfully operate within any given IPX environment, a particular router might need to be configured for multiple IPX encapsulation types.

To illustrate this, we will look at a typical network scenario featuring a basic IPX environment that consists of two Ethernet networks, each with a different network type. Figure 12.6 illustrates this IPX environment.

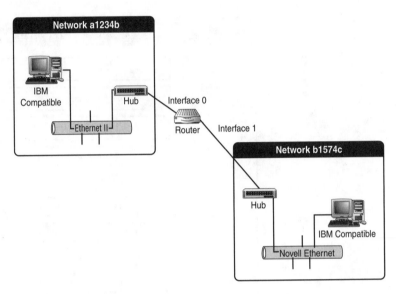

FIGURE 12.6
A two-network IPX environment.

Within this environment is a standard Ethernet II IPX network. This network can be thought of as the new portion of the networking environment. The network was set up to expand the capabilities of the second network within the environment. The second network is an older Novell Ethernet environment that uses the IEEE 802.3 architecture. In this example, a router can be placed between the two networks to allow information to flow from one network to the other.

This hour has given you a general overview of the routed protocol IPX. While we touched lightly on protocol routing in this and previous hours, we will now be moving to more in-depth discussions of the routing process.

Summary

Like IP, IPX is a network layer routed protocol. Routers utilize the services of protocols such as IPX to encapsulate and carry data during the routing process. IPX protocol addresses are represented in hexadecimal format.

Numbers written in hexadecimal format (also known as base 16) are denoted by the 0x notation before the hexadecimal value.

The host portion of an IPX address is composed of the data link layer MAC address of the host device. The uniqueness of the MAC address ensures that two devices will not have the same protocol address. The network portion of the address is shared by every device within the same networking environment. The encapsulation type must be common throughout a network as well, and it must match the network type being used.

Q&A

Q Why are there different encapsulation types for IPX?

A IPX was a proprietary protocol for a long time. Therefore, when Novell changed header formation or protocol versions, it affected only Novell's own devices. As the technology spread, a method was needed to distinguish between the different network types.

Q Why are IPX addresses displayed in hexadecimal format?

A Given the size of the addresses (128 bits), the address is actually smaller when displayed in hexadecimal. Another reason for using hexadecimal format is that the existing MAC address (used in the host portion of the IPX address) is already expressed as a hexadecimal value.

Quiz

1. What is the most common encapsulation type used on Ethernet networks today?
2. How many hexadecimal digits are in an IPX network address?

Answers

1. Ethernet II
2. Eight

12

Hour **13**

Dynamic Versus Static Routing

The routing process can take on two different characteristics: It can be either dynamic or static. In static routing, the process of selecting routes for data to be forwarded across a network is statically defined within the router's memory. In dynamic routing, routing occurs dynamically as a function of the router's own internal calculations.

Each type of routing has a purpose and a place in most environments. Knowing which type of routing is best in any given situation will help you to both understand the routing process and design better routed networks. Most routing environments do not follow a standard template. You must decide for yourself, based on your experience, what type of routing to implement on your network. Whatever you choose, every path and option must be carefully planned to ensure that the correct information is sent to the correct destinations.

However, planning routes is only the first step to implementing a routing type. After you have decided where your network is to be routed, you need to determine how the data will flow through it. Will you define predetermined paths for the router to follow, or will you let the router decide which path is best? Each of these options has advantages and disadvantages.

Static routing allows you to define a set path for data to travel from Point A to Point B. The router cannot stray from this definition at all. Static routes are good in situations where security is a deciding factor in the transportation of information. These defined routes can also work well if you only want the router to use a specific line (for bandwidth reasons). The major problem with using static routes is that if the route becomes unavailable (for example, the line goes down, the device on the other end fails), all the information traveling across that link stops. The router does not have the option of choosing an alternative route. Figure 13.1 illustrates a statically routed environment.

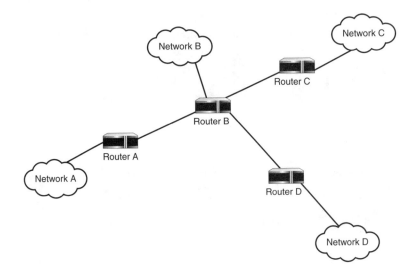

Within the environment in Figure 13.1, if a PC in Network A tries to send information to a PC in Network D, there is only one path the data can take. Traveling from Network A to Network D, information can only move through Router A to Router B and on to Router D. This is an example of a static environment.

Dynamic routing is the default routing type for most routers. When most people think of the routing process, they envision dynamic routing. No predefined paths exist within a dynamically routed environment. The router is free to make decisions, based on environmental factors, about which route is best at the time. Dynamic routes are best suited to large environments where variables constantly change. One of the problems with dynamic routing is that is can be extremely hard to troubleshoot. Because there is not a set definition about what path the router will select for sending data, you cannot predict where a packet is at any given time. This can make the tracking for problems very difficult.

Many routers can handle a mix of dynamic and static routing, allowing you to use dynamic routing for the majority of the network and use static routing only where it is really needed. On the surface, these mixed routing environments offer the best of both worlds—the reliability of dynamic routing with the predictability of static routing. But, as you'll learn in this lesson, mixed networks have some unique problems.

Dynamic Routing Basics

The most common type of routing found on networks today is dynamic routing. From an engineering and administrative point of view, dynamic routing is far easier to work with than static routing. The router, rather than the user, handles the establishment and maintenance of dynamic routes. However, dynamic routing does have its downside. As you will find in this section, troubleshooting dynamic routing issues can be a daunting task.

Some may argue that the purpose of a router is to dynamically move information from one network to another. Although a few low-end routers provide support for only statically defined routers, most routers are dynamic at heart.

 Some manufacturers produce low-end, inexpensive, specialized routers that only move data via static routes. These routers have no support for dynamic routing, and are not widely used.

As you have learned, a router takes a packet from a network, the routing algorithm processes data contained within that packet to determine the best path on which to send it, and the router forwards the packet along that path. (Routing algorithms are discussed in Hour 3, "Routing Algorithms.") This is the basic premise of dynamic routing. The router is left to calculate (for itself) the best path from one network to another. All network route decision making is passed to the routing algorithm.

The routing algorithm is a driving force behind dynamic routing. The algorithm takes in data from each individual network packet and uses it to calculate a custom path that is best for that packet, given the circumstances. This process is repeated for every packet that is moved through the router. Therefore, it is possible that each packet will take a different route, even if they're going to the same destination.

13

> A *packet* is a piece of data, not an entire transmission of information. Every time one PC communicates with another, millions of packets can be involved. In dynamic routing, each of these packets could take a different path to the same destination.

As mentioned previously, dynamic routing is best suited for large environments or environments where the physical layouts and structures are constantly changing. The network in Figure 13.2 is a good example of an environment that is suitable for dynamic routing.

FIGURE 13.2

A good environment for dynamic routing.

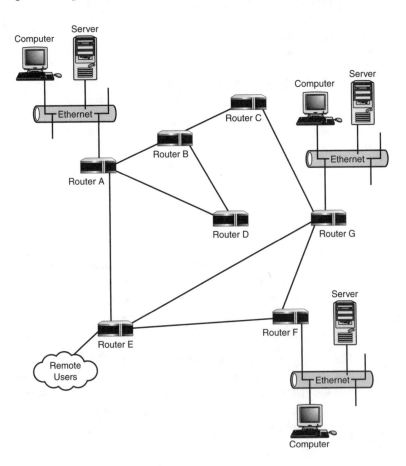

Using the network in Figure 13.2, try to trace the path data would take from Router A to Router F. You should find that there are 10 different possibilities:

- A-B-C-G-F
- A-B-D-C-G-F
- A-D-B-C-G-F
- A-D-C-G-F
- A-B-C-G-E-F
- A-B-D-C-G-E-F
- A-D-B-C-G-E-F
- A-D-C-G-E-F
- A-E-G-F
- A-E-F

Of the 10 possible routes, 6 include the use of Router E. In Figure 13.2, Router E is attached to a group of remote users. These users may not always be available, and therefore it should not be assumed that their router will be available. This means you have the added complication of determining when Router E is (and is not) available and work that into your routing plans.

As you discover more about routing, you will find other situations that can complicate routing plans. Some common complications are

- Routers running incompatible routing protocols
- Inconsistent lines (links that commonly "black out")
- Router load (routers handling more traffic than expected)

Through experience, you will learn how to recognize, plan for, and work around these potential routing hazards.

13

This example shows that dynamic routing environments can be extremely complicated. A packet leaving the Ethernet network that is linked to Router A, bound for the network linked to Router F, is sent to Router A. Router A then passes the packet to the routing algorithm, which, taking into account the current state of the environment, makes a decision about which path to Router F is best. Figure 13.3 illustrates this process.

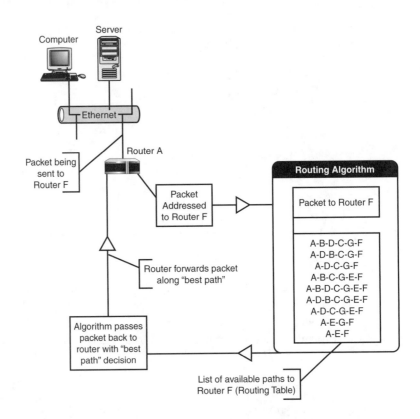

FIGURE 13.3

The dynamic route selection process.

One reason dynamic path selection is so desirable is that it can adapt to changes in the environment. For example, say that Router A chooses the path A-B-C-G-E-F as the best path between Router A and Router F. After transmitting some data, Router A discovers that the link between Router B and Router C has failed. Normally, this would mean that data would no longer be able to flow from Router A to Router F. However, given that this is a dynamically routed environment, Router A can update its path information within the routing table to move data along the route A-D-C-G-E-F. This updated path bypasses the failed link between Router B and Router C, while still getting information to the proper recipients.

In many cases, dynamic routing changes are undetected by network users. Routers will automatically detect changes in the environment and adjust accordingly, with no effect on the workload of the network. However, in some situations problems can occur.

Dynamic environments are susceptible to problems such as routing loops, where a router cannot adjust to a change in the network and sends packets on a continuous loop to itself. Problems such as routing loops are discussed in the next section.

Notice that nowhere in the previous scenario is there mention of any administrator intervention. The most desirable feature of dynamically routed environments is that the routers make all the critical decisions. For an administrator, this can mean the difference between having a life and working 150 hours a week monitoring routers. In large environments especially, dynamic routing is at the heart of maintaining a smooth network.

Problems with Dynamic Routing

Although dynamic routing helps you tame very large environments that can change without warning, it can also lead to some headaches. The large networks that dynamic routing was designed to work with are also the source of its biggest shortcoming. Because there is no user intervention required to determine the path of data between two networks, troubleshooting routing problems in dynamic routing environments can be extremely difficult.

For example, say you have a large dynamically routed environment, such as the one in Figure 13.4. During the course of normal business, you find that traffic from Network A is having trouble reaching Network D. You need to find out where on the network the data is encountering problems.

FIGURE 13.4

A large dynamic routing environment that requires troubleshooting.

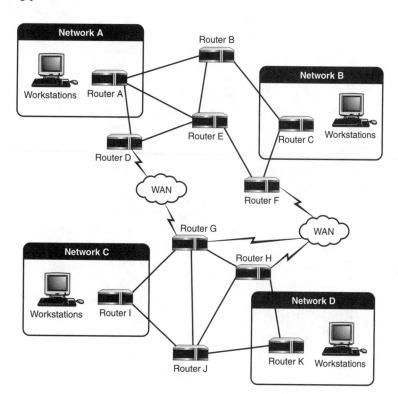

13

Information can travel more than 70 possible routes from Network A to Network D at any one time. Because you do not know which of the many paths data is taking at any given moment, troubleshooting a routing problem can be extremely difficult. To compound the issue, every path from Network A to Network D must traverse a WAN link. In addition, five different WAN links can be used in any path, and each of these links could be causing problems as well.

When you're troubleshooting dynamic routing environments, it is best to approach problems in a very methodical manner. Rather than try to determine where the problem is, it might be better to eliminate potential routes based on where problems are not being experienced. In the example shown in Figure 13.4, just knowing that both Network B and Network C are not having problems allows you to eliminate about 33 routes from the troubleshooting list. You can focus your attention on using tools such as protocol analyzers and ICMP to pinpoint where your issues are.

Using `traceroute` you can send multiple packets through the environment, mapping the path each one takes. This should give you a good idea of the approximate path used by Router A to get to Router F. You can then examine the characteristics of each router in the path. Items such as traffic load, metric value, and link stability are all factors that can pose potential problems on networks. Using tools specific to each brand of router, you can examine and adjust the amount of traffic a router can handle, or the metric value assigned to the router.

Adjusting the traffic load will ensure that routers with less memory take on less traffic. This prevents bottlenecks in the router. Adjusting the metric value will keep routers that are less reliable from being chosen by other routers as the best path.

Another potential problem with dynamic routing environments is security. Many highly sensitive enterprises (for example, the U.S. government, large corporations, businesses that are involved in e-commerce) need to be very aware of the security of their routed environments. One potential security hole with dynamic routing is the use of routing updates.

Dynamic routers use *routing updates* to alert each other when the environment changes. As routing updates can be specific to the routing protocol being used, a more in-depth discussion of these updates occurs in the hours pertaining to the specific routing protocols. These routing updates enable dynamic routing. If a link between two routers fails, the routers send out an update to all the other routers in the environment, stating that the link is down. The remaining routers can then correct their routing tables to establish new routes for sending data.

The security problem arises because each update contains the address of every router involved. If a cracker obtains a routing update (which is not that difficult to do), that person will in essence have the addresses of routers they can then attempt to exploit. For this reason, many high-security facilities rely on routing methods such as static routing that do not involve routing updates.

Routing updates can be easily obtained by listening to the network at any given interval. Most routing updates are sent to a broadcast address, to ensure that every router gets them. Any packet that is sent to a broadcast address is received by every device on the network. If a cracker knows what to do with that packet, security can be compromised.

If routing updates are not monitored, other network-related problems can occur. Because updates are broadcast to every address on a network, the number of updates sent by one router can be in the hundreds. If you multiply this by each router (for every number of seconds in the update interval), you can see that a massive burst of traffic floods the network at one time. These bursts of traffic can cause congestion problems on links that don't have sufficient bandwidth.

> The update interval is the amount of time between each routing update. This amount of time can be adjusted per router, but it is usually set to 30 seconds.

Static Routing Basics

Static routing is much more labor-intensive than dynamic routing. It involves a lot more configuration and maintenance than dynamic routing. For this reason, many users elect to implement static routing on relatively small, inert environments.

Static routing uses predetermined routes between networks. For example, Figure 13.5 illustrates a simple network that is a good environment for static routing. In this network, you could easily configure paths that routers could use to forward data.

In Figure 13.5 you could define a static route on Router A that says, "any information from Network A to Network B should be sent from Router A to Router B to Router C." After that, any information from Network A that is being sent to Network B will follow that exact path.

13

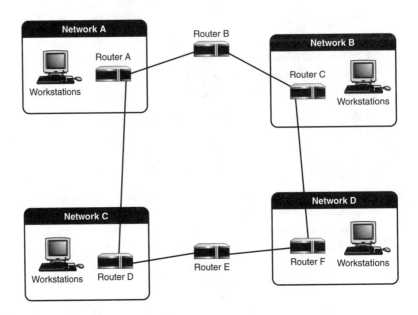

FIGURE 13.5

A good environment for static routing.

You need to configure static routes for every possible path, on every router. Just because you have defined the route A-B-C on a network with three routers does not mean that information from C will get back to A. On Router C, you need to define the route C-B-A, and on Router B you will require routes going to both Router A and Router C in order to have full communication.

You must be careful to fully plan each static routing environment before implementing the network. You should spend a good deal of pre-implementation time on paper, defining every possible route that could occur. This will cut down on the amount of time needed to configure the routers during implementation. Even in relatively small environments, static routes can be overwhelming.

One major advantage of static routing is the speed with which information can be moved. In dynamic routing, the routing algorithm needs to calculate the best path for every packet that comes in, and this process can be very processor intensive. Because a static router does not rely on a routing algorithm for routing decisions, the processor is freed up to move more data. This means that statically routed environments can move data at a much quicker rate than dynamic environments.

Another advantage of static routing environments is the lack of routing updates. Because static routers do not send out routing updates, there is less chance of traffic congestion on the networks. This means that you have a better representation of the line bandwidth used by your data. Not sending routing updates gives static routing a security advantage as well. Because the routers have no need to update each other's paths, no one can intercept any routing updates between the routers. This gives crackers less chance to learn the addresses of potential targets. Many security-sensitive organizations rely on static routing to keep their routers secure.

Problems with Static Routing

The major problem with static routing is the lack of redundancy. When you define static routes on a router, you are telling that router not to forward packets along any paths besides the ones you define. This becomes a problem when a link in a static route fails.

If a link in a static environment fails, the routers have no alternative paths on which to forward data. Therefore, all data that uses the failed link stops moving. The paths remain down until the link is restored, or a new static route that doesn't use the failed link is defined. A routing administrator needs to define new static routes on the routers that utilized the affected link.

This problem can be compounded if more than one router use the failed link. Whereas dynamic routing would automatically determine a new route, static routing is at the mercy of the administrator. If the administrator cannot create a new route in an acceptable time-frame, the network users will experience longer periods of downtime. (Remember, with the link down, all packets bound for any destination on that link will be lost.)

Links can become unavailable for many reasons, including electromagnetic interference, communications outages, advanced cable age, and accidental damage.

13

Many companies use a combination of dynamic and static routing to achieve a balanced environment. You will often find dynamic routing in use on the general network areas, with static links imposed in high-security portions of the networks. Figure 13.6 illustrates a network using a combination of dynamic and static routing.

FIGURE **13.6**

A mixed routing environment.

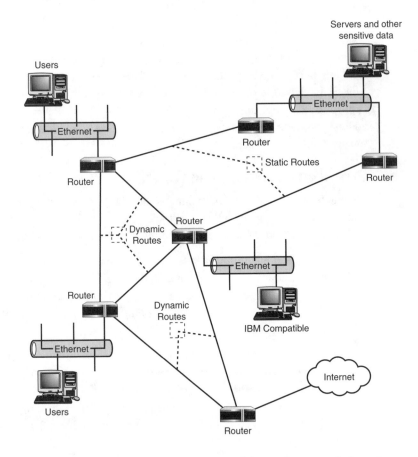

Within the environment pictured in Figure 13.6, the core of the environment (where the general population of users is) is designated with dynamic routes. These routes connect the users with each other and the Internet.

The more sensitive data in the environment is kept in a network that is separated by static routes. These static routes ensure that no routers will create routing updates that disclose the network location of the data. In Figure 13.6, two static routes have been defined to provide a level of fault tolerance—if one router fails, information can be supplied through the second.

Users should never notice whether their information is being sent along dynamic or static routes—the entire process should appear transparent to them.

Summary

Routing environments can be divided into two categories: dynamic and static. Each category has advantages and disadvantages. Dynamic routing allows routers to use routing algorithms to decide which path is best for forwarding data. Static routing relies on the network administrator to define routes between all possible points on the network.

Dynamic routing utilizes routing updates to exchange route information between routers. These updates contain portions of the routing table (a list of addresses and locations of the networks within the environment). These routing updates can pose both security and congestion problems.

Static routing, while posing less of a security or traffic problem, has its own issues. Routers using static routes are unable to recover from link outages without administrative assistance.

Q&A

Q Can all routers support both static and dynamic routing?

A No. Some specialized routers (primarily for small office and home office use) use only static routing. However, you will generally know before you purchase one of these routers that it is meant for static use only.

Q Can both dynamic and static routes be defined on the same router?

A Yes, a single router can utilize both static and dynamic routing. Referring back to Figure 13.6, two of the routers in the figure participate in both the dynamic and static environments. This allows the two environments to be connected.

Quiz

1. Which routing type is best used in large environments?
2. True or false: Static routers have less congestion problems than dynamic routers.
3. Which type of routing uses the least processing time?

Answers

1. Dynamic routing
2. True. Due to their lack of routing updates, they generate less traffic.
3. Static routing

13

HOUR 14

Understanding ISDN

In this lesson you will examine your first WAN protocol: *Integrated Services Digital Network (ISDN)*. ISDN does not run directly on a router in the same way that IP or IPX would. Rather, ISDN runs within the public switched network (PSN), which connects routed networks. Your router serves as a gateway or translation device to present data that originates on your network to the ISDN devices in the PSN. In other words, your routers will not actually run the ISDN protocol (that functionality is reserved for switches). Your routers will be installed with instructions to translate common network packets into the ISDN format. These packets are then forwarded to the ISDN switches.

To perform the function of forwarding packets to and from ISDN areas, your router must understand ISDN architecture and read ISDN packets.

The History of ISDN

ISDN was the first of the consumer-grade broadband products to be widely accepted. Before the advent of ISDN, 56Kbps modems, operating with standard phone lines, were the fastest connection devices available. Offering digital transmission rates over public lines, ISDN caught on very quickly with the general public. However, shortly before ISDN became popular as an in-home technology, it was a burgeoning enterprise technology.

One of the main advantages of ISDN was the price. ISDN offered an inexpensive solution for businesses that needed a high-bandwidth connection between sites but did not need the 100% availability of—or as much bandwidth as—a T1 line. ISDN links could be configured as dial-in pay-per-use links; in other words, you paid for what you used. This feature made ISDN a popular choice for WAN links that were not used as often as links that required a great deal of up-time.

Another feature of ISDN that made it popular is that it was designed to work over existing telephone networks. This allowed ISDN users to utilize their existing telephony infrastructure. Users could also receive telephone calls while using ISDN services on the same line.

Although few businesses still utilize ISDN connections as their main form of WAN connectivity, many SOHO (small office, home office) users still take advantage of the inexpensive access to bandwidth and existing cabling.

Home offices make good use of the pay-per-use nature of ISDN because many home users do not stay connected around the clock. When the home user powers off a PC, he or she stops paying for the WAN services provided by ISDN.

One of the most popular uses for ISDN is connecting a home office to a central location, thus providing true WAN connectivity. This is the type of scenario where you are most likely to find ISDN today. This is also the most common ISDN scenario where a router would be utilized.

ISDN Technology

The term *ISDN* describes a service used to connect WAN links, and it also refers to the suite of protocols used to move data across these links. In the first part of this section you will learn about ISDN as a connection service. Later we will discuss ISDN as a protocol suite.

As a connection service, ISDN is a digital supply link that consists of multiple channels. The most common type of ISDN is known as *Basic Rate Interface (BRI)*. Most routers can work with BRI ISDN. Another form of ISDN is *Primary Rate Interface (PRI)*. While BRI is more common among home users, PRI is mainlys utilized by business consumers.

Before you attempt to configure ISDN on your router, you should confirm that the hardware for ISDN is present.

BRI ISDN consists of three channels: two B (bearer) channels, and one D (delta) channel. Table 14.1 shows the bandwidth of a BRI ISDN line.

TABLE 14.1 Bandwidth of BRI Channels

Type of Channel	Number of Channels in a BRI ISDN Line	Bandwidth
B	2	64Kbps each
D	1	16Kbps

The two B channels are the digital data links. These two channels are used to transfer data from point to point. The D channel is used for signaling. The combination of these channels creates a line that is capable of transmission speeds up to 144Kbps. However, because the D channel is only used for signaling, the actual bandwidth is 128k.

PRI ISDNs consists of 23 B channels and 1 D channel. Because a PRI line can handle more B channels, the D channel is slightly larger to accommodate the greater signaling needs. A PRI D channel is typically 64Kbs, giving a PRI line a total capacity of 1536Kbs (1472Kbs with the D channel).

Because ISDN is a pay-per-use service, most ISDN connections are made through a piece of hardware known as a *dialer*. Similarly to a standard telephone line, ISDN modems are required to dial a central location to initiate service. Most routers include the functionality of an ISDN modem with the ISDN hardware, whether it is onboard or part of an upgrade.

Before you can configure ISDN services on a router, you need to obtain several key pieces of information from the ISDN host. Information such as the ISDN switch type, the service profile identification (SPID), the encapsulation method, and the protocol address is needed to properly configure ISDN services on a router. However, before we can discuss what this information means, or where you obtain it, we need to explore ISDN terminology and functionality.

ISDN Terminology

Like most technologies, ISDN has its own set of phrases and abbreviations. This section illustrates some of the key terminology used regarding ISDN.

14

The following ISDN terms are used to refer to different types of equipment that may appear on an ISDN network, on either the host side or the client side:

- Type 1 terminal equipment (TE1)—TE1 is a piece of ISDN equipment that contains all the components necessary for ISDN communication. Thanks to the TE1, there is no need for a separate modem for the router to interface with.

- Type 2 terminal equipment (TE2)—TE2 uses a separate terminal adapter and modem to establish an ISDN connection.

- Terminal adapter (TA)—A TA is an ISDN interface that does not have modem capabilities. Therefore, a router that is equipped with a TA requires the services of a separate ISDN modem to establish an ISDN connection.

- Type 1 network termination equipment (NT1)—NT1 is used to terminate the ISDN signal at an end system, such as a multiplexer.

- Type 2 network termination equipment (NT2)—NT2 is used to switch or transport the ISDN signal to the TE1.

ISDN equipment types are commonly referred to by their abbreviations, especially in technical literature. Although most routers are equipped with TE1, you should be aware that some scenarios might require the use of TE2 interfaces. Check your specific router's documentation to see what (if any) ISDN terminal equipment is supplied. Figure 14.1 illustrates the different types of ISDN equipment.

Figure 14.1

ISDN equipment.

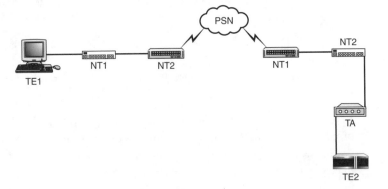

While knowing the terminology used for ISDN services is important, it is only half of the picture. As ISDN is also a suite of protocols, there is a whole set of terms used to refer to each protocol within the ISDN suite.

ISDN Protocol Terminology

ISDN is also a suite of protocols that define operations and functionality on the first four layers of the OSI model (that is, the transport, network, data link, and physical layers). These ISDN protocols can be grouped into the following categories for easy reference:

- Q—Q protocols deal with the signaling of points in an ISDN connection. Generally, these protocols work on the D channel of a BRI link.

- E—The ISDN protocols in the E category are used to carry data across the existing telephone network. These protocols serve as standard network protocols in much the same way that IP and IPX serve as protocols.

- I—The protocols in the I category are used only to define certain concepts related to ISDN. These protocols also define the terms and services of ISDN connectivity in a WAN environment.

One of the major Q protocols in ISDN is *Link Access Protocol D (LAPD)*. Functioning like many of the protocols discussed thus far, LAPD encapsulates ISDN data for transmission. Whereas ISDN functions at the network layer of the OSI model (because it is a routed protocol), LAPD functions at the data link layer. One of the major functions of LAPD is to maintain the addressing capabilities of ISDN as they relate to the devices that are involved in the ISDN environment, including routers on the business end and public telephone equipment on the WAN side.

> This text is geared to cover network layer protocols. However, you should be aware of the role LAPD plays in the ISDN suite. Because LAPD provides the mechanism for establishing connections, the functionality of LAPD is critical to the operation of ISDN.

Several terms describe specific points, called *reference points,* in an ISDN network. Reference points are used to describe the locations within an ISDN loop that are related to a specific function of the ISDN protocol. For example, a reference point can be used to describe the link between two pieces of ISDN-specific equipment. The following are the ISDN reference points:

- R—The link between a TA and any other unrelated equipment
- T—The link between an NT1 and an NT2
- S—The link between an end system and an NT2
- U—The link between an NT1 and the public network

Figure 14.2 illustrates an ISDN network with the reference points labeled.

14

FIGURE **14.2**
*ISDN reference
points.*

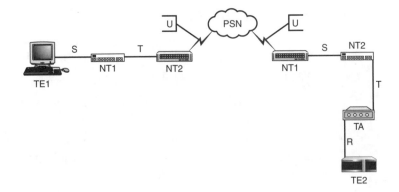

ISDN Functionality

Because ISDN is a WAN protocol, network administrators are responsible for very little of the daily maintenance of ISDN links. However, gaining an understanding of ISDN in its entirety provides insight into the information that routers require when you're preparing for ISDN connections.

To a business, a WAN link should appear as a seamless integration between two geographically separate locations. Figure 14.3 illustrates a business's perceived notion of an ISDN link.

FIGURE **14.3**
*A business's percep-
tion of an ISDN
network.*

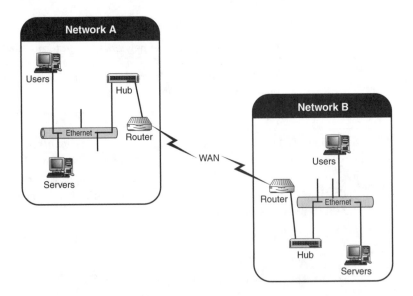

The network illustrated in Figure 14.3 shows the equipment under the responsibility of a typical network engineer in an ISDN environment. When you are configuring a router (or a pair of routers) for ISDN connectivity, this should be your view of the network. The remaining environment that exists between the business and the carrier is the sole responsibility of the host or carrier.

The carrier, who is responsible for the ISDN environment between itself and the business, monitors and maintains the equipment that transports the ISDN signal from each site. Figure 14.4 illustrates the full ISDN environment, from the carrier's perspective.

FIGURE 14.4

A full ISDN environment.

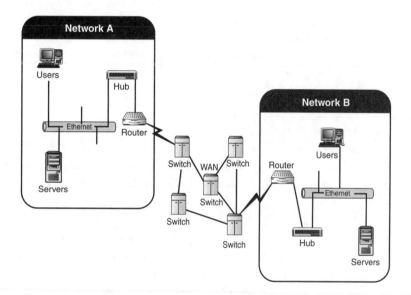

To understand how the environment in Figure 14.4 works, let's trace the path of a data transmission from Network A to Network B.

1. The information originates on Network A, in the form of an IP packet. The IP packet is created and addressed like any other IP packet, with no concern for how to reach the destination.

2. The IP address of the destination, which resides in Network B, is affixed to the packet, which is sent to Router A.

3. Router A compares the destination address of the IP packet with its existing route table. This comparison tells the router that Network B can be reached only through the WAN interface, which is configured for ISDN. The router prepares the IP packet for transportation across the ISDN WAN link.

14

4. The IP packet is framed and encapsulated according to the type of switch the carrier is using. ISDN has been designed to accommodate more than 15 different types of PSNs.

> The term *PSN* refers to the networks of the public telephone companies. Because many PSNs greatly predate the use of ISDN, a standard could not be developed for the PSN. Therefore, ISDN needed to be developed in a way that allowed it to accommodate the various types of PSNs that currently exist.

After the packet has been properly framed, or encapsulated, the router's ISDN interface attempts to open a circuit to the carrier's network. The ISDN interface dials the carrier's network, identifies itself, and passes the ISDN frame(s) to the environment. The PSN is then responsible for ensuring that those frames reach Network B, based on the destination ISDN address.

When the frames reach the router on Network B, the framing fields are stripped off and the data is restored to IP packet form. The IP packets can then be routed to the target system. A router can be configured to convert IP packets (or packets from any other protocol) into frames that are suitable for ISDN transmission.

Configuring ISDN

To this point in the book, when you have configured a router to utilize a specific routed protocol, only basic information has been required. For example, the router might need to know the protocol address assigned to the interface being configured or, in the case of IPX, the encapsulation type might need to be specified. ISDN requires a slightly more involved configuration. With ISDN, you need to configure more information than most routed protocols need in order for the router to operate correctly. In fact, the type of information required by ISDN is similar to that needed by routing protocols. Table 14.2 shows the required information for configuring ISDN.

> You need to obtain some of the information shown in Table 14.2 from your ISDN provider. They will provide you with this information at the time service is established.

TABLE 14.2   Information Required to Configure ISDN

Required Information	Purpose
ISDN switch type	The ISDN switch type tells the router what type of equipment the carrier is using on its network. There are more than 15 types of ISDN switch types (see Table 14.3).
The service profile identification number (SPID)	The SPID is used to identify the type of service to be provided to a certain link. Each ISDN link in a network can have up to two SPIDs.
Encapsulation method	The encapsulation method is used in conjunction with either Frame Relay or X.25.
Protocol address	Because ISDN links route protocol data, they must be configured with an appropriate address.

For the sake of visualization, and because of the level of complexity, the remainder of this section discusses configuring ISDN on Cisco routers.

You can specify the switch type from within the router's configuration mechanism. Most types of routers require that this setting be *global*. That is, it is configured into the router in a way that allows it to be applied to all of the router's interfaces, rather than just one. For Cisco routers, this type of configuration is performed with the *global configuration mode*. Specifying the switch type in global configuration mode indicates that the setting applies to any ISDN interface that may be installed on the router. Table 14.3 shows the switch types for North America. Keep in mind, you will not generally know the type of switch your ISDN provider uses. Therefore, you must obtain the appropriate switch type for your network from your ISDN provider.

It is not important to know the specifics behind using any of the configuration modes on Cisco routers for the examples in this book. However, if you want to know more about using and configuring Cisco routers, try the Cisco Web site at www.cisco.com, or check out *Sams Teach Yourself Cisco Routers in 21 Days* (Sams Publishing).

14

TABLE 14.3 North American Switch Types

Switch Type	Description
basic-5ess	BRI AT&T switch
basic-dms100	BRI DMS-100 switch
basic-ni1	National ISDN-1 switch
primary-4ess	AT&T 4ESS switch (PRI ISDN only)
primary-5ess	AT&T 5ESS switch (PRI ISDN only)
primary-dms100	NT DMS-100 switch (PRI ISDN only)

```
Router(config)#isdn switch-type basic-ni1
```

Next, you need to configure the interface-specific information, including any protocol addresses, SPIDs, and encapsulation methods. The first piece of information we will configure is the SPID:

```
Router(config)#interface bri 0
Router(config-if)#isdn spid 1 123456789
Router(config-if)#isdn spid 2 987654321
Router(config-if)#no shutdown
```

Keep in mind that you may have none, one, or two SPIDs, depending on the service that is being provided to your site. You need to confirm the SPIDs with your carrier. In the preceding configuration examples, we used two SPIDs. If you only have one SPID on your ISDN, you would omit the line

```
Router(config-if)#isdn spid 2 987654321
```

as the 2 after the word spid indicates that this is the second SPID for this ISDN configuration.

Notice that this configuration specifies to the router that we want to configure the interface bri 0. This means that we are configuring the information on the first BRI interface. On most routers, interfaces are numbered starting at 0, rather than 1.

Next, you need to configure the encapsulation method. Your choices for encapsulation are Point-to-Point Protocol (PPP) and High-Level Data Link Control (HDLC). Again, you will need to consult your provider to determine the encapsulation method you need to configure (PPP is the most common). Here's how you configure the encapsulation method:

```
Router(config-if)#encapsulation ppp
```

Finally, you need to configure the routed protocol addresses on the interface that will carry the ISDN data:

```
Router(config-if)#ip address 153.4.16.1 255.255.0.0
```

At this point, you have configured the router's interface to run ISDN. Now, as with the other routed protocols covered so far, you need to establish routes to connect the IP or IPX packets to the ISDN link. For protocols such as IP and IPX, you use static routes to identify the paths to and from the ISDN link.

This step is important because the PSN has no idea what kind of information you plan to send over the ISDN link. Therefore, you must specify to the router that it should forward routed protocol packets to ISDN. The routed protocol is generally IP or IPX.

```
Router(config-if)#dialer map ip 153.4.10.1 name NETWORK_B 234567891
Router(config-if)#dialer-group 1
Router(config-if)#dialer-list 1 list 99
Router(config-if)#access-list 99 permit 153.4.16.0 255.255.0.0 153.4.10.0
255.255.0.0
```

Although this list of commands may seem daunting, it is quite logical if you examine it one line at a time. The first line states that a mapped route is to be configured, and that any ISDN frames are to be forwarded to the IP address 153.4.10.1 (which is presumably not on the local network). This IP address is then related to the name NETWORK_B at the ISDN address 234567891.

The second line creates a dialer group and names it 1. The dialer group acts as a package to hold and refer to the dialer map. The third line creates a link between that dialer group (which has been added to a dialer list) and an IP access list.

> One dialer list can represent many dialer groups.

The last line of the command string creates the IP access list that allows the router to accept packets from network 153.4.16.0 (which is local) and pass them to 153.4.10.0 (which is not local).

These four commands basically state, "Permit this router to take IP packets from network 153.4.16.0 and pass them to network 153.4.10.0 through the ISDN link 234567891 (also known as NETWORK_B)."

14

Summary

ISDN is a WAN protocol that is used to connect geographically separated networks. ISDN exists on the PSN and forwards routed protocol packets from one network to another. ISDN services are generally established in terms of BRI lines. A typical BRI link holds 64Kbps of bandwidth.

When configuring ISDN on a router, you need to know the switch type and the SPID, which are provided by your ISDN carrier. You configure this information into the router in global configuration mode, so that it is recognized by all configured interfaces.

ISDN is a protocol that works hand-in-hand with other, higher-end WAN protocols. The most popular of these protocols are X.25 and Frame Relay.

Q&A

Q Why is ISDN configured on local routers if it only runs on the PSN?

A Even though ISDN as a protocol does not actually run on the router you configure, the router needs to know how to communicate correctly with the ISDN environment. By communicating with the ISDN environment, the router can forward and receive packets through the PSN.

Q Why must static routes be configured between ISDN links?

A When you are configuring two routers on either side of an ISDN link, you must use static routes to connect them because the PSN has no knowledge of your network's topology. Given that the PSN doesn't know the layout of your network, it cannot dynamically move information to or from its routers. Therefore, you need to indicate the exact path ISDN information should use in accessing your network.

Quiz

1. What are the two types of ISDN links?
2. True or false: After an ISDN interface is configured, a routed protocol address needs to be mapped to the ISDN interface.
3. What is the SPID?

Answers

1. BRI and PRI
2. True. The router needs to know what kind of information to send over the link.
3. The service profile identification number, assigned by the ISDN provider to distinguish between ISDN links.

HOUR 15

Learning X.25

This lesson focuses on an important protocol in WAN functionality, X.25. Developed in the 1970s as a suite of protocols for the established ISDN networks of the public switched network (PSN), X.25 has become a strong, proven protocol adaptable to many networks. (X.25 also served as the predecessor of today's Frame Relay.)

 Even though X.25 is a suite of protocols, you will most often see them referred to as "the X.25 protocol". We will cover the major protocols in the suite later in this lesson.

As with most WAN protocols, you are not likely to have many interactions with configuring X.25, which runs on the switches of the PSN. However, you should understand how it works. X.25 networks have two parts: the private network (the company's own network, which you will be working on, commonly referred to as a LAN) and the PSN, which is the carrier side of the network. We will use the terms *carrier* and *private networks* throughout this lesson.

Configuring a router to interface with a WAN protocol and configuring a switch to run a WAN protocol are two very different things. When you configure a router for a WAN protocol (for example, ISDN, Frame Relay, X.25), you are actually configuring the ability for a router's interface to communicate with a device that is running that protocol. The protocol itself does not run on the router.

You will most likely not work directly with X.25, but X.25 introduces several important concepts that apply to most WAN protocols. These concepts specify how protocols establish sessions and maintain connections between systems, and they are common across most WAN protocols. As you will find, though, each protocol has a different way of referring to similar procedures and circumstances. Therefore, although the concepts described in this lesson and in Hour 14, "Understanding ISDN," and Hour 16, "Learning Frame Relay," all sound similar, each protocol has it own terms and functions for dealing with them.

The IEEE and the ITU-T

One central entity is charged with overseeing and maintaining the concepts that make up most protocols. The Institute of Electrical and Electronics Engineers (IEEE) is the governing body that oversees all innovations and developments in the field of protocols.

One protocol that is not in the realm of the IEEE is X.25. X.25 is overseen by the Telecommunication Standards Sector of the International Telecommunication Union (ITU-T). The ITU-T issues all updates and enhancements to X.25.

X.25 has been in use since the mid-1970s. Like most WAN technologies, X.25 started on the PSNs used by the telephone companies. The technology that comprises X.25 predates most WAN technologies by a decade. Therefore, other WAN protocols, such as Frame Relay, are based on the concepts and technologies set forth in X.25.

Some technologies that were introduced in X.25 and are used in other WAN protocols (such as Frame Relay) include *virtual circuits* and *packet framing*. Packet framing is briefly discussed in Hour 16, but we have yet to fully introduce the topic of circuits.

As you learned in Hour 5, "Understanding WAN Protocols," a virtual circuit defines the path that data takes when it moves from one device to another. To ensure that the majority of information being transferred arrives intact, two devices can form circuits between them. The virtual circuits used by X.25 fall into two categories: permanent and switched. Both of these circuit types are described later in this lesson.

Before we discuss the concepts that provide the functionality behind X.25, you need to understand the terminology used in X.25 environments. As you have discovered with every new protocol introduced in this book, each has its own set of terms used to describe conceptually similar elements, including routers, switches, and computers. X.25 is no exception to this rule and has its own terms for network equipment that will be used throughout this lesson.

X.25 Terminology

Many of the terms used in X.25 relate to the equipment used in X.25 environments. The following terms describe the different type of hardware that can be found on an X.25 network:

- Data circuit terminating equipment (DCE)—DCE devices reside on the carrier side of the X.25 network and connect the private network to the X.25 network. These devices include receiving signal modems, switches, and T1 equipment. Because you are working on the private side of the network, you never have to configure or otherwise work directly with DCE.

- Data terminal equipment (DTE)—DTE is the private network equivalent of DCE. DTE devices are the routers and switches that connect the network to the WAN. DTE can also refer to any terminal devices and PCs that interface with DTE or DCE. The majority of an administrator's work with X.25 occurs at the DTE level.

- Packet-switching exchange (PSE)—The PSE is the collection of switches that make up the PSN. These switches are the backbone of the WAN to which you connect. All data movement takes place through the PSE. The switches that form the PSE are the same switches that form the PSN, and are therefore the same switches that form the backbone of the Internet.

- Packet assembler/disassembler (PAD)—A PAD is a device that serves as an intermediary between DTE and DCE. In many cases, you need a secondary device to connect a router to an X.25 network. A PAD provides the services of buffering, packet assembly, and packet disassembly for devices that do not have those capabilities built-in.

These terms describe equipment that can be found on both the PSN and the private side of most X.25 networks. For example, DCE is found on the PSN (that is, carrier) side of the X.25 environment, whereas DTE is located on the private side (that is, your side).

To understand how your routers should interface and interact with an X.25 environment, you need to understand each of these pieces of equipment and how they affect your networks. The following sections explore each of these pieces of hardware and explain where they reside in the flow of data.

15

For the sake of simplifying our discussion of PADs and DTE, all private-side equipment is referred to in this lesson as DTE.

Most routers are designed to perform many tasks. Therefore, a router rarely specializes in any one specific role or duty. Often, when you try to establish a connection to a WAN, you need a secondary device to connect to the router's serial port. A PAD is a device that can do this.

X.25 Concepts and Functions

Knowing what type of equipment you will be dealing with should help you understand the following concepts related to X.25:

- Permanent virtual circuits (PVCs)
- Switched virtual circuits (SVCs)
- Link Access Procedure, Balanced (LAPB)
- Packet Layer Protocol (PLP)

An important feature of X.25 is its ability to utilize virtual circuits. This functionality was carried over to Frame Relay (see Hour 16). These virtual circuits are one of the functions that make X.25 a robust WAN protocol.

The two circuit types used by X.25 are *switched virtual circuits (SVCs)* and *permanent virtual circuits (PVCs)*. The next sections explore the differences between these two circuit types.

PVCs

When electronic data is sent from a PC on a computer network, it is sent out in short bursts. That is, packets are sent out onto the network one at a time. Routers (being dynamic by default) are free to send these individual packets along any path it deems necessary to reach its destination, even if each packet is sent along a different path. However, as the PSN is the same network over which telephone conversations are carried, it wants to deliver all the packets for a specific session over the same path. This not only ensures that the packets arrive in order (something that is not guaranteed on most networks), it means that any protocol utilizing the PSN must be connection-oriented.

Imagine if packets in a telephone conversation were sent in the same way data packets are sent. Every time you spoke a word into the telephone, it would go down a different path to the receiver. Many of the words would arrive out of order, and the conversation would be garbled. Also, because each word would travel across a different line, many different conversations would stream about the wires at the same time. It would be nearly impossible to determine what words were meant for you. Figure 15.1 illustrates two devices involved in packet switching.

FIGURE 15.1

Packet switching.

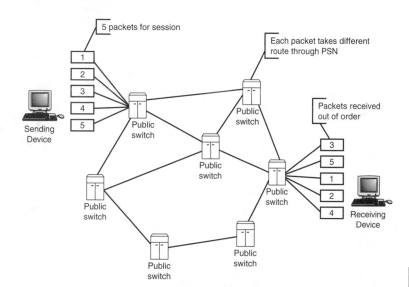

So that telephone communication can be understood by humans, when a telephone call is initiated, the switches that make up the PSN create a static link between the two callers for the duration of the conversation. During the call, every word, sigh, and noise traverses the same dedicated path as the last, thus ensuring that everything arrives in sequence and uninterrupted. More importantly, no other conversations can utilize the same lines that are involved in the link, which is known as a *circuit*. WAN protocols on the PSN have adopted these circuit technologies and learned to use them to their advantage.

A PVC defines a set path that data will traverse from one location to another. This path never changes. Whenever one device initiates a session with another device on the opposite side of the WAN link, the same path, or circuit, is used. PVCs can be thought of as static routes. In much the same way that static routes can be defined on routers to always use the same path between devices, PVCs always use the same circuit between two entities. Figure 15.2 illustrates an X.25 PVC between two networks.

15

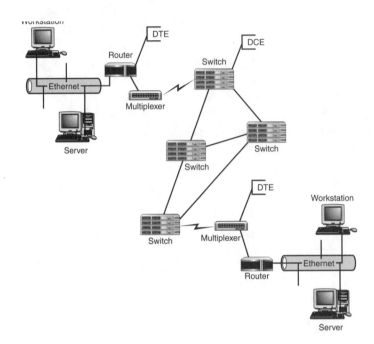

FIGURE 15.2
An X.25 PVC.

Any information sent between Network A and Network B in Figure 15.1 will always travel across the circuit 1-2-3.

There is one major downside to using PVCs: If one cable were to become unusable (for example, Link 2 in Figure 15.1), the whole communication path between Network A and Network B would go down. Whereas a router would simply choose a new path to the destination, working around the bad line, the PVC cannot stray for the set circuit. Therefore, one point of failure makes the WAN unusable.

SVCs

There is one major difference between SVCs and PVCs: Whereas the path of a PVC does not change, the path of an SVC can differ with each new session. That is, when a session is initiated between two devices, one dedicated circuit is used for the duration of the session. At the conclusion of the session, the circuit is torn down. The next time a session is established between the two devices, a different circuit may be used.

An SVC is reliable because the single circuit connecting two devices can utilize a different path each time it is established, eliminating the single point of failure that occurs in a PVC. This makes SVCs an attractive alternative to PVCs. When Frame Relay was being developed, many of the technologies and advances present in X.25 were used and adapted to the newer, increased demands of networking.

The use of virtual circuits of any kind requires the efforts of more than one type of protocol, working on more than one layer of the OSI model. Two main protocols in X.25 have a direct impact on the use of virtual circuits and how DCE and DTE respond to them: LAPB and PLP.

LAPB

LAPB is the X.25 protocol that operates at the data link layer of the OSI model. LAPB is responsible for the following tasks in an X.25 environment:

- Synchronize the transfer of data between DTE and DCE
- Monitor the data transfer to detect errors

These functions are important to X.25 because they have to do with data integrity. LAPB performs data-integrity–related functions to ensure that all the correct data that is exchanged between two devices is sent and received intact.

After a circuit (whether it is a PVC or an SVC) has been established, LAPB synchronizes the two sides of the session. This reduces the amount of talk-over that occurs between the two devices. In other words, LAPB ensures that while one device is sending, the other is receiving and that while one is receiving, the other is sending. Although this might not sound like a big deal, in the computer communications world—especially that of the early 1970s—it was huge. It was not uncommon to have devices talk blindly over each other, causing packet collisions and session disconnection.

LAPB constantly monitors the ongoing transmissions between two devices to perform error checking. LAPB performs consistency checks on the packets that are being sent over the circuit. Then the instance of LAPB running on the sending device numbers each packet. The receiving device reads the packet numbers to ensure that it is receiving the correct information. If a packet number is missing or out of sequence, or if any of the data integrity checks fails, the receiving device notifies the sender, and the data is retransmitted. By performing these functions itself, X.25 (as a protocol suite) does not need the assistance of any other external protocols to perform its functions.

15

PLP

The packet layer is the X.25 equivalent of the network layer of the OSI model. If LAPB is the traffic controller of the X.25 environment, PLP is the brains. PLP is responsible for five major aspects of X.25 functionality (also referred to as PLP modes of operation):

- Call setup
- Data transfer
- Idle

- Call clearing
- Session restart

Of these PLP modes of operation, only data transfer and session restart pertain to PVCs. PLP is mainly used during the complicated tasks of establishing and maintaining SVC sessions. Therefore, our discussion of PLP will assume that the X.25 devices involved are using SVCs.

Before two devices can communicate, a session must be initiated between them. This is done through the use of PLP in call setup mode. When one device wants to establish a session with another, it sends a call request to the other device. If the receiving device is capable of participating in a session, it sends the first device a call acceptance. At this point, the two devices are free to build a circuit between them.

Call request and call acceptance are two specialized packets whose sole purpose is to convey a state. These types of packets generally do not carry any data.

After a circuit has been built between the two devices, PLP switches to data transfer mode, enabling X.25 to transfer data. In data transfer mode, the two devices send and receive any data they want to share. PLP remains in data transfer mode until one or both sides complete their communications.

When communication between the two devices concludes, PLP on the sending device is signaled to enter call clearing mode.

LAPB functions when PLP is in data transfer mode. That is, X.25 does not call on LAPB to perform any of its functions until PLP has been put into data transfer mode. This allows the two protocols to do their work without getting in each other's way.

Call clearing mode is X.25's way of destroying virtual circuits. When PLP is in call clearing mode, a packet known as a *clear request packet* is sent. The clear request is processed by every switch that is participating in the virtual circuit. This ensures that the circuit is cleared cleanly and that no traces of the connection are left open. Any remaining connection fragments could clog the PSN with unused circuits and create a massive congestion problem.

In some cases, although the two devices have finished sharing data, they might not want to destroy the current circuit. The devices might not want to lose the conditions provided by the current circuit, or perhaps more data is in a prepared state, awaiting transmission. In these cases, PLP is put into idle mode. In idle mode, neither side is transmitting data, but the session remains open.

Finally, if a DTE device is powered off, thus breaking all its current connections, the PLP notices the sudden loss of circuits. Upon being restarted, the PLP on the DTE enters session restart mode. PLP then attempts to restart any circuit connections that were in effect at the time DTE was powered off.

Summary

X.25 is a robust WAN protocol that was built to operate on the PSN. X.25 networks utilize many different equipment types, including DTE, DCE, PSE, and PAD. Many routers require the use of an external PAD to participate in an X.25 network.

X.25 uses two protocols to control the exchange of data within its environment: PLP and LAPB. PLP operates at the network layer of the OSI model, and LAPB operates at the datalink layer. These two protocols are one feature of X.25 that set it apart from most other WAN protocols.

Q&A

Q Why does X.25 include separate protocols for handling different tasks?

A The protocols within X.25 allow X.25 to adapt to many situations while not relying on the use of external, LAN-based protocols. With protocols such as PLP and LAPB, X.25 is ensured that no operational conflicts can occur.

Q Why do protocols on the PSN, such as X.25, need to be connection-oriented?

A These protocols are connection-oriented because of the PSN's need for data to arrive in a specific order. Data traveling across the PSN must be sent and received in the same order. To facilitate this aspect of the network, all protocols working on the PSN are connection-oriented.

Quiz

1. What network layer protocol is included with X.25?
2. What X.25 protocol performs error checking?
3. What is the X.25 term for the switches that reside in the PSN?

15

4. What type of packet is sent to signal the end of a SVC session?

5. Which is considered to be more reliable, an SVC or a PVC?

Answers

1. PLP

2. LAPB

3. PSE

4. Clear request packet

5. SVC, because the path used can change for each session.

HOUR 16

Learning Frame Relay

One of the most important WAN protocols to be developed from the IDSN public switched network (PSN) standard is Frame Relay. Frame Relay was developed in the late 1980s as a quicker, more streamlined version of X.25, geared for the new ISDN networks.

One of the major differences between Frame Relay and X.25 is that they operate at different layers of the OSI model. Frame Relay, which is a WAN protocol, operates at the data link layer of the OSI model. X.25 operates on both the network layer (which handles routing) and the data link layer (which handles switching). In an effort to streamline the protocol, network layer support was removed from Frame Relay. The rationale for this was that fewer switches do their job while routers do their jobs.

In the same way that routers operate purely at the network layer of the OSI model, switches operate at the data link layer. Therefore, Frame Relay would seem to be a switching protocol. For this reason, routers are not involved in moving Frame Relay data. Rather, with Frame Relay, as with most WAN protocols, a router's job is to pass preformatted data to the switch for transport to another router. When the information reaches the target router, the WAN data is translated back into routable protocol information.

One of the problems with Frame Relay is that it does not have built-in flow control or the ability to check the integrity of data. Frame Relay discards any packets it needs to discard in order to handle congestion and other housekeeping issues. For example, if a Frame Relay link becomes overly congested, it begins to drop any packets that it cannot handle. The downside to this situation is that these packets are not reported as lost and they are not requested again.

What Frame Relay lacks in "bells and whistles" it makes up for in speed. Frame Relay can operate at speeds more than 50 times faster than X.25. This may be of little consolation, though, to people who need the extra features they are used to seeing in most protocols.

For these reasons, upper-layer protocols are always used in conjunction with WAN protocols such as Frame Relay. For example, protocols such as TCP/IP can be used to handle error checking of the data that originates from Frame Relay links. Upper-layer protocols can also be used to recover packets that are discarded by Frame Relay.

An *upper-layer protocol* is one that operates at one or more of the top four layers of the OSI model (that is, the application, presentation, session, and transport layers).

Frame Relay Technology

The goal of this section is to introduce you to some of the technology and terminology you encounter when you establish a Frame Relay connection.

The hardware required in maintaining and completing a Frame Relay circuit is grouped into two categories:

- Data circuit terminating equipment (DCE)
- Data terminal equipment (DTE)

Figure 16.1 illustrates the two major categories of equipment in a Frame Relay circuit. The DCE comprises the switches that make up the PSN. You will never find a DCE as part of a business-level Frame Relay network; they will only exist in the PSN.

FIGURE 16.1

Frame Relay equipment.

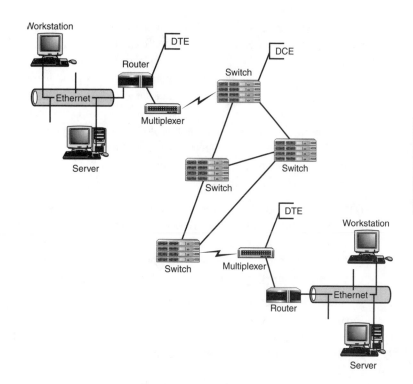

16

DCE switches are the core of the PSN. DCE switches move data into and out of the PSN. In fact, the PSN is a collection of large-scale DCE switches that move data from location to location. Frame Relay uses these same switches to move data between dedicated networks.

The consumer or the private network portion of a Frame Relay circuit never needs to configure or maintain anything that resides on a DCE. The Frame Relay carrier is responsible for the handling and control of all information that comes in contact with DCE switches. This can be both a help and a hindrance for administrators.

If a problem occurs on the DCE portion of a Frame Relay link, you do not need to worry about fixing it. The telecom provider (or Frame Relay carrier) should have its own staff of experts who are capable of troubleshooting and repairing switches. Troubleshooting and fixing DCE equipment is a very large chunk of responsibility that the network administrator therefore does not have to cover.

However, when you use Frame Relay, the network and the network administrator are at the mercy of the Frame Relay provider. No information can flow into or out of the network until the provider finishes its job. This can leave an administrator feeling very helpless and unsure about the state of the environment. Due to this great feeling of uneasiness, many providers offer up-time guarantees that relate to the state of their Frame Relay equipment. These contracts are likely to state that in the event of a network blackout, service will be restored within a given amount of time. The job of handling the traffic on a Frame Relay link and guaranteeing a specific throughput is referred to as *Quality of Service (QoS)*. For more information on this very large topic, check out `http://www.webopedia.com`.

DTE is the Frame Relay equipment that resides on the consumer side of the WAN (see Hour 5, "Understanding WAN Protocols"). Therefore, a router connecting to a Frame Relay link would be considered DTE. However, most routers do not have an interface geared specifically for Frame Relay. To accommodate a Frame Relay connection, additional equipment—that is, a multiplexer—would be needed.

A multiplexer/demultiplexer splits a T1 line (or another larger telecom pipeline) into separate channels. These channels are then sorted into two groups: those that contain Frame Relay data and those that do not. The channels that contain Frame Relay data are then sent to the router's serial interface.

Most routers include serial interfaces, but you should always check your hardware's equipment before attempting to establish any connections.

The Serial Interface

The serial interface is like the Swiss Army knife of router interfaces. Most router connections that cannot be made directly through an Ethernet port attach to the serial interface. Since the early days of computer networking, the serial interface has been the interface of choice for communications developers. The serial port is a stable interface with a fairly strong, consistent throughput.

Interfaces like Ethernet and SCSI are specialized interfaces that, while having their own good points, are not as versatile or universally accepted as the serial port.

A high-bandwidth line such as a T1 line is composed of channels that can carry voice and/or data. A T1 line contains 24 separate channels. These channels can be used as data or telephone connections, so one T1 line could carry a combination of data and voice. Multiplexers are used to separate these channels for use for the Frame Relay equipment. Generally, the T1 provider or the Frame Relay supplies equipment such as multiplexers.

The DCE and the DTE are the two major pieces of equipment you should be aware of. Anything you work with is DTE, and everything else is generally DCE.

A number of software terms are associated with Frame Relay operation. One term commonly used in Frame Relay configurations is *DLCI (data link connection identifier)*. The DLCI is the number assigned to the Frame Relay circuit. This number is unique and is used by the routers at each end of the WAN to establish a connection. A Frame Relay DLCI is similar to an ISDN SPID (covered in Hour 14, "Understanding ISDN"). When configuring a router for Frame Relay, you need to know the DLCI assigned to your particular circuit before you begin to work.

Another piece of optional information you might need when configuring a Frame Relay interface is the *LMI (local management interface)*. When LMI is in use on a Frame Relay circuit, special packets known as LMI packets are sent out periodically across the network. These packets can relay optional information to and from the Frame Relay equipment about the status of the environment. Several LMI options can be configured into a router, but your specific carrier needs to support the LMI you want to use. One popular LMI is known as a *virtual circuit status LMI*.

Frame Relay uses two circuit types (as discussed in Hour 15, "Learning X.25"):

- Permanent virtual circuits (PVCs)—PVCs are logical circuits that are statically mapped from network to network. Given the nature of a switched network, there is no guarantee that packets will ever be sent over the same path twice. A PVC ensures that information flowing between two networks traverses the same path. PVCs reduce the risk of data loss and congestion by eliminating the unknown element of switching.

- Switched virtual circuits (SVCs)—An SVC changes path with each new session. When you use SVCs, packets are always sent along the same path for the duration of a session. After the session has ended and a new session has begun, the packets can be sent over a different path.

The virtual circuit status LMI provides an alert to the routing equipment if a PVC link becomes unavailable. PVCs have a single point of failure. If one link in a PVC fails, the entire circuit is useless. By using the virtual circuit status LMI, the PSN can notify the router in the event of such a failure.

Frame Relay Configuration Basics

One of the first pieces of information you are required to configure on your router is the Frame Relay encapsulation method. The encapsulation method specifies how the Frame Relay packets are formatted. Unless you are certain that all the equipment (that is, the DTE and the DCE) is Cisco based, you should use Internet Engineering Task Force (IETF) encapsulation. The examples in this lesson will use IETF encapsulation.

If all the equipment in use on your Frame Relay network is Cisco based, feel free to use the Cisco default encapsulation. Cisco provides its own Frame Relay encapsulation method that allows its equipment to move data efficiently.

The encapsulation method must be configured identically on both ends of the network. The following example illustrates the commands used to configure a Cisco router for IETF encapsulation. Notice in this example that the configuration occurs on the serial interface:

```
Router(config)#interface serial 0
Router(config-if)#encapsulation frame-relay ietf
```

Because the router communicates through one interface (the serial interface) to a multi-plexer, it is conceivable that one serial interface could be the communication point for multiple Frame Relay links. There is no rule that says every channel of a T1 line (in the multiplexer) can't be a separate Frame Relay circuit. Therefore, many routers support serial interfaces that can be configured with subinterfaces.

A *subinterface* is a logical division of a single physical interface. In the same way a group of apartments can share one physical address within an apartment building, such as 105A, 105B, and 105C, serial interfaces can be configured with subinterfaces (S0.1, S0.2, and S0.3).

Any number of subinterfaces can be configured on one serial interface. If your configuration calls for using multiple Frame Relay circuits, use the following command to configure the subinterfaces on a Cisco router:

```
Router(config)#interface serial 0.1 point-to-point
```

The subinterface number is separated from the interface number by a decimal point. Therefore, by requesting `interface serial 0.1`, you are configuring the first subinterface of serial interface 0. The keyword `point-to-point` indicates that the circuit is a point-to-point circuit. This keyword should be used unless otherwise indicated by your provider. The following configuration command should be repeated for all interfaces.

```
Router(config-if)#encapsulation frame-relay ietf
```

This command establishes the encapsulation type for the (sub)interface. At this point in the configuration, the DLCI, which is provided by the Frame Relay carrier, should be configured into the router. The DLCI identifies your Frame Relay circuit on the network and distinguishes it from other Frame Relay circuits. Although the majority of these steps can be performed in any order, the DLCI is needed when you are establishing Frame Relay route maps, and therefore it should be configured next.

When configuring the DLCI, the routed protocol address of the interface should also be configured. You configure the DLCI and the routed protocol address the same way you configure ISDN. The interface's protocol address (IP or IPX) is used to route data to and from the interface. The following commands configure both the DLCI and the routed protocol address (The first command shown configures the DLCI, while the second established the routed protocol address):

```
Router(config-if)#frame-relay interface-dlci 56
Router(config-if)#ip address 198.156.82.1 255.255.255.0
```

When all the applicable addresses are configured, you can configure the static mappings. The format of this command is similar to that of the `dialer-map` command in ISDN. The command used to create the Frame Relay static maps is `frame-relay map`:

```
#frame-relay map <protocol> <protocol address> <dlci number>
```

For example, the `frame-relay map` command can be used as follows to basically state, "Route all IP data from network `198.156.81.0` to Frame Relay circuit (DLCI) 56":

```
Router(config)#frame-relay map ip 198.156.81.0 56 Cisco
```

The Frame Relay map acts as a route guide, informing the router where data should be sent. The router then passes the map information along to the PSN. A Frame Relay map is a static route mapping ensuring that your Frame Relay data will be routed over the correct circuit.

Summary

Frame Relay was developed to be a quicker, more streamlined version of the X.25 protocol that is used on ISDN networks. Although Frame Relay is a very fast WAN protocol, it has drawbacks. Most notable among Frame Relay's problems is its lack of error checking and flow control.

Frame Relay equipment is categorized by one of two types, DTE or DCE. DCE is equipment that resides on the carrier side of a Frame Relay circuit. DCE equipment commonly includes the PSN switches. DTE equipment is located at the business end of the circuit, and includes all the routers used in the network. When configuring Frame Relay, you need only be concerned with setting up the DTE. The DCE is configured by the Frame Relay provider.

When configuring a router for Frame Relay, you need to know the encapsulation type being used on the circuit and the DLCI number. The encapsulation type (usually IETF) determines the formation of the data being sent across the circuit, while the DLCI identifies the circuit on the network. Both pieces of information are available from your Frame Relay provider.

The next hour will introduce you to your first routing protocol. The Routing Information Protocol (RIP) was one of the first routing protocols developed for use in networking environments. Still used widely today, RIP is an important topic for anyone learning the routing process.

Q&A

Q Why use Frame Relay at all if it requires the added use of an upper-layer protocol?

A Frame Relay is not the only protocol that requires the added use of an upper-layer protocol; all WAN protocols require them. You cannot run a routed (or otherwise networked) environment without the use of routed (that is, upper-layer) protocols.

Q Why are Frame Relay mappings needed?

A If the Frame Relay data was not statically mapped, there would be no guarantee that the information would travel over the correct circuit. The paths are statically mapped to tell the router exactly which path to use.

Quiz

1. What Frame Relay encapsulation type do you need to use if all your equipment is not Cisco branded?

2. What is the Frame Relay term for the equipment that resides on the corporate end of the network?

3. What type of router interface is generally used for Frame Relay?

Answers

1. IETF

2. DTE (data terminal equipment)

3. Serial

Hour 17

Understanding RIP

So far in this book you have learned a number of topics and concepts related to routing. You have also learned about the major routed and WAN protocols. Beginning with this lesson, we will focus on the core process of any router: the routing protocol.

Routing protocols are responsible for the successful transfer of data from one location to another over the best possible path. Therefore, you should spend more time designing for and implementing routing protocols than doing any other router maintenance duties.

Routing Information Protocol (RIP) was one of the first routing protocols used in private-sector environments. Originally released in 1982 for Unix environments, the technology in RIP can actually be traced back to a Xerox protocol called PUP (PARC Universal Protocol) GWINFO (Gateway Information Protocol). RIP as a routing protocol can be classified as an *interior gateway protocol (IGP)* because RIP is designed to work within one homogeneous environment.

Keep in mind that one environment can consist of multiple networks. RIP will function correctly within an environment using multiple networks as long as no WAN links are involved. If your environment has networks that are separated by WAN links, RIP will not function over those links.

> Another category of routing protocols, known as exterior gateway protocols (EGPs), is used to connect and route between environments. One such EGP is Border Gateway Protocol (BGP), which is covered in Hour 23, "Understanding BGP."

RIP was designed during a time when routing environments were not as large as they are today. Therefore, it cannot handle some of the complex, large environments that tend to be used in enterprises today. However, because of the protocol's focus on small to mid-sized networks, it remains extremely popular.

RIP was not designed specifically for small- to medium-sized networks. When RIP was first released, it was used within some of the largest networks of the day. Of course, as technology progressed, the capabilities of networking did as well, and network environments grew larger and larger. The larger networks that were once the domain of RIP are quite small by today's standards. RIP is now classified as a smaller protocol compared to its original purpose.

> Other routing protocols that function well on smaller networks are OSPF (Open Shortest Path First) and IGRP (Interior Gateway Routing Protocol). Although both of these protocols are good in smaller environments, they are *scalable*. This means that these protocols also function on networks that are larger than anything RIP could handle.

RIP Technology

RIP was designed during the early 1980s by one of the more innovative companies in networking technology, Xerox. RIP was originally designed to run on PCs, Unix servers, and other computing devices that could be networked together in a single environment resembling a bus network.

Because RIP was designed to run on computers rather than on routers, the engineers had to develop it in such a way as to allow the sharing of processor time. The same processor that handled requests from the protocol also needed to handle requests from the computer. Therefore, RIP had to be streamlined so that it would not use all the available processing time.

The computers that ran RIP also had very limited resources (for example, memory space, drive space). To work around this, RIP needed to be very lightweight. RIP does not take up as much memory as other modern routing protocols (such as OSPF). This allows it to be a quick protocol that does not require a lot of overhead.

> Protocols that are defined as *lightweight* do not consume many system resources and may not require as much RAM or processor power to run. However, to make a protocol lightweight, many designers leave out functions that "heavier" protocols have.

17

The initial designers of RIP also tried to build in some safety features to protect networks from potential routing problems such as routing loops. A *routing loop* occurs when devices are connected in such a way that protocols can become confused and continue around in a never-ending journey across the environment. Figure 17.1 illustrates a simple routing loop.

FIGURE 17.1

A simple routing loop.

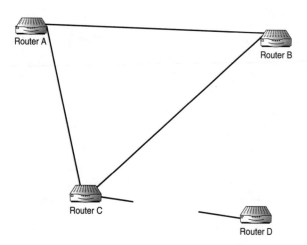

In Figure 17.1, if Router A sends a packet to Router D, the packet will get caught in a routing loop because the link to Router D has become unavailable, but each device still thinks Router D is accessible through the other remaining devices. The packet will move from Router A to Router B to Router C, looking for the target. Router C will forward the packet to the next hop, Router A, and the loop will continue indefinitely.

To prevent routing loops, the designers of RIP wrote into the protocol a type of kill switch called the *hop count limit*: a limit on the number of hops that, if exceeded, would cause the packet to be labeled undeliverable and be dropped. Aside from the hop count limit, RIP introduced three other technological routing advances:

- Route poisoning
- Split horizon
- Hold-down timers

Each of these advances has been used in one form or another in most routing protocols introduced since RIP. They are important features for engineers to understand because they can greatly affect the overall routing process. Learning about these widely used routing protocol concepts will help you in future troubleshooting processes.

RIP produces a routing table that stores all of the information a Cisco router needs to move data from one location to another. This table is normally stored in the router's DRAM (Dynamic Random Access Memory). The design of DRAM allows devices to access its contents quicker than standard RAM. This allows the router to access the table quickly and make changes as needed.

The contents of the routing table depend on the routing protocol being used. Figure 17.2 illustrates a sample network from which the routing table in Table 17.1 is based. Table 17.1 illustrates a typical routing table on a RIP router named Router D.

TABLE 17.1   A Sample Routing Table

Network	Next Hop	Metric	Timer	Flags
153.19.88.0	Router A	2	30–180–240	None
198.63.35.0	Router B	6	30–180–240	None
153.19.89.0	Router C	1	30–180–240	None

FIGURE 17.2

A RIP environment with four networks.

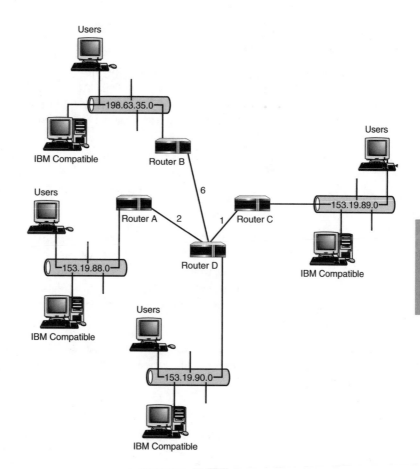

The routing table holds the information that the router needs in order to make informed routing decisions. The following are the fields in the routing table:

- Network—The Network field holds the destination network address.

- Next Hop—The Next Hop field holds the address of the router that is the next direct link to the destination. For example, in the example shown in Table 17.1, Network 153.19.88.0 might be attached to Router G. The path from Router D to Network 153.19.88.0 is Router D to Router A, to Router G, to Network 153.19.88.0. Because Router D is not directly attached to Router G, it cannot send data straight to Router G. Therefore, the next hop is to move information from Router D to Network 153.19.88.0 through Router A.

- Metric—Also known as *cost,* the Metric field represents the number of hops from the next hop that are required to reach the destination.
- Timer—The Timer field represents three different timers used by RIP. The *routing update timer* is used to mark the interval between routing updates. RIP generally sends a routing update every 30 seconds. The second timer is the *route timeout timer.* If a routing update is not received from a particular network within 180 seconds, the route timeout timer marks this route as inaccessible. The final timer is the *route removal timer.* This timer deletes any route in the routing table that has not been updated in 240 seconds.
- Flags—The Flags field holds any optional RIP features. This field is not commonly used.

From the routing table illustrated in Table 17.1, we can deduce that Router D is two hops away from Network 153.19.88.0 through Router A, six hops away from Network 198.63.35.0 through Router B, and one hop away from Network 153.19.89.0 through Router C. When Router D receives a packet addressed to Network 153.19.88.0, Router D uses RIP to examine the routing table and concludes that the packet should be sent through Router A.

Routers running RIP send copies of their routing tables to their neighbors every time the routing update timer expires. This allows routers to keep abreast of changes in the network's topology.

A router's *neighbor* is any router that is directly linked to it. In other words, two routers that are directly linked to each other are considered neighbors. However, routers that are separated by a third router (or another connectivity device such as a switch) are not considered neighbors.

The purpose of routing updates is to give each router an opportunity to inform its neighbors of the current number of hops from one location to another. One problem that can arise from this process is that routers sometimes incorrectly report the state of networks they do not have direct knowledge of. The cure for many common routing problems can be found in the four special features of RIP—hop count limits, route poisoning, split horizon, and hold-down timers—that are described in the following sections.

Hop Count Limits

The most debated feature of RIP is the hop count limit. When RIP was designed, a limit of 15 hops was imposed on all RIP environments. But this feature is a double-edged sword: Although hop count limits are an effective tool against routing loops, they also severely limit the size of the environment that can use RIP. The hop count is a measure of how many routers (hops) a piece of data must travel through to reach its destination.

Packets that are sent from a PC begin with a hop count of 1. Each time the packet passes through a router, the hop count, which is stored in a field of the RIP header, is incremented by 1. When a packet reaches its 16th hop, the device discards the packet as undeliverable. Therefore, if a loop were to occur, it could only last for 15 hops. Figure 17.3 illustrates a packet that must travel three hops to reach its destination.

FIGURE 17.3

Three router hops.

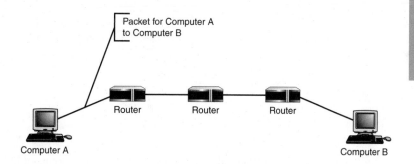

The router tracks the number of hops a packet has made through the fields in its header. Every time a packet passes through a hop, a counter in the packet header is incremented. When the number hits 16, the packet is discarded. (The fields of the RIP header are discussed later in this lesson, in the section "Routing Updates in RIP." By examining these header fields, you can better understand how hop count limits are implemented.)

This section focuses on one field in the header: the Metric field. (As this lesson progresses, we will discuss the other header fields and their functions.)

Every time a packet reaches a RIP router, the routed protocol header is stripped off. The router determines the best path for the data to traverse, and then the RIP-adjusted protocol header is reapplied. When the header is reapplied, the TTL (Time to Live) field (among others) is adjusted to illustrate the number of hops the packet has already encountered. Therefore, when a packet reaches a router and the header is examined, the router can immediately see if the packet has reached the hop count limit. Any packet that has reached the limit can be discarded. Figure 17.4 illustrates this process.

FIGURE **17.4**

A packet modified by RIP.

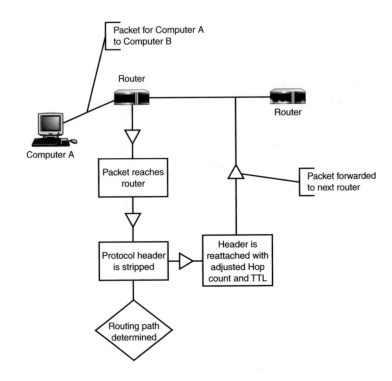

The designers of RIP could barely imagine a single environment that would encompass more than 15 hops. Many of the large environments at the time did not even have 10 networked devices. Therefore, to conceive of an environment that could surpass 15 routing hops was far-fetched.

As technology progressed and networks became larger, it grew evident that routing environments would quickly surpass the RIP hop limit of 15. It would have been easy to simply abandon the old RIP routing protocol in favor of a newer, more up-to-date version. However, instead of redesigning RIP to meet the needs of modern networks, new protocols were based on the architecture of RIP, without the limitations of RIP. Routing protocols such as OSPF (discussed in Hour 20, "Exploring OSPF") were created to meet some of the enterprise needs that RIP could not address.

Hop count limits are a valuable tool in combating routing loops. Although imposing hop limits does control the size of a routing environment, it is more of a help to administrators than a hindrance. Keep in mind that most routing loops are created unintentionally. Therefore, you might not notice them right away, if at all. RIP's hop count limit is an important tool that engineers can rely on to help control these common problems.

Route Poisoning

RIP's feature, *route poisoning,* occurs when a particular path in a routing table is assigned a hop count of 16. Because RIP routers can not forward data to a destination that is over 15 hops away, assigning a hop count of 16 to a path within the routing table causes the path to become unreachable. Any packets addressed to that destination will be discarded. This poisoning of a route can quickly prevent routing loops.

The following scenario describes a situation in which a router would choose to poison a path. If a router continuously receives updates in which a particular path's metric is incrementing, the router deduces that a routing loop has occurred. The router then sets the route's metric to 16 in its own routing table and triggers a routing update. This update alerts all neighboring routers that the path is poisoned and should not be used. Figure 17.5 illustrates a network where route poisoning has occurred.

17

FIGURE 17.5

A network with a poisoned route.

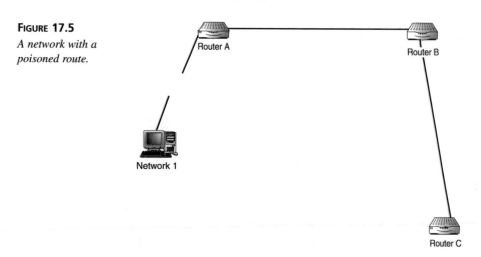

In Figure 17.5 the link between Network 1 and Router A has become unavailable. During an update, Router B tells both Router A and Router C that it can reach Network 1 in two hops. Router A, realizing that it can no longer reach Network 1 by itself, changes the metric for Network 1 in its own routing table to 3 (1 for itself plus 2 for the metric from Router B) and sends out an update. Router B receives the update, notices that Router A has changed its metric from 1 to 3, and adjusts its routing table to reflect a metric of 4. This is a classic routing loop.

When it receives the updates from Router B, Router C realizes that the loop has occurred and immediately sets the path to 16. When Router A and Router B receive the update, the path is poisoned and becomes ignored.

Split Horizon

The concept of *split horizon* is another tool RIP uses to prevent routing loops. The rule of split horizon states that a router cannot send an update back to the device it was received from. By eliminating these redundant updates, routers are not misled into believing that links that do not exist are actually fully functional. For example, Figure 17.6 illustrates an environment where the split horizon rule could make a difference.

FIGURE 17.6

An example of split horizon.

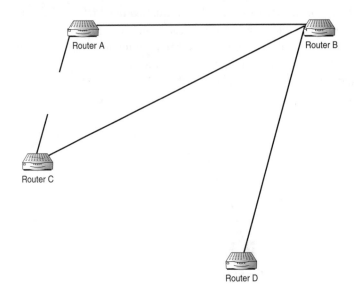

The scenario depicted in Figure 17.6 shows four routers (A, B, C, and D). The link between Routers A and C has failed. Router A therefore adjusts its routing table to show that it no longer links to Router C. Router A sends an update to Router B, notifying it of the unavailable link. However, before Router B can send out another update, it receives an update from Router D, stating that the link from Router A to Router C is still operational. Router B then corrects its routing table and notifies Router A that the link between Router A and Router C is functional, even though it is not. This creates a routing loop between Router A and Router B.

When split horizon occurs, a router cannot send an update to a router that it has received an update from until it has updated its remaining neighbors. Therefore, the router can be assured that the correct information will be sent to all the routers involved.

Hold-down Timers

Hold-down timers are used in conjunction with other RIP features such a split horizon. A *hold-down timer* indicates an amount of time during which a particular path cannot be updated. For example, during a split horizon scenario, a hold-down timer would be used to prevent an inactive route from becoming falsely reactivated.

When a router detects an unavailable link, it initiates a routing table update. Then the router places a hold-down timer on the route to prevent it from receiving a false update from a neighboring router. After the hold-down timer expires, the router is free to update the unavailable path as needed.

How RIP Works

RIP works like any routed or WAN protocol: It is a common language that all routers in a single environment can speak in order to facilitate the movement of data from one network to another. When you're dealing with routing protocol such as RIP, it is important to recognize that all the routers within that environment need to use the same routing protocol.

> Although all the routers within a given environment need to use the same routing protocol (like RIP, OSPF, or EIGRP), they do not necessarily need to use the same routed protocol (such as IP, IPX, or AppleTalk). Routers can connect networks that use dissimilar routed protocols. However, for information to be passed from one router to another, all the routers need to use the same routing protocols.

When a packet of data reaches a router, it has already experienced a few changes. (As you learned in Hour 4, "Understanding Routed Protocols," the packet has been segmented and encapsulated so that the data represents the routed protocol that is being used.) The router receives the data and begins to read the protocol header information. Until this point, the routing protocol has yet to be used.

The router looks mainly at one field in the protocol header—the Destination field. The router compares the Destination field data with the entries in its routing table, which is a product of the routing protocol. Keep in mind that the router has not even made a decision to route this packet; no protocols—routing protocols or other protocols—have been called into use by the router. At this point, the router is simply determining where the packet is trying to go.

After it determines that the packet is addressed for a destination that is reachable through one of the router's interfaces, the router hands the packet over to RIP. RIP then takes a closer look at the router's routing table to determine exactly what path the packet needs to be sent down. Still working from the packet's original protocol header destination, RIP compares that value to a list of possible known destinations. If more than one path is returned as a matching destination, RIP then looks to the routing table metrics.

Table 17.2 shows a sample IP packet header. This sample header gives RIP the information it needs. Table 17.3 illustrates a sample routing table. Using these two tables, you can easily see the process RIP uses to route data.

TABLE 17.2 An IP Header

IP Header Field	Value
Version	4
Header Length	6
Type Of Service	0
Total Length	16
Segment ID	1
Flags	0
Fragment Offset	0
TTL	1
Protocol	17
Checksum	1024
Source Address	153.85.23.15
Destination Address	153.85.26.85

The data in the packet header is compared with the router's routing table, which is illustrated in Table 17.3. After the router compares the destination address of the header file with the networks listed in the routing table, two possible matches are produced.

TABLE 17.3 A Routing Table for Comparison

Network	Next Hop	Metric	Timer	Flags
153.85.23.0	Router B	4	30–180–240	0
153.85.24.0	Local	0	30–180–240	0
153.85.23.0	Local	0	30–180–240	0
153.85.26.0	Router C	2	30–180–240	0
153.85.26.0	Router D	3	30–180–240	0
203.152.0.0	Router C	2	30–180–240	0

The router now has a choice to make: Which path is the packet sent down to reach Network 153.85.26.0? According to the routing table, the router can reach Network 153.85.26.0 through Router C or Router D. The router looks to RIP's routing algorithm to decide which path to choose. The algorithm looks at the metrics for both—the path to Router C (a metric of 2) and the path to Router D (a metric of 3)—and determines that the packet should be sent through Router C (having the lowest metric value).

Now RIP's focus shifts from determining the best path to moving data across that path. The IP protocol header is reattached, but some of the fields are changed. Table 17.4 shows the fields of the reattached IP header.

TABLE 17.4 The Reattached Protocol Header

IP Header Field	Value
Version	4
Header Length	6
Type Of Service	0
Total Length	16
Segment ID	1
Flags	0
Fragment Offset	0
TTL	2
Protocol	17
Checksum	1024
Source Address	153.85.23.15
Destination Address	153.85.26.85

After determining the best path with which to route the packet, RIP attaches the modified IP header to the packet. The IP header now has an incremented TTL. If this TTL value reaches its threshold before the packet reaches its destination, the packet will be discarded.

Routing Updates in RIP

Besides its duties to move data around the network, RIP is also responsible for updating the routing tables of the routers on which it runs. RIP facilitates the updating of routing tables and the successful convergence of the environment through automated updates.

Every 30 seconds, every router on the network sends RIP updates. However, unlike most link-state protocols (discussed in Hour 3, "Routing Algorithms"), RIP routers send updates only to their neighboring routers. Depending on the update trigger, each of these updates can contain either the entire routing table or a portion of the table.

An *update trigger* is an event that either starts or requests a routing update.

Three events can trigger a RIP routing update: the expiration of an update timer, the state change of a link, or a direct RIP update request. In a RIP routing table, the routing update timer expires every 30 seconds. When this timer expires, the router sends a copy of its routing table to each of its directly connected neighbors. These neighbors use the information to update their tables and produce their own routing updates.

If a link between two routers (or one router and a network) fails, the directly attached router updates its table and sends out an immediate update. During an update that is triggered by a network change, only the affected portion of the routing table is sent to the neighboring routers. The neighboring routers update the related portions of their own tables and continue to propagate updates.

Finally, a router running RIP can request an update from a specific router. This is typically done after the expiration of a hold-down timer. When a router receives a request for an update, the entire routing table is sent to the requesting router.

Regardless of the event that triggers an update, routing tables are sent out as part of RIP header information attached to an RIP update packet. Like most routed protocols, routing protocols encapsulate data within header fields that are specific to that protocol. However, the only data that routing protocols tend to encapsulate is routing table updates. Table 17.5 illustrates the fields RIP uses to disseminate routing update information.

RIPv1 Versus RIPv2

There are two versions of RIP commonly in use today, RIPv1 and RIPv2. In the examples provided I will try to show you both RIPv1 and RIPv2 information. RIPv2 was designed to offer some features not available in RIPv1. RIPv2 enables the passing of subnet mask and next hop information between RIPv2 routers. Routers running RIPv2 could only use the subnet mask that was assigned to the router, so all routers within a RIPv1 network needed to share the same subnet mask.

TABLE 17.5 RIP Header Fields

RIP Header Field	Purpose
Command	Indicates whether the packet is a request for an update or a response to a request
Version	Indicates the version of RIP being used (typically version 2)
Zero	Populated with zeros (unused)
Address Family Identifier	Represents the address family (typically IP)
Zero or Route Tag	Populated with zeros (unused) for RIPv1; a route tag identifier for RIPv2
Address	Specifies the protocol address of the route
Zero/Subnet Address	Populated with zeros (unused) for RIPv1; the Subnet Address of the above IP address for RIPv2
Zero/Next Hop	Populated with zeros (unused) for RIPv1; indicates the Next Hop address for RIPv2
Metric	Specifies a metric (to be used by the routing algorithm) associated with the address. This metric is used to calculate the best path.

17

In the RIP header, the Address through Metric fields can be repeated multiple times to represent an entire routing table. (The limit is 25 addresses within a single update.) If the packet represents a link change, the packet appears as shown in Table 17.5, with only one address field.

RIP continues to send updates to each of its neighboring routers until convergence is achieved. If the network is ever out of convergence, serious problems—such as routing loops—can occur. When you're using RIP on your router, if you find that you are not achieving convergence cleanly or quickly enough, you can adjust certain elements such as timers to help meet the overall network goals.

Configuring RIP

This section focuses on configuring RIP on a Cisco router. Again, we are using Cisco routers for all the configuration examples because of their prevalence in today's environments.

To enable RIP on a Cisco router, you must use the `router` command. The `router` command allows you to start router-specific processes within the router. The `router` command tells the router to enable its RIP capabilities:

```
Router(config)#router rip
```

After enabling RIP on the router, you must set the network of the router. This gives the router a point of identity on the network and tells the router its location within the environment.

```
Router(config-router)#network 198.124.0.0
```

> Especially with routing protocols, setting a network address for protocols to associate with is a common part of the setup of a router.

Most routers allow RIP to run with just this simple information. However, you can manually configure and adjust any of the features and parameters associated with RIP to suit the needs of almost any environment. Some of these adjustable parameters include the following:

- Setting RIP timers
- Setting the version of RIP to be compatible with other vendors and implementations

If you become familiar with the uses of these options you will be able to better manage routers and maintain clean, efficient routing environments.

Setting RIP Timers

As discussed earlier in this lesson, RIP uses four timers over the course of normal routing: the routing update timer, the hold-down timer, the route timeout timer, and the route removal timer. All four of these timers relate to the manner and interval in which a routers deals with table updates. Each of these timers has default values but can be manipulated to fit the specific needs of any network.

The command used to configure the RIP timers is `timer basic`. With the `timer basic` command you can configure all four RIP timers at once. The syntax of the `timer basic` command is as follows:

```
#timer basic <routing update timer> <route timeout> <hold-down timer> <route
➥removal>
```

Therefore, to set the RIP timers to 30, 180, 45, and 270 respectively, you would use the following command:

```
Router(config-router)#timers basic 30 180 45 270
```

So, in the previous example the routing update timer was set to 30 seconds.

- If the update timer is set to 30, the specific router will send its table updates every 30 seconds.

- The route timeout timer, which controls the amount of time before a particular route is set to be removed, is normally set to about 180 seconds. This means that any routers for which an update is not received in 180 seconds are marked for routed removal.

- The hold-down timer specifies an amount of time during which a router cannot apply any updates. It should be staggered so as not to correspond with any existing update timers. In other words, if the update timer is set to 30 seconds, the hold-down timer should be set to about 45.

- Finally, the route removal timer controls the amount of time before a specific route is actually removed from a router's memory. Any router for which an update is not received within the specified amount of time is considered to be unavailable and is removed from the routing table.

Because these timers control updates that are sent to a router's neighbors, you might want to manually inform the router about the location and address of its neighbors.

Working with Multiple Versions of RIP

Using RIP in an environment where multiple router hardware vendors are used may cause some problems. For example, most routers use RIPv1 as the default RIP version. Some brands of routers may use RIP version 2.

RIPv1 and RIPv2 are incompatible with one another. Therefore, if you have an existing routing environment and change one router to use RIPv2 (while the others are running RIPv1), that router will not work. You need to ensure that all your routers are using compatible versions of RIP before changing settings.

When you're configuring RIP versions at the interface level, you should be particularly aware of the send and receive properties of the interface you are working with. Many routers allow one interface to use a different RIP version for sending data than for receiving.

The ability to change either the send or the receive properties of a RIP interface is useful if you are participating in route redistribution.

17

Route redistribution occurs when a router is permitted to advertise its routes to a network that it is not directly related to. However, in doing so, you run the risk that the new network does not use the same version of RIP that you do.

You can choose to receive updates for only RIPv1 routers and send those updates to RIPv2 routers. If one version of RIP is running in an environment where you do not want table changes to affect the network, specifying the send and receive RIP versions of a particular interface can be incredibly useful.

Summary

RIP was one of the first routing protocols developed for use in the private sector. RIP is a lightweight protocol that can be used on small- to medium-sized networks. One reason that RIP is only used in smaller environments is its self-imposed 15 hop count limit. RIP contains specific abilities that allow it to combat certain network issues, such as routing loops. Several features that help RIP deal with routing loops are split horizon, hold-down timers, poison routes, and hop count limits. These timers specify when RIP updates are sent out, and how RIP deals with networks that do not reply to those updates.

Q&A

Q Why is RIP still used if it is limited to 15 router hops?

A Because RIP is limited to 15 router hops within a single environment, it is great for small environments. As demonstrated in this lesson, there are very few commands needed to configure RIP. Therefore, RIP is a good protocol for administrators who do not have a lot of time to devote to router management.

Q Why are versions 1 and 2 of RIP incompatible?

A RIPv2 deals with information that RIPv1 just doesn't understand. The router's subnet mask and the next hop address are not used by RIPv1. Because of this, RIPv2 routers can make assumptions about the state of a path that RIPv1 routers cannot.

Quiz

1. A sample routing environment consists of five routers, two of which are connected to Router A. Every 30 seconds, how many routing table updates will Router A receive?

2. What happens after the expiration of a route removal timer?

3. Which timer controls the amount of time between RIP updates?

Answers

1. Two (one from each directly-connected neighbor)

2. Any routes marked for deletion after no updates have been received are removed from memory.

3. The update timer

17

HOUR 18

Routing with IGRP

Building on the discussions in Hour 17, this lesson explores the realm of IGRP. For the first few, mostly experimental, years of computer internetworking, RIP was the king of routing protocols. IGRP was developed to meet the needs of networks requiring quicker, more stable convergence, and more room than the RIP 15-hop count limit allowed.

The Internet age was looming on the horizon, and a new breed of routing protocol was needed to meet the growing demands of corporate infrastructures. However, because routing itself was still a burgeoning technology, the new routing protocols needed to be as easy to understand, maintain, and configure as RIP. However, the core technology of RIP would not withstand being tweaked to the extent that was needed to handle the increasing traffic.

As the Internet became popular, the need to find a routing protocol that expanded beyond the capabilities of RIP was becoming obvious. Cisco began developing the *Interior Gateway Routing Protocol (IGRP)* in the mid-1980s. IGRP is a protocol found only on Cisco devices that expands on the core technology of RIP. IGRP allows routers to function as gateways, and can handle larger, more complex environments than RIP.

A *gateway* is used to connect networking environments. They are a key element in *inter-domain* routing, or the moving of information between unrelated environments. Gateways enable the passing of information between unrelated networks.

Not long after the introduction of IGRP, its successor Enhanced IGRP (EIGRP) was introduced. Together, the two protocols would become a key factor of interdomain routing.

> EIGRP is covered in Hour 19, "Learning EIGRP."

By comparing the technical concepts of RIP and IGRP, you will gain a stronger knowledge of their proper function within routing environments. On the surface, it would seem that the only thing these protocols have in common is their algorithm. RIP, IGRP, and EIGRP all use the Bellman-Ford distance vector routing algorithm (distance vector algorithms are covered in Hour 3, "Routing Algorithms"). However, after some simple examination, we will uncover and discuss a few other common elements among the protocols.

Discussing the similarities and differences between RIP, IGRP, and EIGRP will help you better understand how each works. As you have learned, most protocols are not easily interchangeable; they tend to have their own specialized function in the routing world.

IGRP Versus RIP

As discussed in Hour 17, RIP is an interior gateway protocol (IGP). As an IGP, RIP's purpose is to move data within single networking environments. That is, the technology that lies under the functionality of RIP was not designed to handle the addressing and operational needs of routing data among multiple, uniquely addressed environments.

Because RIP was designed to be quick and lightweight as well as functional, some advanced features were left out. RIP's designers chose to narrow the amount of add-in parameters and options for the protocol. Doing so created a fairly fast protocol that was easy to maintain, but also lacked some functionalities that administrators would later look for in routing protocols, such as the ability to handle interdomain routing.

It is nearly impossible to design a protocol that is everything to everyone. As networks became larger and more sophisticated, network administrators and designers needed protocols that could grow with them and their networks. Cisco and a few other key organizations began to work on IGRP to meet these new needs. IGRP would pick up where RIP left off.

Like RIP, IGRP is an IGP, but its capabilities greatly outweigh those of RIP. IGRP works on a much larger scale then RIP, allowing multiple environments to seamlessly share data among their individual devices. IGPs such as RIP, IGRP, and EIGRP work within the networking environments without being able to move data among them. IGPs and exterior gateway protocols (EGPs), such as the Border Gateway Protocol (BGP), work hand-in-hand to provide routing functionality for large, multinetwork environments.

IGRP, and later EIGRP, introduced a few new terms into the vocabulary of routing and network engineers. Large, common-purpose environments became known as *autonomous systems (ASes)*. An AS is a collection of networks or environments that have a common routing element. These environments are grouped into ASes for addressing purposes. ASes can be addressed as individual entities, allowing data to be easily routed to entire networks at one time.

Another term that was introduced into the routing vocabulary is gateway. Gateways, as conceptual devices, will become increasingly important in choosing a routing protocol as we move into the later lessons of this book. The use of or interaction with gateways defines the functionality of many routing protocols. Gateways are devices that route information from within a specific, addressed network to devices that belong to and are addressed by environments that do not reside within the origin network. In other words, a gateway is usually a router that sits on the border of a network and routes data into and out of that network. For example, Figure 18.1 illustrates an environment that has a gateway.

18

FIGURE 18.1

An example of a gateway.

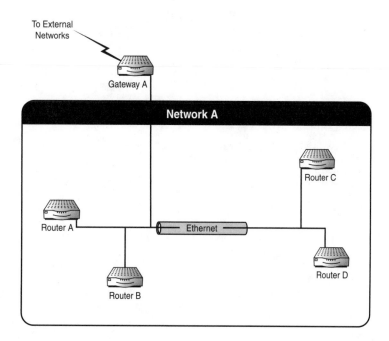

The most common gateways in environments today link corporations with the Internet. The Internet is fundamentally a large routed environment. Therefore, any router that connects a local environment with the Internet is a gateway. However, when we start talking about routing and the Internet, we enter into a very large and complex subject. Let's build some background information first by examining how gateways function in smaller environments.

A simple multinetwork environment might consist of two networks (each with its own routers) and two gateways. The two networks could exist within the same building or across the country; either way, a gateway on each side of the environment would connect them. The routers within each network (excluding the gateways) would route information around the network as described in the lessons so far in this book. When the routers within the smaller network discover a packet for which they have no address information, they forward the packet to the gateway. The gateway examines the packet and sends it to the corresponding gateway at the other network. The packet is then passed to the routers in the other network, and the process continues. Figure 18.2 illustrates this simple two-gateway environment.

FIGURE 18.2

An environment with two gateways.

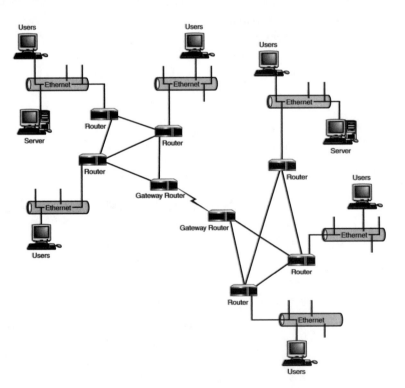

When environments are connected with each other through the use of gateways, they can be categorized into two groups. The portion of the environment that contains the network (and the routers within that network) is considered the *interior*, and the part of the environment that connects the gateways is known as the *exterior*. The interior and the exterior each have their own specialized routing protocols. IGPs such as RIP, IGRP, and EIGRP are used to route information within the interior portions of the environment, and EGPs such as BGP are the backbone protocols that connect the gateways with each other.

IGRP Technology

IGRP was based strongly on the same technology that forms RIP. Many core elements of this technology were not changed; rather, the capacities of the elements were increased. This section discusses only the elements of RIP that were expanded on during the design of IGRP.

The major elements of RIP that were modified in IGRP are the metrics used in the distance algorithm and the number of achievable hops. IGRP also implements an unequal-cost load balancing technology. When Cisco was designing the standards for IGRP, it had one luxury that the designers of RIP did not—the ability to design the protocol for specific routing hardware. Therefore, some elements needed to be tweaked in ways that would accommodate the new hardware platform. Whereas RIP was adapted to routers, IGRP could be written directly for them.

18

IGRP Metrics

IGRP uses a variety of metrics to calculate the best path from one network to another. Remember that RIP uses only one metric—hop count. IGRP abandoned hop count as a metric in favor of the following more definitive and accurate variables:

- Internetwork delay
- Bandwidth
- Load
- Reliability

Internetwork delay is the amount of time from when a packet is released by a router to when it reaches its destination (that is, another router). Delay can be represented by any number from 1 to 16,777,216 (in tens of microseconds). The delay factor of a path represents a more abstract value than the other metrics because there are many reasons one particular line might have more delay than another. Some factors are network congestion and electrical interference. Although the source of the delay cannot be pinned to any one factor, monitoring the delay of a line will help you improve your network's performance.

Bandwidth is the cumulative speed of a link, and its value can range from 1200bps to 10Gbps. The bandwidth of a link is a little less abstract than the delay. Most administrators should have a good idea of the bandwidth of their lines. The administrator sets the bandwidth metric for each line. If a particular link is set with low bandwidth, the chances of that line being chosen as a best route are slightly diminished.

If you configure the bandwidth metric of a particular link to reflect an incorrect value, it could cause some potential problems. For example, setting the bandwidth metric of a 56k line to 1Gps would tell the router to send 1Gps worth of data across that line. Not only would this cause a traffic bottleneck, packets would begin to get discarded as they waited for the router to move them. Conversely, if a 1Gps line is configured with a metric of 128k, the line would not be used as often, resulting in a waste of bandwidth and possibly putting undue traffic onto other lines on the network.

The *load* of a line is a figure that shows how much a line is being used. Load can be expressed as a value from 1 to 255. If a line is being used very heavily, the value jumps. Load is also used if the router has been configured for load balancing. *Load balancing* distributes the number of packets that flow between given links so that one link is not used more than another.

Finally, *reliability* represents how often packets are lost when a line is being used. Reliability is a value between 0 and 255. A reliability value of 255 indicates that a line is 100% reliable—that is, it never drops a packet.

A metric such as reliability is one that takes some time and experience to configure. As you work with networks and routers more, you will begin to recognize which lines are giving you more trouble than others. You can then make a judgement as to how reliable that line is. You may need to change the reliability metric of a line a few times to get it just right.

These four metrics are combined to accurately calculate the best path over which to transmit data from one network to another. Each line connected to a router that runs IGRP has these metrics associated with it. Therefore, IGRP needs a place to store the expanded base of metrics that are used during route calculation. To accommodate this data load, IGRP has a larger routing table than RIP. The IGRP routing table includes the same fields as the RIP routing table, as well as the fields Delay, Bandwidth, Load, and Reliability.

IGRP Routing Updates

IGRP routing table updates contain the same basic information as RIP routing table updates. With the exception of the added fields in the IGRP header, the update information in IGRP is the same as the information in RIP. IGRP routers, like RIP routers, periodically send local updates of their routing tables to any directly connected neighbors.

IGRP routing updates are sent every 90 seconds. This is a big increase from the 30 seconds used by RIP. The reason for the extra time is simple: IGRP can handle much larger networks than RIP. Therefore, enough time must be allotted to ensure that every router in the environment is updated before the routers begin another update.

Due to the increase in time between updates, the amount of time used to discard unused routes is greater in IGRP than it is in RIP as well. If an update pertaining to a specific router is not received within 270 seconds, the route is marked as inactive. Inactive routers are not used, but they remain in the routing table for future use. After 630 seconds of no updates, the routes are removed from the routing table.

Compared to updates in RIP, routing updates in IGRP tend to be larger (due to the number of fields) and they tend to take longer (due to the number of hops). Therefore, the designers of IGRP expanded the dictated time intervals between important IGRP update functions.

IGRP uses an update feature that RIP does not use: the *flash update*. IGRP's routing updates are sent out once every 90 seconds, but some of the metrics used by IGRP can change in realtime. Therefore, the flash update mechanism was put in place to allow IGRP to notify its neighbors in the event of a drastic metric change. If an IGRP metric changes, IGRP can initiate a flash update. During a flash update, the new metric values for the affected route are sent to the router's direct neighbors. Flash updates help keep IGRP tables current while keeping to a minimum the traffic caused by full updates.

IGRP Configuration Information

This section describes the commands needed to configure a Cisco router to use IGRP. Many of the commands look similar to those used to configure RIP. However, Cisco built in more control over the operation of IGRP than is available with RIP.

When configuring IGRP, one very important piece of information is the AS number (ASN). One of the first configuration parameters required by most routers during IGRP configuration is the number that will identify the router within the environment. With IGRP, the ASN is used to differentiate one AS from another. A valid ASN is any number from 1 to 65,535. Unless otherwise indicated, the ASN can be any number in this range that the administrator deems appropriate.

18

Some routing protocols, such as BGP, use ASNs that are assigned from a central agency, much the same way IP addresses are assigned. Therefore, you should always check with the appropriate governing bodies, such as the American Registry of Internet Numbers (ARIN) before assigning ASNs.

Here's the syntax you use to begin configuring a Cisco router for IGRP:

```
#router igrp <asn>
```

After you assign the ASN, you need to assign the network address, which is the IP network address for the router that is being configured and will be used for all routing table updates. This is the syntax for the network command:

```
#network <ip address>
```

Specifying the ASN and the network address are the only required configuration tasks for implementing IGRP. The following code segment shows an example of implementing IGRP on a Cisco router:

```
Router(config)#router igrp 210
Router(config-router)#network 198.10.0.0
```

These commands should successfully configure a Cisco router to participate in an IGRP network. You can configure several optional parameters if you want to tweak the performance of IGRP. These optional parameters include modifying update timers and disabling features such as split horizon.

Modifying Update Timers

Like RIP, IGRP uses four timers to initiate and track certain events that are related to routing updates: the route update timer, the route timeout timer, the hold-down timer, and the route removal timer. Each timer has a default value, but you can configure the default values in order to tweak a timer for a particular routing environment. Table 18.1 shows the default values of the IGRP update timers.

TABLE 18.1 IGRP Timer Default Values

Timer	Default Value, in Seconds
Route update	90
Route timeout	270
Route removal	630
Hold-down	280 (The hold-down timer should equal three times the route update timer plus 10 seconds)

You use the `timers basic` command to change the default timer values with the Cisco IOS (Internetwork Operating System). You can change a timer in order to encourage quicker updates or remove a failed router from the routing table more rapidly. The overall goal of adjusting any IGRP timers is to achieve a quicker and more reliable convergence. The syntax for the `timers basic` command is as follows:

```
#timer basic <routing update timer> <route timeout> <hold-down timer>
➥ <route removal>
```

In an attempt to achieve a greater convergence rate for the network as a whole, you can adjust timers so that they yield more favorable results. However, you need to be careful when adjusting any timers, because your changes can cause longer, more inaccurate updates just as easily as they can create faster ones. The following code illustrates the use of the `timers basic` command:

```
Router(config-router)#timers basic 75 200 76 550
```

This code sets the Cisco router's timers to the following values:

- The route update timer is changed from 90 to 75.
- The route timeout is changed from 270 to 200.
- The hold-down timer is set at 76.
- The route removal timer is changed from 630 to 550.

Enabling/Disabling Split Horizon and Hold-down Timers

A convenient feature of IGRP is the ability to enable or disable the split-horizon and hold-down timer features that are often used to prevent routing loops. In small environments with very little dynamic change, these features might not be needed. On the other hand, an administrator might want to use only one feature rather than both of them.

A router can use the hold-time timer to mark suspect routes (routes that may be invalid or not functioning correctly). A router can place a route in hold-down if it has recently learned the route or if the route fails unexpectedly. In either case, the router would not re-advertise the route for the period of time during which the route is in hold-down. When the route comes out of hold-down, the router can tell other routers about it as normal.

A router "learns" about routes during router updates. The router has no direct knowledge of the route; it simply knows what other routers tell it about the route.

18

On a Cisco router, you can disable the hold-down timer by using the no keyword, as shown here:

```
Router(config-router)#no metric holddown
```

The split horizon feature restricts routers from sending updates to the routers from which those updates are received. For example, say that Router B sends an update to Router B, informing Router A that one of Router B's links has failed. If split horizon is in use, Router A cannot send an update of its own to Router B. This reduces the risk of Router A learning incorrect information from a third router about Router B's link and passing it back to Router B.

You can enable or disable split horizon at the interface level. Many routers allow the feature to be used on a per-interface basis. To disable the feature, with the router in interface configuration mode, you enter the following command:

```
Router(config-int)#no ip split-horizon
```

Summary

Cisco developed IGRP in order to improve on RIP. Compared to RIP, IGRP has improved control timers, more metrics, and a larger hop count limit. These improvements make IGRP a vast improvement over RIP. Due to the nature of many of the new IGRP parameters, the protocol is better suited to large networking environments than RIP.

You will find that many of the configuration and conceptual elements explored in this lesson also apply to EIGRP, which is examined in greater detail in the next hour.

Q&A

Q Why does IGRP use more metrics than RIP?

A So that it can be more accurate than RIP, IGRP uses more than one metric to calculate the best path. As with any mathematical formula, the more options you have to base a calculation on, the more reliable the results will be.

Q How do I obtain an autonomous system number?

A One governing body, the American Registry of Internet Numbers, has been charged with assigning and tracking all ASNs. To obtain one, you need to make a petition to ARIN and provide any information supporting your need for an ASN. To find out more about obtaining ASNs, visit ARIN's Web site at http://www.arin.net.

Quiz

1. What units are used to segment an IGRP network?
2. What is the hop count limit in an IGRP network?
3. Which IGRP metric represents the current usage of a line?
4. What keyword is used to disable a timer?
5. What is the default value for the update timer (in seconds)?

Answers

1. ASes (autonomous systems)
2. 255 hops
3. Load
4. no
5. 90

18

Part III

Advanced Routing and Protocols

Hour

19 Learning EIGRP

20 Exploring OSPF

21 Exploring PNNI

22 Using IS-IS

23 Understanding BGP

24 Basic Router Security

Hour 19

Learning EIGRP

Enhanced Interior Gateway Routing Protocol (EIGRP) is a Cisco-proprietary routing protocol. Because there is no guarantee that you will be using the information in this book only to learn Cisco-based products, the discussion of EIGRP is fairly short. All the configuration examples provided in this lesson are shown for a Cisco router (as EIGRP only runs on Cisco routers), to illustrate the different configuration parameters used by the protocol.

Cisco developed EIGRP as a successor to the popular IGRP routing protocol. One of the major enhancements to EIGRP was the addition of Diffusing Update Algorithm (DUAL), which is an algorithm that can achieve extremely fast convergence times. DUAL is also used to process *replacement routes*, which are routes that are held in memory as potential stand-ins should a primary route become unavailable.

The use of DUAL gives EIGRP an edge over IGRP. Because routing updates are only partial views of the network, EIGRP can process them quicker and with fewer CPU cycles, as well as using less bandwidth by sending them to other routers.

EIGRP is also one of the only routing protocols that is capable of *multiprotocol routing*. This means that EIGRP is able to route many different protocols, such as IP, IPX, and AppleTalk. This capability is a big deal in the routing world, where the majority of the existing routing protocols are designed to route only IP.

Learning about EIGRP will enhance your knowledge of the most prevalent routing protocols in use today and give you a better understanding of one of the two protocols that are used specifically by Cisco-brand routers. Even if you do not intend to learn to use Cisco routers specifically, the majority of routing equipment in use today (especially on the Internet) is Cisco-based.

Many of the concepts and functions of EIGRP are directly extended from IGRP. The descriptions of these redundant functions are not repeated in this lesson; to learn more about those functions, refer to Hour 18, "Routing with IGRP." This lesson focuses on the unique features of EIGRP.

EIGRP Technology

Multiple changes were made to IGRP in order to design its successor, EIGRP. The first point that designers wanted to work on was achieving faster convergence times. To do this, they had to re-evaluate the routing algorithm used by IGRP. The designers felt that the update technology that was developed for use with RIP was being stretched to its limits within IGRP. Therefore, to accommodate EIGRP, a new modification of IGRP's distance-vector algorithm (DUAL), was developed.

DUAL consumes a lot of processor time to achieve an extremely quick convergence time. Whenever a router learns a new path, DUAL determines with a good degree of certainty whether the path can be considered loop-free. From that point on, only updates pertaining to changes within the environment are processed and applied to the routing table.

Because the acts involved in processing the route calculations for DUAL are very intensive, EIGRP routers do not process every update. DUAL is configured to process an update only if that update pertains to a physical or logical change that effects one of the router's paths. Thus routers that use EIGRP are able to achieve much quicker convergence times than those that use other protocols.

DUAL router calculations are processed only when the route being used has changed, which in an optimal environment is very rarely. This is the only processor-intensive task in EIGRP. Therefore, the router is extremely processor-efficient as it goes about its normal daily business.

By processing only the packets that pertain to changes in the router's route configuration, the router is free to devote the maximum possible processor time to packet routing. When an update arrives at the router, the router makes a quick determination about whether the update will affect the router's current route configuration. If the update does affect the router, the update is processed. Then, only the part of the route that has been affected is re-sent in another update. This process of sending and processing the smallest possible updates makes EIGRP one of the fastest converging protocols in use today.

The other major enhancement made to IGRP during the EIGRP design process was the addition of the hello packet. Many routing protocols use hello packets to discover their neighboring routers. These hello packets are normally protocol independent and are used to keep dynamic environments under control.

Hello packets are used for an EIGRP process known as *neighbor discovery*. A router's neighbor is any other router that is directly connected to it. A router uses hello packets to assess the current state (that is, online or offline) of the router's neighbors. Figure 19.1 illustrates the neighbor discovery process.

FIGURE 19.1
The neighbor discovery process.

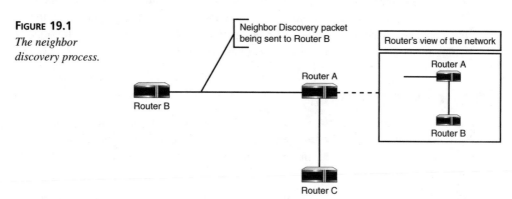

An EIGRP router periodically sends a hello packet to each of its neighbors. The neighbors process the hello packet and respond with an acknowledgement. The sending device, having received the packet, assumes that because a response was received, the neighbor is online and functional.

If the neighbor does not send a response, or if the sending device does not receive the response, after a given amount of time (determined by the hello packet interval), the neighbor is marked as suspicious, and the router flags any routes that utilize that neighbor. The router also makes a note to resend a hello message to that device after a random amount of time has elapsed. If the second hello message does not bring a response from the neighbor, the router is assumed to be offline, and all routes that include the neighbor are deleted from the router's memory.

Hello Packet Intervals

Hello packets are distributed at varying intervals, depending on the bandwidth of the link being used. Hello packets are sent out every 5 seconds by default on high-bandwidth links; they are sent out every 60 seconds by default on low-bandwidth links. They are sent out at a longer interval on slower lines because of the amount of congestion that can be produced by these packets. If the packets are sent at a longer interval on low-bandwidth links, there is less possibility that the line will be clogged with needless information. While the hello packet interval is set by default by the Cisco IOS, the administrator can adjust it to fit the needs of a specific environment.

When a router that has been marked as offline (that is, all routes have been deleted from its neighbor's memory) comes back online, it contacts its neighbors. At this time, the router is again added to its neighbors' routing tables as an online neighbor. All normal routing functions can then continue through this router.

Configuring EIGRP

The Cisco IOS commands used to configure EIGRP are almost identical to those used for IGRP. Logically, none of the command-driven configurations changed from IGRP to EIGRP. Rather, most of the changes occurred under-the-hood. However, a few of the optional parameters did change.

With an EIGRP router, as with IGRP routers, you need to specify a network address and an autonomous system number (ASN). Therefore, the same basic command structure can be used to enable both IGRP and EIGRP on a Cisco router. The following code sample shows the commands used to enable EIGRP on a Cisco router:

```
Router(config)#router eigrp 578
Router(config-router)#network 10.0.0.0
```

One optional parameter that can be configured within EIGRP dictates how much bandwidth EIGRP can utilize on any given line. By default, EIGRP uses 50% of the available bandwidth of every link in a route. Cisco allows administrators to adjust this percentage per interface. If you know that a particular line has very low bandwidth and that losing half of that bandwidth would render the link unusable, you can adjust the bandwidth usage in the interface configuration mode. The syntax to adjust the usable bandwidth percentage is as follows:

```
#ip bandwidth-percent eigrp <percentage>
```

For example, if you use the following commands, EIGRP is allowed to use only 25% of the bandwidth:

```
Router(config)#interface ethernet 0
Router(config-int)# ip bandwidth-percent eigrp 25
```

Summary

Cisco developed EIGRP as an enhanced form of the IGRP routing protocol. The major enhancements to IGRP include the addition of DUAL and an advanced neighbor discovery mechanism. DUAL enables EIGRP to achieve very fast convergence; EIGRP can converge quickly because DUAL allows a router to process only the updates that pertain directly to the router's own paths. Any update that contains information that does not relate to one of the router's paths is ignored.

EIGRP uses hello packets to determine the existence of neighboring routers. When a router receives a hello packet, it sends an acknowledgement to the sending device. This exchange proves to both routers that the other exists and is operational.

Q&A

19

Q Why was EIGRP developed, if IGRP was already an improvement over RIP?

A By the time EIGRP was developed, technology had advanced to a point where a quicker, more reliable version of IGRP could be designed. EIGRP made such an improvement on convergence times that it was quickly accepted by companies that had previously adopted IGRP.

Q How does EIGRP know if a neighboring router is online?

A EIGRP uses packets known as hello packets. These packets are sent to all neighboring routers. Any router receiving a hello packet that does not send an acknowledgment for the hello packet is assumed to be offline.

Quiz

1. What two numbers do you need to specify when you configure EIGRP?

2. What is DUAL?

3. True or false: To be considered for load balancing, a path metric must equal the product of the local metric times the variance.

4. By default, how much bandwidth does EIGRP use on any given line?

5. True or false: DUAL calculations are processed every 60 seconds.

Answers

1. The autonomous system number and the network address

2. The Diffusing Update Algorithm, used by EIGRP for loop-free route calculation

3. False. The path metric must be less than the product of the local metric and the variance.

4. 50%

5. False. To conserve CPU usage, DUAL calculations are only processed when there has been a change in a route.

HOUR **20**

Exploring OSPF

Open Shortest Path First (OSPF) is a link-state interior gateway protocol (IGP) that can work in environmental conditions similar to those of RIP, IGRP, and EIGRP. Like RIP, IGRP, and EIGRP, OSPF is used to route data within the boundaries of border gateways. However, OSPF is extremely popular because of its natural ability to converge networks rapidly. Unlike EIGRP, OSPF is available on routers other than Cisco routers. This makes it popular in networks where equipment brands may be mixed.

In the late 1980s the Internet Engineering Task Force (IETF) developed OSPF as a replacement for RIP. However, rather than use the same core technology as RIP, the IETF choose to start from scratch. The IETF realized that a link-state routing protocol would be a better choice for intragateway routing than a distance-vector protocol.

The IETF began developing OSPF during the same time frame in which Cisco and its partners were developing IGRP, which is discussed in Hour 18, "Routing with IGRP."

Since its release, OSPF has become one of the most popular IGPs for large environments. The following are some of the key factors that make OSPF such a popular routing protocol:

- OSPF is a link-state protocol, and link-state protocols have quicker convergence times than distance-vector protocols.
- Even though OSPF is an IGP, it can send and receive routes to other autonomous systems (ASes) through an exterior gateway protocol (EGP).
- OSPF can route based on IP subnet addresses.
- OSPF can perform load balancing across equal-cost links.

Many features of OSPF are not necessarily present in other routing protocols. OSPF was designed to meet a specific need within the routing world, and it was not based on any one particular existing platform, as IGRP was. OSPF is one of the leading large-environment IGPs today.

> **OSPF's Open Nature**
>
> OSPF is considered an open protocol due to the fact that its specifications are readily available to the public. Having an open standard allows any developer to port it to a specific operating system or platform. The specifications for proprietary protocols, such as IGRP, tend to be closely guarded secrets. Such protocols are usually released on fewer systems and are tightly controlled.

OSPF Technology

For the most part, the protocols we have examined to this point share a common set of terms and functions. However, OSPF is a new technology that has a unique set of terms.

To successfully define all the terms associated with OSPF technology, we will be referring to them in context. We will examine how an OPSF network is formed and operates so that you can easily learn the important terms and concepts related to OSPF.

The largest routable area in OSPF is an autonomous system, which is a group of networks that share the same IP addressing scheme. Figure 20.1 illustrates a sample OSPF AS. One AS can contain one or several smaller networks. The end of an AS is defined by the placement of the border gateway routers. A border gateway router is used to connect ASes with other entities, such as the Internet or other ASes. Because OSPF is an IGP, it can only run on routers that are contained within a single AS. Usually such IGPs cannot be installed on border gateway routers (border gateway routers are normally reserved for EGPs). OSPF, however, can be installed on the border gateway router.

FIGURE 20.1

An example of an OSPF AS.

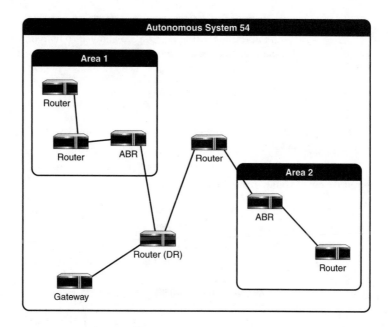

 OSPF was designed to work implicitly with IP. Therefore, OSPF network addresses are always in IP form.

Although OSPF will run on a border gateway router, the border gateway router does not use OSPF to communicate with other gateways. That is the job of EGPs such as Border Gateway Protocol (BGP). The gateway uses OSPF to collect route information about the AS. Then, using an EGP, the gateway redistributes those routes to other OSPF ASes.

One OSPF AS can contain many border gateway routers. But regardless of the number of gateways within an AS, they all serve the same role. OSPF uses gateways to distribute routes to external locations that OSPF itself has no knowledge of. These routes are distributed through the AS via link state advertisements (LSAs). An LSA contains a portion of a router's routing table that indicates the state of the router's directly connected links. These LSAs are sent to every router on the network, through a process called *flooding*. (Distance vector protocols, on the other hand, send updates only to their neighbors.) Each router uses these LSAs to build a database of the network's current state.

Within an AS, several smaller entities, known as areas, can exist. An *area* is a network or group of routers that share the same topological database. Each router within an area shares the same view of the other portions of the AS. Each area within an AS is configured with an area ID that is used to identify all the routers within that area.

20

All the routers within an area are allowed to hold only topological data that
relates to that area. Although they know what addresses lie outside the
area (through LSA floods), they do not know the exact topology of those
addresses.

OSPF areas fall into two categories: stub areas and not-so-stubby areas (NSSAs). Both
stub areas and NSSAs are used only in ASes that have connections to external routes.
That is, a specialized area can be used only if the AS connects to other ASes and receives
redistributed routes from those ASes.

A *stub area* is an area within an AS that does not allow external routes to be redistributed
into it. To keep down the amount of network traffic, an administrator might use a stub
area in order to not allow external LSAs. Stub areas must originate from the backbone of
the AS. Figure 20.2 illustrates an area that could be a stub area (Area 1).

FIGURE 20.2

*A stub area within an
OSPF network.*

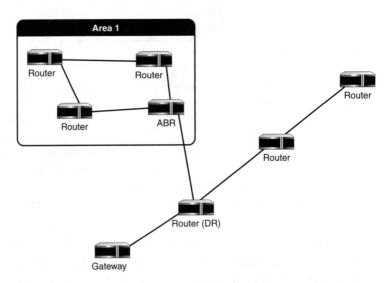

The routers in OSPF areas that connect directly with other parts of the environment outside of the router's own area are known as area border routers (ABRs). To qualify as a
stub area, an area's ABR must connect directly to the backbone of the AS (as shown in
Figure 20.2). An area like Area 19 in Figure 20.3 could not be a stub area because the
ABR for the area is attached to another area—not to the AS backbone.

Figure 20.3

An area that cannot be used as a stub area.

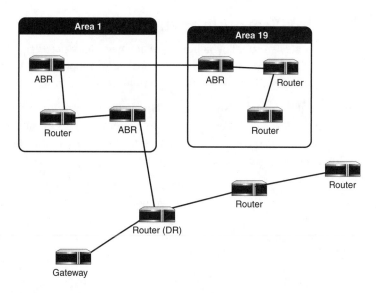

An *NSSA,* like a stub area, is an area that does not allow external LSAs. However, whereas stub areas must forward all their externally targeted packets to the backbone, NSSAs can use default routes to reach certain destinations. This allows for a more versatile area while still reducing LSA traffic.

Within OSPF ASes, one router is voted to be the *designated router* (*DR*). The DR oversees the LSA flooding process and is the only router that keeps an entire routing database. That is, the DR keeps the topographical database for the entire AS.

When the routers within the AS elect a DR, they also choose a backup DR (BDR). If the DR fails, the BDR already has a complete database. This eliminates the need for a massive LSA flood to populate the DR's database.

20

Now that we have defined some of the terms that are used in OSPF, let's examine exactly how the technology works. The following sections describe the following OSPF technologies:

- The link-state algorithm
- Stub areas
- NSSAs
- Route redistribution
- OSPF updates

The Link-State Algorithm

The link-state algorithm, which is also known as *Dijkstra's algorithm,* computes the shortest path between two points. It is capable of computing all the distances within any area at one time, which allows OSPF to route information very quickly.

However, the process of simultaneously calculating every route within an area at once does have a downside: It is very processor intensive. This means that routers that run OSPF tend to use more processing power than routers that use other protocols. However, OSPF does have many good points as well.

Like all routing algorithms, the link-state algorithm requires the use of a metric to determine the shortest distance between two points. OSPF uses a metric that is set by the local router. Using the detected bandwidth of its interfaces, the local router applies a calculation to determine the metric for a particular link. This is the equation that routers running OSPF use to determine the metric for a link:

Metric = 10^8/Link Bandwidth

When this formula is applied, the links with the highest bandwidth have the lowest cost. For example, a 128Kbps line has a cost of 781, whereas a T1 (1.544Kbps) line has a cost of 64. This ensures that the links that have the most available bandwidth are used more than those that might not be able to handle the traffic.

Because routers automatically calculate the OSPF metric, the administrator doesn't have to intervene much and is thus free to focus on other tasks. However, just because a particular link may have the most bandwidth does not make it the best choice. For example, the highest-bandwidth link to a destination might be a leased line for which the company must pay by the byte used. The administrator would want the OSPF router to purposely not use this line as often as a free link to the same target. In this situation, the administrator can manually override the router's metric with one of her own. The engineer could give the leased line a higher metric than the free lower-bandwidth line, to ensure that it will not be used as often. This kind of metric override is also useful when an administrator needs to sculpt or influence the flow of data through a specific area. The administrator can avoid trouble areas and exploit more favorable ones, while maintaining the dynamic nature of OSPF.

OSPF Updates

The information that OSPF needs to calculate the shortest path is distributed through the use of updates that are shared among the routers within an area. They help the devices create an overall picture of the environment at any given time.

Updates in OSPF networks are periodically sent to all routers within an area. However, unlike distance vector updates (which include the entire routing table in every update), an OSPF update includes only the portion of the routing table that deals with the sending router's direct neighbors. Figure 20.4 illustrates a typical OSPF area during an update.

FIGURE 20.4

An OSPF area during an update.

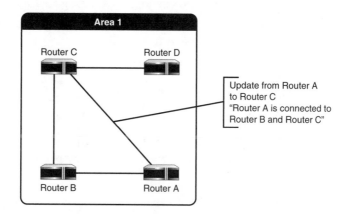

In Figure 20.4, Router A broadcasts only the part of its routing table that deals with the link between itself and Router B. Router C broadcasts information about its links with Router B, Router A, and Router D. This allows the routing updates to be as small as possible, thus enabling the network to converge as quickly as possible.

There are five types of updates in an OSPF area, and each of them has a specific purpose:

- Hello message—OSPF routers use hello messages to determine the current state of their links. Routers regularly send hello messages to each of their directly connected neighbors. When a router receives a hello message from a neighbor, it assumes that the link between itself and that router is functioning. If a router does not receive a hello message within a specified amount of time, the link is marked for removal.

- Database description—A database description is a specialized update that is used between two routers, which are known as *adjacencies*. When two routers in an area have identical topographical databases, the DR can mark them as adjacencies. When two routers are linked as adjacencies, they exchange database descriptions to ensure that their databases stay in sync.

- Link-state request—A router uses a link-state request to initiate a link-state flood before the update timer has expired. Some routers send out link-state requests when they are powered on to cause an update flood that helps the new router build its routing table.

20

- Link-state update—The link-state update is used to flood the network with topographical data. Every router within an OSPF network uses link-state updates to keep and maintain the most accurate view of the environment.
- Link-state acknowledgement—Every link-state update sent over a network requires that an acknowledgement be sent to the originating device. The router compares this list of acknowledgments to the routing table, to determine whether all the routes being reported are actually working.

OSPF routers use a combination of these update types to create the most accurate picture of the network possible. Updates, regardless of type, are sent from router to router as an OSPF packet. The packet's header contains information that pertains to the type of packet. Figure 20.5 illustrates the fields of an OSPF update packet.

The second field of the packet header indicates the type of packet. From this field, the receiving router can immediately determine whether the packet is a hello message or another type of update.

Many updates are sent only within a single area. Keep in mind that there can be many areas within one AS. Therefore, to understand the flow of OSPF packets through a network, you must understand the formation of areas.

OSPF Areas

As you have learned, OSPF ASes are subdivided into areas, and areas are small networks within an AS that share the same topological database. These areas are addressed independently of the AS they belong to, and independently of each other. Three types of areas can be formed within an OSPF AS: a standard area, a stub area, and an NSSA.

A fourth type of area is known as the *backbone.* The backbone of an OSPF AS is actually not an area in the sense that standard areas, stub areas, and NSSAs are. Rather, the backbone is made up of the routers that are not in a particular area. The purpose of the backbone is to connect the areas of the AS with each other and with any external networks. (All routers within the backbone are assigned an area number of 0. Area 0 can only be used for the backbone of an OSPF network.)

FIGURE 20.5

An OSPF update packet.

Version 1 byte
Type 1 byte
Packet Length 2 bytes
Router ID 4 bytes
Area ID 4 bytes
Checksum 2 bytes
Authentication ID 2 bytes
Authentication 8 bytes
Data variable length

20

An area dictates the overall functionality of the devices that are contained within it. Routers within an area can share information only with each other. At least one router in an area functions to connect that area with other areas, or with the backbone. Such routers are known as ABRs.

The routers within an area have only direct knowledge of each other. However, they can forward packets to their ABRs for delivery outside the area. The routers within an area have direct knowledge of the routers in their area, and they have indirect knowledge of the routing environment outside the area. Using these different types of information, the area routers can properly address packets targeted for other areas within the AS.

If an area needs to be connected to the AS backbone but is behind another area, virtual links can be established. A *virtual link* is a connection from an ABR to an intermediary ABR that then terminates at the backbone. Figure 20.6 shows an example of a virtual link.

FIGURE 20.6

A virtual link.

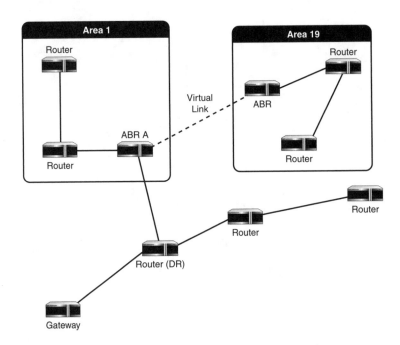

In Figure 20.6 Area 19 has established a virtual link to the backbone through Area 1. This allows routers in Area 19 to send packets directly to the backbone.

 When you're configuring a virtual link, the transit area (the area that is between the backbone and the area establishing the virtual link) cannot be a stub area.

The routers within an area receive information concerning external routes through a process known as *route redistribution*. During route redistribution, the AS gateway (using an EGP) gathers the LSA information for external ASes. The AS gateway then forwards this information through the backbone to the ABRs. The ABRs broadcast the redistributed routes to the routers within each area. The area routers use this information to send data outside the AS.

Route redistribution can burden areas by creating extra traffic and LSAs. Therefore, if an area is directly connected to the AS backbone, the administrator can shield it from the extra traffic of route redistribution by making it a stub area.

Stub Areas

As mentioned previously, a stub area is an area that is specifically designated not to receive redistributed routes from areas that are external to the AS. Creating stub areas can help reduce the amount of traffic within an area and free up resources that would otherwise be needed to process the extra updates. The key criterion to forming a stub area is that the area itself needs to be directly attached to the AS backbone.

The routers on the AS backbone have implicit knowledge of routes that are outside the AS. Therefore, the routers in the stub area can send information to external routes, by forwarding those packets directly to the backbone. However, this process can cause additional burden on some of the busiest routers in an AS.

NSSAs

An NSSA is a stub area that has been programmed with direct routes to external ASes. As with a stub area, the routers in an NSSA are shielded from the added traffic of route redistribution. However, they can still reach some external routes through predefined paths. The routers in an NSSA are configured with the information needed to reach certain routes that are external to the AS.

NSSAs do not need to be directly connected to the AS backbone. Because the routers have the information needed to properly address packets, these packets can be forwarded through other areas. However, the downside to NSSAs is that they may not be able to reach every external route. The routers within an NSSA can reach only the routes for which they have predefined route information.

Route Redistribution

What separates NSSAs and stub areas from other areas is their inability to receive and process redistributed routes. ASes communicate their internal structures to other ASes through the process of route redistribution, which enables AS intercommunication.

20

Route redistribution occurs when a border router advertises routes externally. These routes can be static routes, routes that are learned from other routers, or routes that are obtained from other IGPs (such as RIP). Redistributing an AS's routes allows devices in neighboring ASes to communicate directly with devices in the local AS.

EGPs that connect two or more ASes move the redistributed routes.

> Hour 23, "Understanding BGP," focuses on one such EGP—BGP—and describes the route redistribution process in detail.

In OSPF users have the ability to configure which routes they want to redistribute to external sources and where they want to send them. Border gateways can advertise all, part, or none of their local routes to external sources. The next section discusses how to configure a Cisco router to participate in an OSPF AS. During this discussion, the topic of configuring route redistribution is examined.

OSPF Configuration

Compared to IGRP or EIGRP networks, OSPF ASes can be quite complicated and involved. I strongly recommend that you have a diagram of the finished environment before you begin configuring OSPF routers.

The configuration of an OSPF router depends on the role of the router within the AS, so it is important to know the details about each router you configure. Area routers are configured differently from backbone routers, and backbone routers are all configured differently from one another, depending on the type of areas being used. Therefore, you should have a precise knowledge of how the environment is going to look and where the router you are configuring fits into that environment before you begin configuring. The `router ospf` command is used to configure the device for OSPF, and its syntax is shown here:

```
#router ospf <process ID>
```

As with most of the IGPs we have covered thus far, a process ID or another form of identifier is required to uniquely identify the environment. The ID can be a number ranging from 1 to 65,535:

```
Router(config)#router ospf 349
```

You must have IP configured on the router before you begin configuring OSPF. In most cases, the router's OSPF router ID is based on its IP address.

If you are configuring a router to participate in an area, you need to supply the area ID and the IP scheme for the area. On a Cisco router, the command used to configure this information is network. The syntax for the network command is as follows:

```
#network <ip address> <wildcard bits> area <area address>
```

In the syntax for the network command, notice that after the IP address for the network, the router requests a set of wildcard bits. These wildcard bits act as a reversed subnet mask. Whereas a subnet mask uses bits to indicate network addresses, the wildcard bits are used to represent hosts. When combined with the network IP address, the wildcard bits indicate the range of addresses available to the area. For example, the Class C IP network 225.65.34.0 would use a wildcard mask of 0.0.0.255 to include all the IP addresses in that network.

The following example establishes an area with the area number 1 and a Class B addressing scheme:

```
Router(config-router)#network 198.56.0.0 255.255.0.0 area 1
```

To configure a router as a member of the OSPF backbone, you use Area 0. Also, to ensure that the backbone routers can handle all the potential traffic for the network, the IP range should be 0.0.0.0 255.255.255.255 (that is, the IP broadcast range):

```
Router(config-router)#network 0.0.0.0 255.255.255.255 area 0
```

When you configure any ABR, it must have at least one interface configured to the backbone and one interface configured to the area. For example, an ABR for Area 3, would have one interface configured with an IP address in the acceptable range for Area 3, and one interface addressed for the backbone. This ensures that all the areas will have proper communication with the backbone.

To configure a stub area or an NSSA on a Cisco router, you must use some additional commands. For example, you use the area command to create both NSSA and stub networks.

You execute the area command on the ABR that separates the area from the backbone. The syntax of the area command is as follows:

```
#area <area number> <area type> <area specific params>
```

20

To create a stub area known as Area 3, you would execute the command as follows:

```
Router(config-router)#area 3 stub no-summary
```

The no-summary parameter indicates that no IP route summaries are to be sent into the stub area. This keeps the traffic volume as low as possible in the stub area.

You also use the area command to create virtual links between areas and the backbone. *Virtual links* allow areas to communicate directly with the backbone, through a transit area. The ABR of one area is virtually linked to the ABR of the transit area, which is directly linked to the backbone. In Figure 20.6, Area 1 is a transit area between Area 19 and the backbone. This creates a transparent virtual link to the backbone. The syntax for creating a virtual link is as follows:

```
#area <local area ID> virtual-link <router ID> <optional parameters>
```

The following example configures a virtual link in Area 3:

```
Router(config)#router ospf 45
Router(config-router)#area 3 virtual-link 123.1.1.2
```

On some routers, you might need to change the default metric of a particular link. OSPF automatically computes the metric of a route as 10^8 divided by the bandwidth of the link. However, this calculation may not always produce the desired results. For example, the largest bandwidth an OSPF metric can accommodate is that of an Fiber Distributed Date Interface (FDDI) link, which always produces a metric of 1.

> FDDI is a high-speed ring architecture capable of supporting 100Mbps of data.

If a router has more than one FDDI interface, or if technology has surpassed the FDDI bandwidth, the calculation used to figure the metric might need to be expanded. You can use the auto-cost command to change the value used to calculate the default metric:

```
Router(config-router)#auto-cost reference-bandwidth 4294967
```

> The value that is specified with the auto-cost command is a representation of the maximum number of bits per second. This value can range from 1 to 4,294,967.

Summary

This lesson introduced you to the concepts and commands behind one of the most popular routing protocols in use on large networks—OSPF. OSPF offers a great amount of flexibility for configuring areas and sculpting traffic flows.

OSPF networks, known as autonomous systems, are divided into areas. These areas can be classified as standard, backbone, stub, or NSSA. The type of area an OSPF router is in determines its role on the network.

As a link-state protocol, OSPF can achieve much faster convergence times than most distance vector protocols. These quick convergence times are due to the link-state protocol's ability to only distribute link information to its neighbors, making for smaller updates.

Q&A

Q Why do link-state protocols converge more quickly than distance vector protocols?

A Link-state protocols maintain detailed routing information only for their directly connected neighbors, whereas distance vector protocols share table data across all the routers in an environment. Because link-state protocol updates are smaller than distance vector protocol updates, the router can converge more quickly.

Q Why is the backbone area always 0?

A Every OSPF network needs a backbone area. Even if there is only one router on the backbone, it still must be configured as a backbone area. The backbone is the OSPF network's connection to the outside world. Therefore, to ensure that the backbone is quickly identified by the remaining routers on the network, it is automatically assigned the area number of 0.

Quiz

1. What is a stub area?
2. What is the formula for computing the OSPF default metric?
3. What parameter is required in order to enable OSPF?

Answers

1. An area that does not receive redistributed routes
2. Cost = 10^8/Link Bandwidth
3. The process ID, which requires IP

20

HOUR **21**

Exploring PNNI

The *Private Network-to-Network Interface (PNNI)* is a protocol used to pass data between ATM-switched networks. This hour's lesson will focus on the major concepts of PNNI and how it relates to routed networks.

Some literature from the ATM Forum refers to PNNI as Private Network to Node Interface. This further expresses the intent of PNNI to provide connectivity for large ATM switches and private networks (nodes).

PNNI handles the routing of information to and from multiple ATM groups on a local or worldwide scale. The term *PNNI* itself actually represents a logical interface through which multiple ATM networks can connect and communicate with each other. However, PNNI as a specification includes suggestions and regulations for the routing of data between large networks of ATM systems.

The ATM Forum created PNNI in 1996 as an efficient way to route information between ATM environments.

The ATM Forum (formed in 1991) is an alliance of corporations who work together toward a greater acceptance of ATM technology in business. The member companies of the ATM Forum set and accept standards and advances in ATM switching technology.

When the ATM Forum set out to create the standards that would later become PNNI, they looked to pre-established technologies to base the specifications on. By first looking to existing technologies, the members of the ATM Forum could save themselves years of work trying to create something that might not work, or developing a technology that may already have been developed.

PNNI is actually divided into two main functions. The first function is fulfilled by the PNNI routing protocol. The purpose of the PNNI routing protocol is to move data from one ATM cluster or group to another. To route the very fast-moving ATM cells efficiently, the ATM Forum based the designs for the PNNI routing protocol on other link-state routing protocols.

The PNNI routing protocol is based on link-state protocols. That is, through the use of update packets, a node on the network can update other nodes as to the state of its links. In general, these link-state protocols tend to route data in a quick and efficient way.

The second function of PNNI is a PNNI signaling protocol. The signaling protocol is used to build and tear down connections between switches. This function is critical in ATM networks. Before PNNI could work in an ATM environment, it needed to handle requests for connections between two or more switches.

The PNNI signaling protocol was based on another ATM Forum specification—*the User-to-Network Interface (UNI)*. The UNI signaling protocol had been developed by the ATM Forum to be a quick, adaptable signaling protocol between public and private networks. With a few minor revisions, UNI was modified to become the PNNI signaling protocol.

This chapter will introduce you to the technology behind PNNI and the two PNNI protocols. However, before we can discuss how PNNI works, you need to understand the basics of ATM networking.

ATM Architecture

PNNI functions on the ATM networks of the PNNI. Let's examine exactly what ATM is and how it works. *Asynchronous Transfer Mode (ATM)* was developed to enable the high-speed transfer of data, voice, and video over public data lines. Figure 21.1 illustrates a typical ATM architecture.

FIGURE 21.1

An ATM network.

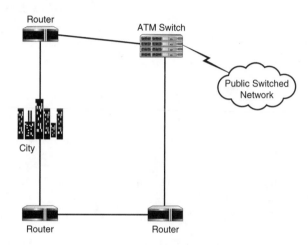

ATM, unlike many networks that people are familiar with, is a *switch environment*. A connection-oriented protocol is used to create circuits between switches for the reliable transfer of data. ATM supports the connectionless transfer of data; however, it is seldom evoked. ATM efficiently transfers data over public lines at rates up to 1GBps and above.

Unlike ATM, most of the technologies that are common on networks today are connectionless (IP being the most popular). The overall inescapable problem with connectionless transfers of data is that there is no guarantee that the data will reach its intended destination. ATM, being connection-oriented, builds *session length* circuits between switches. After the session is completed (that is, all the data has been transferred between the two switches), ATM then tears down the circuit. This allows another session to use one or both of the ports for another connection. Figure 21.2 illustrates the process of building and tearing down ATM connections.

21

FIGURE 21.2

An ATM connection.

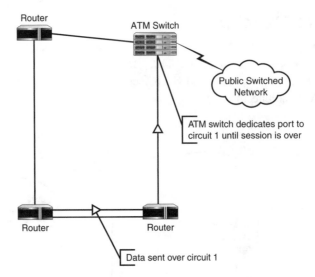

ATM is far from the only architecture to use connection-oriented transfers of data. In fact, TCP, IP's protocol relative, is a connection-oriented protocol. However, ATM is without a doubt the best example of functional connection-oriented data transfer.

The key to ATM's quick transfer rates is in the underlying format of its data. ATM does not transfer variable length packets like most protocols. Protocols such as IS-IS (discussed in Chapter 9, "Discovering IP Router Configurations") transfer packets that can vary in size depending on the data being transferred. Therefore, the receiving device must scan the header of the packet, determine the size of the data, and process the packet. With variable length packets, the amount of time needed to process each packet will change from packet to packet. The larger the packet is, the longer it will take to process.

However, ATM transfers in a fixed length format known as a *cell*. ATM cells are always the same length, no matter how much data needs to be sent. Figure 21.3 illustrates an ATM cell.

FIGURE 21.3

An ATM cell.

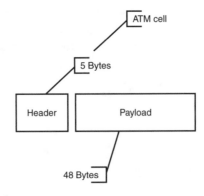

ATM cells, regardless of the amount of data being moved, are always 53 bytes long. As shown in Figure 21.3, ATM cells consist of a 5 byte header and a 48 byte *payload*, or data segment.

> Even though ATM cells are a fixed length (eliminating the need for a header length field), they still need a header. The header of an ATM cell specifies the source and destination of the payload.

The fixed length of ATM cells makes them perfect for carrying digital audio and video. Because receiving ATM devices do not have random bursts of slow and fast processing (dependent on packet size), the signals are received evenly and quickly. Any slowdown in the digitizing of the signal will most likely equal the sample rate of the video or audio and go unnoticed.

Another factor in ATM's success is the fact that it is asynchronous. This means that ATM switches can both send and receive signals at the same time. Therefore, a pair of switches communicating on the same circuit can send each other data at the same time, cutting the transfer time in half.

Again, ATM's asynchronous nature is a result of its fixed cell format. Because the ATM cells are a fixed 53 bytes in length, each switch knows how long it is going to take to receive a packet. Therefore, in between sending cells, the switch can open itself up to receive any cells arriving from the switch on the other end on the circuit.

Before we can further explore how ATM switching and signaling work, we need to look at the layout of a typical ATM network. Because PNNI was not only created to work on ATM networks, but based on an existing protocol (UNI v3), we need to better understand the architecture of ATM switched sites.

ATM Network Layout

There are two types of ATM networks: public and private. A public ATM network exists in the *public cloud*. That is, somewhat like the Internet, a public ATM network is a group of public access ATM networks, usually managed by a public telecom firm. A private ATM network, on the other hand, exists completely within the domain of one enterprise.

> Keep in mind, public ATM networks are comprised almost entirely of ATM switches, known as *public switches*.

21

Of course, as with everything in life, the lines of definition are not always that clear. In fact, you can have two private ATM networks connected by a public network. In this case, each network is its own group and not viewed as a single entity. The private networks are private, and the public networks are public.

ATM networks are relatively simple in design, but not in technology. The devices in ATM networks are split into two categories—ATM switches and ATM end systems. The *ATM switch* is the device that connects to the "mesh" of the network. It's the device that moves data to and from the ATM network. The *ATM end system* is any device on an ATM network that is not an ATM switch. Therefore, all PCs, routers, and printers are considered end systems (ESes). Because ESes have no switching capability, they forward all data to the ATM switch for transmission over the network.

When ATM was first developed, these two device classifications made designing ATM environments fairly easy. The first uses for ATM were in public switched networks. In other words, the company's local network connected to an ATM switch. The information from this ATM switch was then carried over the public switching network, usually a public telephone company. The public switched network carried the data to the ATM switch at the destination network. Figure 21.4 illustrates an ATM public switched network.

FIGURE 21.4

An ATM public switched network.

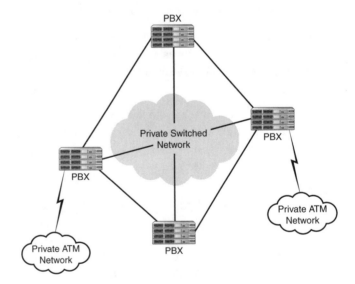

For the first ATM public networks, a set of protocols was developed—UNI and NNI. These protocols were created solely for the purpose of signaling to the public switches that another ATM switch had data to transmit. Figure 21.5 illustrates where the two different protocols are used.

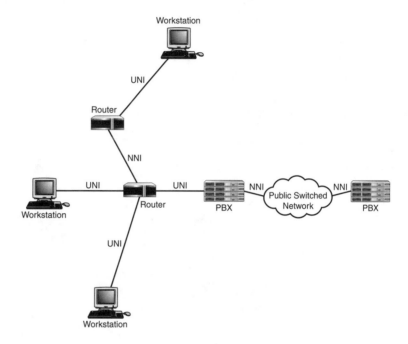

As Figure 21.5 illustrates, because there are two types of ATM networks (public and private), there are two types of UNI and NNI protocols.

UNI was developed to allow the ATM switch (or end system) on a private network to signal to an unknown public switch that it had data to send. UNI would then create a circuit between the two switches. After the session between the two switches was done, UNI would tear down the circuit. The private version of the protocol (P-UNI) could be used to connect ESes with private ATM switches.

As ATM networks began to grow, a protocol needed to be developed to handle the intense communication load of switch-to-switch signaling. NNI and its private counterpart PNNI were developed just for this purpose. NNI would be modeled after UNI, to ensure that proper communication standards were adhered to.

Let's look at how UNI was developed and how it works.

21

The UNI Signaling Protocol

UNI is a signaling protocol that enables the establishment of communications between either ESes and private switches, or private switches and public switches. Signaling protocols send specially formatted messages to switches. The receiving switch then allows for an open line (circuit) of communication between the devices.

UNI can signal for two types of circuits to be open in an ATM environment: point-to-point or point-to-multipoint. Figures 21.6 and 21.7 illustrate point-to-point and point-to-multipoint communications.

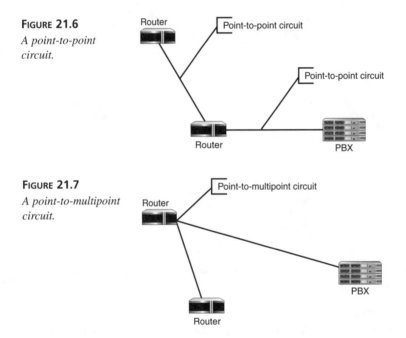

FIGURE 21.6
A point-to-point circuit.

FIGURE 21.7
A point-to-multipoint circuit.

When UNI opens a point-to-point circuit, one system contacts another and requests a session. After the receiving system accepts the signal, a circuit is opened between the two. Acting much like a direct cable connection, a point-to-point circuit enables communication between two systems or points.

The major advantage to a point-to-point circuit is the use of asynchronous ports. A point-to-point ATM connection can establish bidirectional communication between systems. This is very desirable in a networking environment.

A point-to-multipoint connection is established when one system needs to open a circuit with multiple systems. One possible reason for opening a point-to-multipoint circuit would be for multicasting. The major disadvantage to ATM point-to-multipoint connections is that they are not asynchronous.

A point-to-multipoint circuit will only enable communications in one direction (from the point to the multipoints). This is not an issue with the UNI protocol, as the fields within the ATM cell do not allow for the needed entries to open an asynchronous point-to-multipoint (known as multipoint-to-multipoint) circuit. Let's look at the fields within a UNI ATM cell to see how a point-to-point circuit is established.

A standard ATM cell has a 5 byte header. This header contains the required information for any system to determine what kind of cell it is, who it is intended for, and who sent it. The header itself contains different fields depending on the type (that is, a UNI cell header contains different fields than a NNI cell). Figure 21.8 illustrates the fields within a UNI cell header. The fields within the header can be seen in Table 21.1.

FIGURE 21.8

The fields within a UNI cell header.

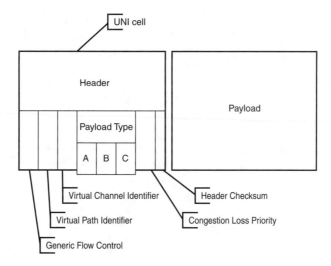

21

TABLE 21.1 UNI Cell Header Fields

Field Name	Size	Purpose
Generic Flow Control	4 bits	Generally unused.
Virtual Path Identifier	8 bits	This field identifies the next hop toward the cell's indented destination. (A cell might need to travel through multiple switches before reaching its destination.)
Virtual Channel Identifier	16 bits	This field also helps the current switch identify the next switch to receive the cell.
Payload Type	3 bits	Identifies the contents of the cell.
Bit A	1 bit	If this bit is 1, the payload is data. If this bit is 0, the payload is not data.
Bit B	1 bit	Indicates congestion.
Bit C	1 bit	Marker used to signal the last in a series of cells.
Congestion Loss Priority	1 bit	This field is used by the switch to discard any cells that have taken too long to reach their destination.
Header Checksum	variable	Used to calculate the size of the header.

As the cell is passed through the network, each switch modifies the Virtual Path Identifier and the Virtual Channel Identifier fields to aid in the successful routing of the cell. As each switch passes the cell along, the path taken by the cell is marked as shown in Figure 21.9.

FIGURE 21.9
UNI cell being routed.

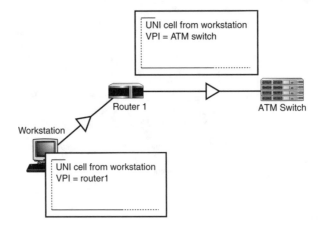

When the cell reaches its final destination, the last switch decides to either accept or reject the circuit. If the switch accepts the cell, the path the cell took to reach its destination is turned into a UNI circuit, illustrated in Figure 21.10.

FIGURE 21.10
A UNI circuit.

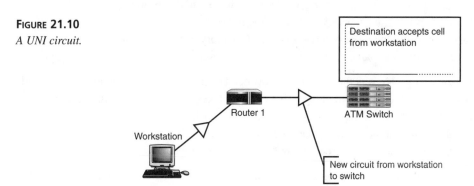

UNI is a good protocol for moving information around an ATM network. However, when the communication requirements dictate that a circuit be opened between two private switches, a different protocol is needed.

UNI does not have the routing or signaling capacity needed to fully handle the task of establishing and tearing down circuits, as well as advertising routing paths. When the members of the ATM Forum set out to create a protocol to do just that, they started with UNI.

By modeling the new private network-to-network interface after UNI, they were ensured of a good base on which to build the protocol. The following sections describe the PNNI protocol, how it works, and why it was modeled as it was.

PNNI Hierarchy

PNNI networks, like those of most protocols, follow a hierarchy. Certain systems or groups of systems are granted precedence over others in the hierarchy to establish optimal paths. In much the same way that IP networks are supernetted and subnetted to establish a relationship between groups of devices, PNNI networks have a hierarchical order of groupings.

If PNNI did not accommodate a routing hierarchy, the networks would be formed in a flat manner—every group or cluster of systems would be equal to every other. Having networks that are flat from a routing perspective can hurt a network in a couple of ways.

21

The first way a flat routing environment can hurt a network is by increasing the amount of memory and processing power needed to make routing decisions. If every system of the network is on the same level, there is no way for a router to separate them into smaller groups. Therefore, a router using an algorithm to calculate a routing path will need to compute that path using every system on the network as a variable. Keeping track of such variables would take a very large amount of memory. Crunching the numbers required for calculating the paths of that many systems would take even more processing power.

The second problem is the reduction of speed. The more variables a router must consider when making a decision, the longer that decision takes. Therefore, on a flat network where every system is the same, every system must be considered by the router as a possible variable. On a larger network, the processes of routing data could require the use of so many variables that network speed would be unbearably slow.

PNNI guards against problems associated with flat networks by implementing a hierarchical network scheme. PNNI places every system into a group, and those groups are then placed into larger groups, creating an endless possibility to the size of the hierarchy that can encompass a network. The smallest group, also considered the base for everything else in the hierarchy, is known as a peer group.

PNNI Peer Groups

PNNI networks are divided into *peer groups (PGs)*. Every peer group has its own address on the network. This address, known as a PG number or group address, is unique for every group, and is shared by all the members of the PG.

How the ESes are separated into peer groups depends on the address of the switch. The separation of the PGs relies on the addressing of the switches because a PG is designated by the common address of its members, and a member's address is derived from the switch to which it is attached.

The purpose of a PNNI PG is purely for routing. Within these PGs, the ESes and their switches pass data among themselves and the other members of the same PG. This limits the amount of traffic that is passed from switch to switch. Being the lowest member of a hierarchy has its advantages.

For PNNI routing purposes, the members of a PG can only have topographical knowledge of the systems within their PG. Systems for any given PG will never know the specific composition of any other PG. By creating a lowest-level group like this, PNNI can control the amount of data that border nodes need to process.

A *border node* is an ATM switch that connects peer groups. By routing data through a border node, information can be sent from one peer group to another.

Let's explore the process of addressing PNNI end systems and peer groups.

PNNI NSAP Addressing

Most private ATM networks use the NSAP addressing format. (Other protocols, such as IS-IS, also use the NSAP address format, or a modified version of it.) The 20-byte NSAP address for ATM is comprised of some network-specific fields, and the host device's MAC address. Figure 21.11 illustrates the fields that make up an NSAP address.

FIGURE 21.11

A NSAP address for an ATM network.

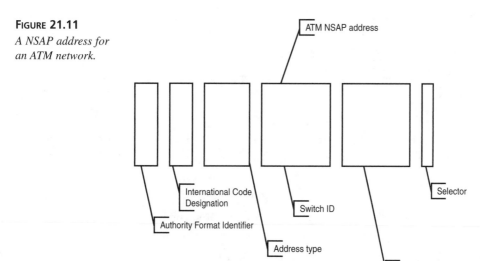

The fields of the NSAP address in PNNI are as follows:

- Authority Format Identifier (1 byte)—Specifies the authority assigning the address.
- International Code Designator (2 bytes)—This field is specific to the addressing authority (used for international uniqueness).
- Address Type (4 bytes)—Signifies whether the address is ICD, NSAP, or DCC.
- Switch ID (6 bytes)—The MAC address of the switch.
- End System Identifier (6 bytes)—The MAC address of the end system.
- Selector—Unused.

21

Therefore, a typical ATM switch address could look like this (the example used supplies the AFI and ICD of Cisco Systems, as the AFI and ICD are unique to the system running them). Figure 21.12 illustrates a populated ATM switch address.

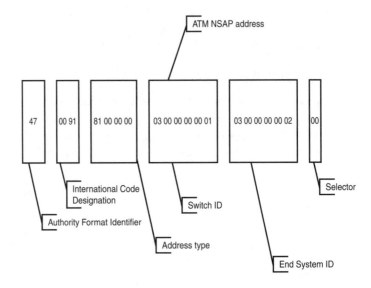

In a peer group, all the systems share a 12-byte identifier. This 12-byte identifier is actually the first 12 bytes of the switch's 13-byte ATM address. The 13th byte is the *switch identifier*.

Therefore, because the first 12 bytes of the ATM address are going to be constant for every ES in the PG, these 12 bytes are the peer group number. In essence, the PG identifier will be the penultimate byte of the switch's ATM address.

One unique aspect of the ATM switch address format applies to the ATM switch itself. According to the preceding logic (The MAC address of an ATM switch is the end system ID of all other devices in the same peer group), the address fields End System ID and Switch ID are identical on an ATM switch within a peer group.

When a new ES is attached to the switch, it adopts the switch's End System Identifier as its Switch ID. The ES's MAC address is then used to populate its own End System Identifier field.

Using this logic, PNNI can dynamically create peer groups. Whenever an ES is connected to an ATM switch, it dynamically assigns the NSAP address, and is adopted into the peer group. These peer groups are at the heart of the PNNI hierarchy model. The following example (Figure 21.13) shows three ATM peer groups.

FIGURE 21.13

Three ATM peer groups.

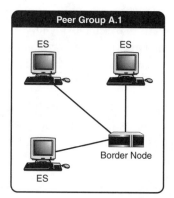

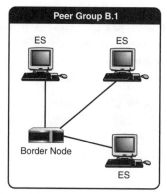

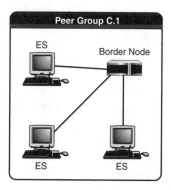

As illustrated in Figure 21.13, the new peer groups are identified by the peer group numbers. Notice that the structure of the address appears to be different from the previous example. The reason is simple. Because the first 12 bytes of the ATM address are the same for every node in the peer group, a letter can be used to represent them (in our example, the letter A). The number after the dot is the 13th bit of the ATM address of the ATM switch. This number is unique to the switch, and completes the representation of the peer group number. The MAC address of each node is then attached to this peer group number to represent each individual end system.

Before routing can begin between the new peer groups, one more step needs to be taken. Each peer group switch needs to be assigned a PNNI level. This level determines the peer groups standing in the PNNI hierarchy. The group with the lowest PNNI-level number is considered the dominant group. The dominant peer group is given routing priority over other peer groups. A PNNI level can be any numeric value from 0 to 104.

21

A peer group with a configured level of 104 is going to have a very low routing priority compared to a peer group with a level of 0. By employing levels, the peer groups can be continuously combined into larger and larger entities. For example, in Figure 21.13, the Peer groups A.1 and A.2 can be considered one larger group. The peer group with the lowest level ID handles the routing decisions in this larger group.

By continually combining the peer groups into larger entities, PNNI eliminates the problems of a flat routing network. Even though the members of a peer group only have knowledge of the topography of their peer group, the lower-level switches have topographical knowledge of each peer group above them.

> The topology of a peer group refers to the location of the end systems in relationship to the switch. In other words, this is the physical layout or design of the environment.

To keep the routing traffic between switches to a minimum, each peer group acts as a self-contained network. Therefore, if an end system in Peer Group A.1 needs to send data to an end system in Peer Group A.2, it must follow a few steps to get there. The switch in A.1, not having direct knowledge of the end systems in A.2, determines that the cell is not meant for the local peer group. The switch then forwards the packet to the switch for Peer Group A.2, and routing protocols take over from here.

As these groups grow in size, the amount of memory needed to keep track of the topology and handle the routing requests grows as well. A division mechanism is needed to permit the potential limit of the PNNI architecture to be circumvented.

> One of the keys to the success of the PNNI network structure is its capability to scale to networks of almost any size. The PNNI hierarchy model, with its use of peer group numbers and peer group levels, can be adapted to most any network.

Through the use of PNNI levels, Peer Groups A.1 and A.2 can be considered a single higher-level peer group. The switch with the lowest level will handle the routing for the higher-level group. Figure 21.14 illustrates a PNNI network with peer groups that have been divided into levels. The structure of the figure has been modified into a pyramid to better illustrate the concept of PNNI leveling.

FIGURE **21.14**

PNNI levels.

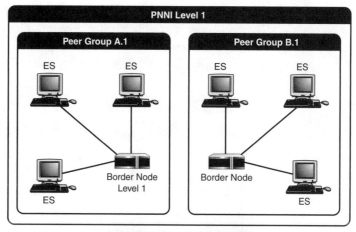
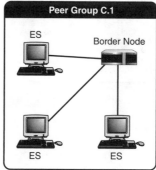

By taking the logic of PNNI levels and expanding it to hundreds of switches, PNNI networks can be scaled to almost any size. After the PNNI levels have been determined, the environment is ready for routing. PNNI will handle the passing of data from switch to switch.

As we briefly discussed earlier in the chapter, PNNI is actually split (by function) into two different protocols. The process of routing data on an ATM network requires special considerations on the part of the protocols being used. Therefore, in addition to the routing protocol of PNNI, a separate signaling protocol needs to be added.

After the data is sent from an end system to a switch, the first job of the PNNI signaling protocol is to notify the destination switch that a session is being requested. The signaling protocol will then build a circuit between the two points. (This process is described in detail later in this hour, in the section "PNNI Signaling Protocol.")

21

After the circuit is open, the second function of PNNI kicks in. As described in the next section, the PNNI routing protocol will handle the actual moving of the data from switch to switch. Figure 21.15 illustrates a PNNI network. The notation in the figure shows what protocols work in certain areas of the ATM environment.

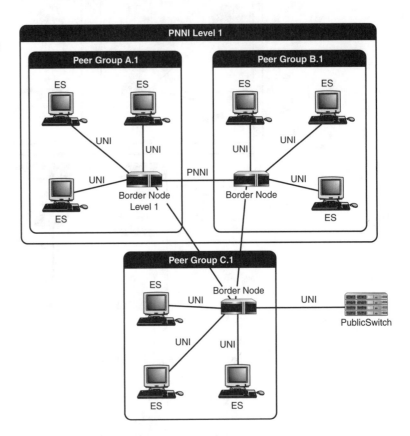

FIGURE 21.15

An ATM environment map with protocols.

Following the flow of data via protocols on an ATM network can be rather confusing if you have never seen it before. Even though the signaling portion of PNNI might seem a little foreign, the routing part is pretty straightforward.

PNNI Routing Protocol

The PNNI routing protocol is based on the very successful link-state category of protocols. Let's quickly review link-state protocols before discussing the technology behind the PNNI routing protocol.

Every switch on an ATM network will advertise the state of its links through hello messages. These messages are distributed to every other switch in the ATM environment regardless of peer group. The receiving systems digest the information in the hello message and formulate an overall picture of the network. Figure 21.16 illustrates the passing of a hello message on an ATM network.

FIGURE 21.16

ATM hello messages.

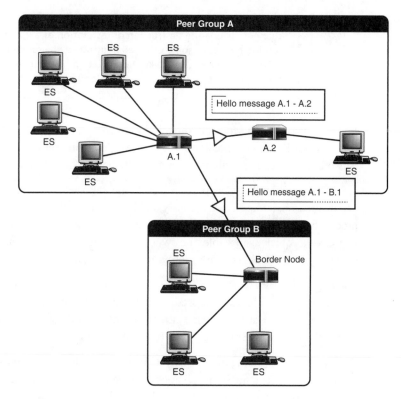

Switch A.1 advertises to Switches B.1 and A.2 the statuses of all end systems directly attached to it. In other words, Switch A.1 will tell Switches A.2 and B.1 that the five end systems connected to it are up and functional. Included with this hello message will be all the metrics needed to associate the particular systems with a path.

When Switch A.2 receives the hello message from A.1, it will realize from the peer group ID that Switch A.1 is in the same peer group. The two routers will then form a link between each other establishing that they are within the same peer group.

21

The process of sending hello messages is know as a *link-state flood*. During this process, every system involved will flood the network with hello messages, advertising the state of its links. These messages are digested by all the switches on the network. Link-state floods have a tendency to be very bandwidth- and processor-intensive.

> Link-state floods are initiated by a change in the ATM environment. These changes include the destruction or restoration of a link, the change of a routing metric, or some other administrative environmental change. However, some changes, like those to certain QoS metrics, might not be great enough to initiate a link-state flood.

Because every switch sends out the advertisements, link-state floods will be worse on larger networks than on smaller ones. However, no matter how many switches are on the network, one precaution will make a lot of difference in how the switches handle the floods.

An ATM switch will always process a hello message before processing a cell for routing. For this reason, adding more memory and processing capability to a switch will help it process hello messages quicker, thus expediting the routing process. By processing the hello messages as quick as possible, the switches can return to normal operation. This process of obtaining the latest network routing information quickly is known as convergence.

Convergence occurs when every switch is operating with the same picture of the network. That is, every switch has processed the hello messages and agreed that the contents of those messages describe the current network topology. In general, link-state protocols like PNNI have a faster convergence time than others.

Routers, no matter what protocols are being used, need to have the most up-to-date topology information to make the best decisions. Link-state protocols use the information in the hello messages (which create the switches-routing table) to calculate the shortest path between systems. Like other link-state protocols, PNNI works on a *shortest path* basis. This means that a PNNI device will always try to choose the shortest possible path between two systems.

Deciding which path is the shortest is the job of the routing algorithm. The routing algorithm is a formula used by the PNNI device to calculate the metrics found in its routing table to produce the best path to a destination. PNNI devices are configured with different metrics to indicate a device's likelihood for being chosen as the shortest path. To understand the algorithm used on PNNI networks, we need to know what variables or metrics are used to calculate the paths.

The metrics that can be used on a PNNI network to describe a device are as follows:

- Administrative Weight (AW)—An administrator-assigned cost. The metric is purely arbitrary, and has a default value of 5040.

- Available Cell Rate (AvCR)—A metric that represents the bandwidth of an unused portion of a line that can accommodate cells. In other words, if a 56k line only has 5k of traffic on it, the AvCR of that line is 51k.

- Maximum Cell Transfer Delay (MaxCTD)—The delay experienced in transmitting cells over a particular link.

- Cell Loss Ratio (CLR)—The number of cells typically lost over a particular link.

- Cell Delay Variation (CDV)—A combined metric representing the link's CLR minus the average CLR for the environment (CLR–Average CLR).

- Maximum Cell Rate (MaxCR)—The maximum cell capacity of the line within a given service category or traffic class.

Each of the preceding metrics has an assigned value, either dynamic or statically. The values are used by PNNI's routing algorithm to calculate the overall value or usefulness of a particular link in reaching the cell's ultimate destination. If the combination of the metrics proves that the current link is the ideal link for routing, the cells are forwarded across the line.

All the metrics listed here, with the exception of Administrative Weight, are considered QoS metrics. QoS routing is a standard set forth in RFC 2386.

The Relationship between PNNI and QoS Metrics

PNNI adheres to the QoS specifications for ATM. ATM, like every QoS-compliant architecture, supports the same metrics for providing a consistent level of routing service to the end systems. Although many protocols have been adapted or enhanced to meet QoS standards, PNNI was designed to handle QoS natively. No extra hardware or software to implement the metrics is required for QoS ATM routing.

Metrics such as MaxCR and CLR are used to ensure that a cell is going to be forwarded over a link that can handle it. The QoS metrics Maximum Cell Transfer Delay, Cell Loss Ration, Cell Delay Variation, Maximum Cell Rate, and the administrative metric Administrative Weight are all statically defined. They rarely change without the administrator's intervention.

21

The QoS metric Available Cell Rate is a dynamic metric that can fluctuate depending on the current link traffic. However, because this metric is dynamic, a change in this cost will generally not cause a link-state update. A change in the Available Cell Rate needs to surpass a preset threshold to trigger a network-wide update.

When a cell needs to be routed on a PNNI network, the signaling protocol will request a minimum value that the circuit will need to successfully route the cells and meet the minimum QoS.

> Depending on the switch being used in the ATM environment, a different QoS algorithm can be used to help determine the available paths. PNNI allows for two different QoS algorithms—simple Generic Call Admission Control (GCAC) and complex GCAC.
>
> Simple GCAC weighs only the available cell rate metric when making a decision whereas complex GCAC uses Available Cell Rate and two new metrics: Cell Rate Margin and Variance Factor.

For example, the PNNI signaling protocol might request that the circuit have a certain bandwidth. In that case, only links that fall within that QoS bandwidth metric can be considered by the algorithm as a possible path. Figure 21.17 illustrates a QoS circuit request.

FIGURE 21.17
QoS routing.

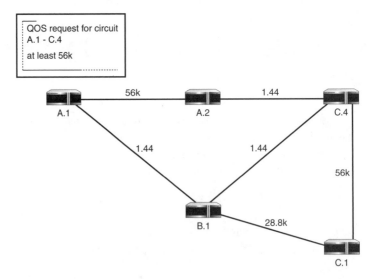

In the figure, data is attempting to be routed from A.1 to C.4. The signaling protocol requests that a link with at least 56k of constant bandwidth be opened to route the cells. This request automatically leaves the link between B.1 and C.1 out of consideration for carrying the cells.

PNNI determines what paths are used for routing data by weighing each link's metrics against a routing algorithm. This algorithm examines the cost associated with every link and determines which is the best to use.

The algorithm of choice for many link-state protocols is Dijkstra's algorithm. PNNI is no exception. While calculating the shortest path, the routing algorithm must ensure that all of the requirements for QoS are met before choosing the optimal path.

Dijkstra's algorithm uses the metrics assigned to each link to determine the shortest path between all possible points on a network simultaneously. It dynamically calculates the costs of every link on the network at the same time. This makes the algorithm a very quick and reliable way to determine paths.

Combining native QoS and shortest path routing is one of the attributes that makes PNNI an attractive protocol, especially for the ATM environment. However, the PNNI routing protocol is only half of the picture.

ATM as architecture is circuit-based. Circuits need to be established before data can be routed over them. The job of establishing these circuits goes to the PNNI signaling protocol.

PNNI Signaling Protocol

The PNNI signaling protocol is the portion of PNNI required to establish and tear down connections between devices. The signaling protocol takes into account any metrics, including QoS, to request that circuits be opened for routing purposes. After the signaling protocol has successfully built a circuit between two points, the PNNI routing protocol can take over.

When an end system on an ATM network needs to send data, the PNNI signaling protocol starts the process by contacting the closest directly-connected ATM switch and notifying it of the request. Figure 21.18 illustrates an ATM end system with a routing request.

The PNNI signaling protocol contacts Switch A.1 on behalf of the end system. The signaling protocol notifies the switch that the end system is requesting that it open a circuit to an end system in the D peer group.

21

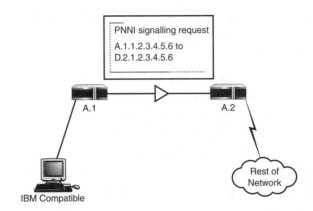

FIGURE 21.18

An end system pre-paring to request a circuit.

Even though the end system knows which specific end systems it needs to contact in Peer Group D, it has no topographical knowledge of that group. Therefore, it would simply request the circuit to the border node of the peer group. Peer Group D's border node would then route the cells to the correct end system.

The signaling protocol also sends along a set of QoS requests. These requests (or minimum requirements) are passed from switch to switch. When a switch receives the QoS requirements, it first finds the links that can meet those metrics. The remaining links are exempt from consideration. The request is then passed down the optimal link to the next switch. If no links are found that meet the QoS requirements of the signaling request, the request is denied. The information from the source end system is then discarded.

Eventually the signaling request reaches the destination border node. Here, the switch can either accept or deny the circuit. If the circuit is accepted, the border node passes the cells to the destination end system, and a circuit is established between the two systems. If the destination border node refuses the request, the data from the end system is discarded.

Figure 21.19 illustrates an ATM network with all the metrics populated. Let's look at the path the signaling protocol would take from end system A.1.X.X.X.X.X to end system D.1.X.X.X.X.X.

The signaling protocol would send the request to Switch A.1. The QoS requirements want a line with at least 56k of bandwidth. When A.1 receives the signaling request, it evaluates all its links to determine which have 56k of bandwidth. In this case, there is only one link, and it does have 56k. The signaling request is then forwarded to B.1.

At B.1, the switch has two choices: The cells can be sent over the B.1—C.1 link, or the B.1—C.2 link. Because the B.1—C.2 link does not meet the QoS requirements, the link is not considered for the path. The request is therefore forwarded to C.1.

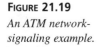

Figure 21.19

An ATM network-signaling example.

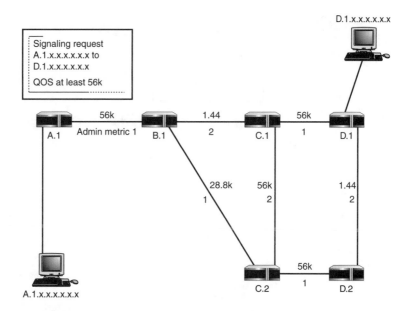

When C.1 gets the request, it also has two choices. The links C.1—C.2 and C.1—D.1 both meet the QoS requirements for the circuit. The switch then turns to its routing algorithm, which determines that the shortest path is the link C.1—D.1. Therefore, the signaling request is forwarded to D.1.

D.1 recognizes that the end system D.1.X.X.X.X.X.X is within its peer group. Switch D.1 can then either accept the circuit request by forwarding it to end system D.1.X.X.X.X.X.X, or it can reject the request. If D.1 accepts the request, a circuit is established between the two end systems. Figure 21.20 illustrates this completed circuit.

If the signaling request is rejected by D.1, the switches C.1, B.1, and A.1 are notified with a return message. This message cancels the circuit's requests on the switches and discards any cells pertaining to the circuit that the switch might have processed.

When the end system A.1.X.X.X.X.X.X completes its session with D.1.X.X.X.X.X.X, the PNNI signaling protocol tears down the circuit, leaving the links clear for routing.

Because some of the QoS metrics are dynamically assigned, there is a chance that they might change during a transmission. PNNI has a built-in mechanism to deal with such an event. PNNI can implement its crankback mechanism if QoS metrics change unfavorably during a transmission.

21

FIGURE **21.20**

A completed ATM circuit.

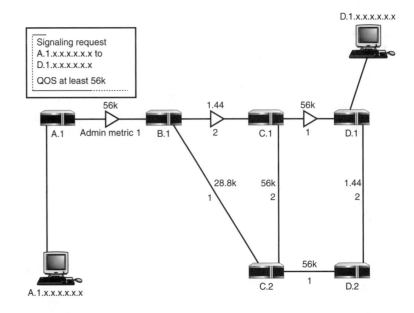

PNNI Crankback

Another feature of PNNI is known as the PNNI *crankback*. Look at the circuit in Figure 21.21.

FIGURE **21.21**

A completed ATM circuit with QoS metrics.

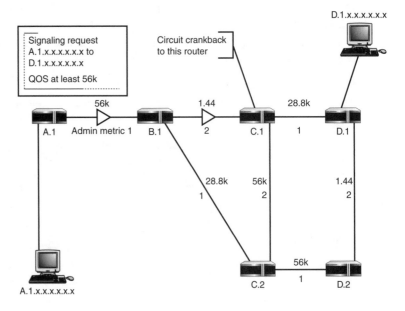

During the lifespan of a circuit, the QoS metrics, such as Available Cell Rate, may change. If a QoS metric changes to the detriment of the circuit (for example, the circuit requires a delay of 10ms, and the delay jumps to 200ms), the PNNI protocol will perform an action known as a crankback.

During a crankback, the protocol rolls the circuit back to the last ATM switch that still meets the QoS requirements. Figure 21.22 shows a circuit during a crankback operation.

FIGURE 21.22

A circuit crankback.

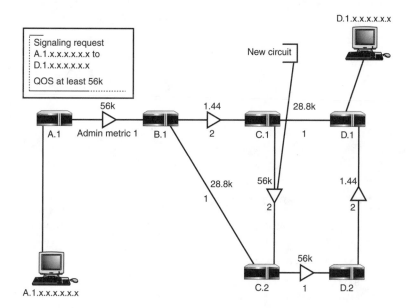

The circuit is then rebuilt from the last good switch. While rebuilding the circuit, the QoS requirements are re-evaluated. When a circuit is involved in a crankback, information pertaining to the crankback is added to a cell. This cell is sent back to the originating switch. The switch can then use the information to rebuild a new circuit. The rebuilt circuit would then look like the circuit in Figure 21.23.

Now that we have discussed the concepts behind ATM switching and PNNI routing, let's examine the commands needed to configure PNNI routing on a Cisco switch.

21

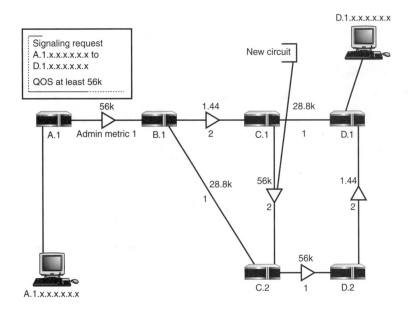

FIGURE 21.23

A rebuilt circuit after a crankback.

Configuring PNNI

PNNI is a protocol that is not actually configured on your router. Because PNNI functions in ATM environments, it has to be configured on switches. The following configuration examples were taken from a Cisco switch:

```
Switch(config)#atm router pnni
Switch(config-atm-router)# aesa embedded-number left-justified
```

There are two commands featured here. The first enables the ATM protocol PNNI, while the last command is used to enable PNNI version 2 encoding. The command aesa (which stands for "atm end system address") ensures that all E.164 address prefixes are translated automatically.

These commands enable PNNI routing. However, there are some peripheral commands that you should be aware of. For example, to specify the ATM address of the switch, use the atm address command:

```
Switch#configure terminal
Switch(config)# atm address 52.000a.c001.034b.000.06a7.0001.
```

Given their name, the main function of switches is not routing. However, they do offer the capability to utilize a very effective routing protocol. Unfortunately, there are many more commands related to and associated with ATM and PNNI than can be covered in one lesson of a book focused on routing.

Summary

PNNI is an effective protocol used to route information across ATM networks. Even though ATM networks are built upon the technologies of switches rather than routers, PNNI is still a routing protocol. PNNI consists of several smaller protocols, each with a specialized function (for example, signaling).

PNNI follows a hierarchical structure where end systems are placed into peer groups. These groups form a routing structure that makes PNNI a very efficient protocol. Other devices within peer groups include Level 1 routers and Level 2 routers.

All devices with a PNNI environment derive their address structure from the MAC address of the ATM switch. Having a common address to map across an entire area gives PNNI a point of reference when routing data to and from the environment.

Q&A

Q Why does PNNI run on switches rather than routers?

A Switches can perform many of the same tasks as routers. Therefore, networks comprised of switches need protocols to assist in the routing process, just as routers. PNNI was designed with the specific needs of switched networks in mind. Keep in mind that switches function on the data link layer of the OSI model, whereas routers function of the network layer. (PNNI actually utilizes the ATM equivalent of the data link layer.)

Q Why is PNNI crankback a desirable feature of PNNI?

A PNNI crankback allows switches to destroy and rebuild circuits that no longer meet QoS standards. This function allows PNNI to consistently utilize the best possible networking conditions.

Quiz

1. What protocol became the PNNI signaling protocol?
2. What are the two QoS algorithms used by PNNI?
3. What is CLR?
4. What is the advantage of point-to-point circuits?

Answers

1. UNI (User-to-Network Interface)
2. Simple GCAC and complex GCAC (Generic Call Admission Control)
3. Cell Loss Ratio
4. Point-to-point circuits allow bidirectional communication between switches.

21

Hour **22**

Using IS-IS

The *IS-IS (Intermediate System-to-Intermediate System)* protocol is a link-state routing protocol developed by ISO to work with the CLNP (Connectionless Network Protocol). The main focus of this hour's lesson will be the general concepts behind IS-IS, and how it complements routed networks.

Unlike the other protocols discussed in this book, IS-IS was originally developed for a proprietary topology from Digital Equipment Corporation (DEC) known as DECnet. It did not necessarily conform immediately to the same OSI standards as protocols like IGRP and BGP. Therefore, some of the structures and concepts within IS-IS may seem foreign.

IS-IS and DECnet

The Digital Equipment Corporation (DEC) developed DECnet as a protocol suite in 1975 for their popular VAX line of computers. Each version of DECnet is known as a phase (Phase I, Phase II, and so on).

IS-IS was based on DECnet Phase V, but much of what made DECnet Phase V work was actually implemented in DECnet Phase IV.

Like all protocols, DECnet needed to follow a specific architecture to move information from one system to another. Therefore, a protocol model was put in place to illustrate how data would move from the user interface of one system, through the PC, over the transmission media, and into the destination system. Most protocols today adhere to OSI model architecture. However, with the first four phases of DECnet, DEC followed their own proprietary architecture for moving data.

DECnet was (and still is) a proprietary system used to enable communication between DEC equipment. The first four phases of DECnet did not adhere to the OSI model, but were instead based on the Digital Network Architecture (DNA).

All phases of DECnet are designed to be backward compatible. Therefore, DECnet Phase III is backward compatible with Phase II. When DEC began developing the OSI-compliant DECnet Phase V, it realized that the protocol needed to be implemented in such a way to be backward compatible with the DECnet DNA architecture. This would later become a very important feature of IS-IS.

DECnet Phase IV DNA was comprised of eight layers that more or less correlated to the seven layers of the OSI model. Figure 22.1 shows the eight layers of Phase IV DNA and how they relate to the OSI model.

You will notice some small differences between DEC's DNA architecture and ISO's OSI model. The main difference is in the upper layers of the two protocols. Many of DNA's upper layers span multiple OSI layers. However, the lower layers (those crucial for routing) are relatively the same. This helped DEC make an easier transition from DNA to OSI.

Because of the differences in the upper and lower layers between the two architectures, DECnet addresses are structured differently then those in other protocols. DECnet addresses are comprised of two parts: an area and a node. This is a concept that would later be carried over to IS-IS.

FIGURE 22.1

The eight layers of the DECnet Phase IV DNA architecture.

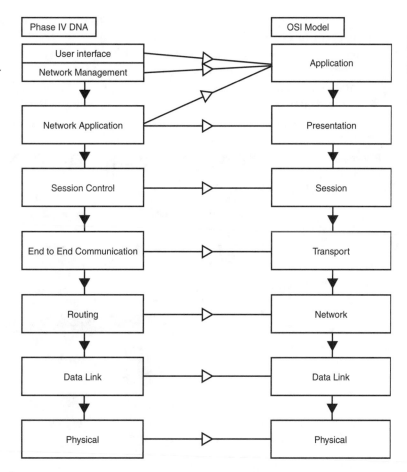

22

DECnet Areas and Nodes

DECnet addresses are 16 bits long. Figure 22.2 illustrates a common DECnet address.

FIGURE 22.2

Dissection of a DECnet address.

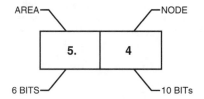

The first six bits of a DECnet address are known as the *area*. The area can be any valid number between 1 and 63 (64 bytes, 0 being invalid). The last 10 bits of the address are the node, addressed as the numbers 1 through 1023 (1024 bytes, 0 being invalid). This creates a total pool of 64,449 possible nodes on a DECnet network. For example, if one DECnet network is comprised of three areas (5, 6, and 7) and each area has 4 nodes (1,2,3, and 4), the network would be addressed as shown in Figure 22.3. Figure 22.3 illustrates a DECnet network with multiple area and node addresses.

FIGURE 22.3

An addressed DECnet network.

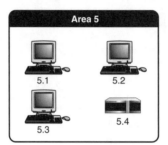

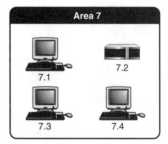

Another feature of DECnet addressing that would need to be ported to IS-IS is the manner with which DECnet deals with MAC addresses.

> The MAC address, or *burned-in address*, is a generally static number assigned by an Ethernet vendor to ensure uniqueness in large networks. It is possible (however unlikely) to manually change this number to fit the needs of certain networks.

Systems on a DECnet network have a MAC address dynamically assigned to them based on their area/node address. For example, the MAC address for a host with an area/node address of 4.2 would be AA-00-04-00-02-10. To arrive at this address DEC follows this convention:

22

First the DECnet address is converted to binary (remember that the address format is six bits and ten bits):

`4.2 = 000100.0000000010`

However, MAC addresses are essentially a series of eight-bit segments, so our new binary area/node address needs to be divided into two eight-bit sections:

`00010000  00000010`

These sections are then flipped:

`00000010  00010000`

The flipped binary sections are then converted to hexadecimal format:

`02 10`

Finally, the new hexadecimal pairs are appended to the DEC Ethernet MAC vendor code `AA-00-04`. A null pair of `00` is placed between the vendor code and the area/node to fill out the address.

The end product is the MAC address `AA-00-04-00-02-10`.

These dynamic MAC addresses were used by DECnet (and later IS-IS) to both route information and send update packets to other nodes. For anyone who has experience with IP addressing or routing, the DECnet address scheme at first seems to be a little unconventional. However, understanding that DECnet provides the base upon which IS-IS was formed is the key to understanding how IS-IS works.

DECnet Nodes

DECnet nodes can be defined as one of three entities:

- An end system
- A Level 1 router
- A Level 2 router

An end system (ES) is defined as anything that is not a router. The most common ES node is a user's PC; however, ESes can include printers, scanners, and other networked devices. The key is that end systems have only one addressable interface and can only communicate with Level 1 routers. In a common network environment, there should be more ESes than any other node on the network.

Logically, a PC on a network cannot send data to any other PC without some assistance. Whether the data flows through a hub or router, another device is required to enable communication between more than two PCs. (The exception to this is when you only want to provide communication between two PCs. In that case, you can connect the two devices with a crossover cable.) Therefore, PCs do not provide any routing capabilities, making them ESes.

ESes can be considered the routing system on the network. The majority of data being routed around the network either starts at or terminates at an ES. Even though they perform no routing duties, the ESes are a very important part of the routing process in a DECnet environment.

The second category of node on a DECnet network is known as a *Level 1 (L1)* router. A Level 1 router is an intra-area router, meaning that it can only route within its own area. In routing terms, L1s have no knowledge of any network topology outside their own area. This is a very important feature that was later ported to the IS-IS protocol. By not routing outside their own area, L1s dramatically cut down on the amount of network traffic in any given environment.

When a router is charged with routing between multiple networks, complex factors need to be taken into consideration. If a router has multiple interfaces for multiple networks, it has to send multiple broadcast messages to complete certain tasks. For example, if a router has four network interfaces (A, B, C, and D) and receives a message for Network C, the router will generally send a broadcast message to each interface. This broadcast message will ask each interface what network it's on. Once the router receives an answer from Network C, it will send the message along. This process can result in an abundance of broadcast messages.

By dictating that L1 routers can only service one area, DECnet eliminated the overflow of broadcast messages.

The routers pictured in Fig 22.3 (area/node addresses 5.4, 6.3, and 7.2) would be considered Level 1 routers. As such, router 5.4 can only route data around Area 5.

Another important feature of L1 routers is in the way they are addressed by DECnet. Level 1 routers can have multiple interfaces; however, they will only have one area/node address. This means that every node interface, or port, on an L1 router will generally have the same address. Therefore, if L1 router 5.4 has four ports, and each is connected to a different ES, each port will be addressed as 5.4. To illustrate this, let's take a detailed look at Area 5. Figure 22.4 illustrates the connections within Area 5.

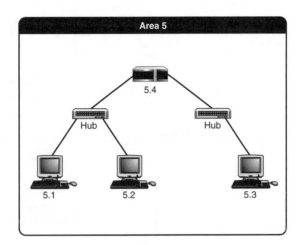

FIGURE 22.4
Router 5.4 with multiple connections and one address.

Notice how each hub in Area 5 is connected to a different interface on Router 5.4. However, each interface is still addressed as 5.4.

Router 5.4 can only communicate to end systems 5.1, 5.2, and 5.3. If ES 5.2 wanted to send data to ES 7.4 in Fig 22.3, it would require the services of Level 2 routers.

Level 2 (L2) routers are routers that can communicate with other Level 2 and Level 1 routers in different areas. To transmit information between two different areas, you need at least two L2 routers. Figure 22.5 illustrates the paths information can take when travelling from system to system across two areas.

As shown in Figure 22.5, there are three possible paths that information can take when being routed from ES to ES across areas.

The first option is to send the data from the ES to a Level 1 router in the same area. The Level 1 router will then route the packets to a Level 2 router in the target area. The Level 2 router can then pass the packets to the intended recipient.

The second option is essentially the first option in reverse. The data leaves the ES and is sent to an L2 router in the end system's home area. The L2 router then forwards the data to a Level 1 router in the target area. Finally the data is sent along to the receiving ES.

The final option is to transmit the data from the ES to an L2 router in the same area. The L2 router then forwards the information to another L2 router in the intended recipient's area. The recipient L2 router then sends the data along to the final ES.

FIGURE 22.5

Data flow across areas.

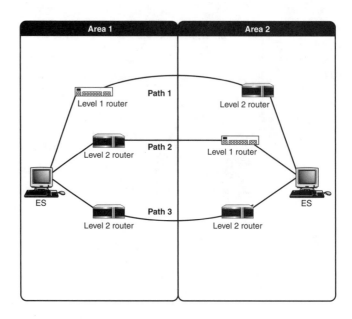

As you can see, Level 2 routers can also interact with end systems, giving them the added capabilities of a Level 1 router. Also, like Level 1 routers, Level 2 routers have only one address to share across all its interfaces. Figure 22.6 illustrates a fully addressed, routable, DECnet network with three areas.

FIGURE 22.6

A routable DECnet network.

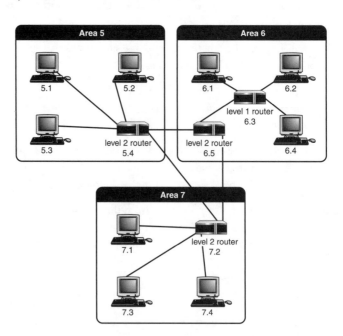

DECnet Routing Basics

The precursor to IS-IS was DECnet Phase IV's DRP (DECnet Routing Protocol). DRP worked by routing packets between systems in an orderly manner. At the heart of DRP was the hello message. By passing around these hello messages (HMs), routers learn the status of the links and routers around them. An ES will send an HM to any L1 or L2 router it interfaces with. Figure 22.7 illustrates the life cycle of an intra-area HM.

FIGURE 22.7

The life cycle of a hello message.

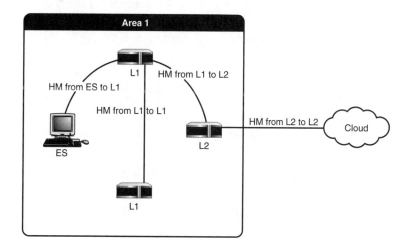

An ES will send an HM to an L1 router. This HM will signal to the L1 router that the ES is functioning on the network and able to receive packets. The L1 router will use this information to build a picture of its home area. By assembling the HMs from the ESes and the other L1s, any particular L1 router can create an up-to-date picture of the network's topology.

Even though the L1 router will not send an HM directly back to an ES, the ES will listen to the L1-to-L1 router messages to formulate its own picture of the current network topology.

L1 routers will send hello messages to other L1s and L2s. These hello messages serve the same purpose as those sent by end systems. The L1 router will alert all other L1 and L2 routers in the same area as to its current state on the network.

Level 2 routers will only send hello messages to other Level 2 routers. Remember, L1 routers and end systems only have knowledge of their own areas, and because L2 routers have routing information for other areas, they cannot share hello messages with either.

When an ES has a packet to send to another ES, there are steps it must follow. The following outline shows the steps an ES follows to get a packet routed on a DECnet network.

Most protocols, including DECnet, enable PCs to keep a routing cache. A *routing cache* is a portion of memory on a PC that has been set aside for storing the addresses of devices that packets are frequently sent to. In other words, every time a PC successfully sends a packet to another device, the destination address and the address of the router that the packet had to be sent through are recorded in the PC's routing cache. The next time a packet needs to be sent to the same destination, the PC need only look in its cache to find out where to forward the data.

An ES will always check its own routing cache before releasing a packet onto the network. This routing cache contains a table relating a destination address with the address of the router that can get the packet there. If the ES cannot find the router it needs in its cache, it adds the destination MAC address (see the formula in the section "DECnet Areas and Nodes" earlier in this chapter) to the packet and forwards it to the closest L1 router (or L2, as the case may be).

The receiving router digests the destination information and, using its routing table formulated from various hello messages, forwards the packet on to its final target. If that target is in a different area, the L1 router will send the packet to an L2 router that can reach the foreign area. In some cases this process may involve more than one L2 router.

If a packet needs to be sent from an ES across multiple areas, it will first reach an L2 router in its own area. Once the data reaches this L2, the router will look in its routing table for the location of the L2 router attached to the target area. Because L2 routers can share information across areas, the L2 in the home area should know the location of the L2 in the target area, regardless of the number of areas between them. The data can then be forwarded along to its intended recipient.

DECnet Phase V

When DECnet Phase V came along, DEC decided to adopt the OSI model as the basis for their protocol. Because all phases of DECnet are backward compatible, DECnet Phase V needed to adhere to OSI and DNA standards.

Because the two architectures were very similar, DEC was able to successfully port the DECnet architecture to the OSI model. However, DEC needed a routing protocol that could route in either the OSI or DEN architectures, and route the DECnet protocol as well as IP. The solution DEC came up with is the Intermediate System-to-Intermediate System (IS-IS) routing protocol, an OSI-compliant routing protocol that was adopted as the routing protocol of choice for DECnet Phase V networks.

How IS-IS Relates to CLNP

As DECnet Phase V was being developed, ISO was developing the *Connectionless Network Protocol (CLNP)*. CLNP is a purely OSI-routed protocol that enables the connectionless transfer of data between two end systems. CLNP is quick, relatively small in size using little network overhead, and is the OSI equivalent of the IP protocol.

> A connectionless protocol, as opposed to a connection oriented one, does not require the acknowledgement of packet receipt. Because these protocols do not require an acknowledgement for every packet sent, they tend to be faster than their connection-oriented counterparts. However, they are also considered somewhat unreliable. IP is a connectionless protocol.

When DEC began developing DECnet Phase V OSI/DNA, they needed a fully OSI-compliant routed protocol to work on the third layer of the OSI model.

> The third layer of both the OSI and DNA models are the layers used for routing network data. In the OSI model, this is called the network layer, and in DNA it's called the routing layer. Such similarities made the transition from DNS to OSI fairly easy for DECnet.

CLNP was the protocol DEC was looking for. However, there was one drawback to using CLNP in the backward compatible OSI- and DNA-based DECnet environment. At this time, there was no routing protocol flexible enough to handle the mixed architectures of OSI and DNA and yet robust enough to work in a large connectionless environment.

This is where the two histories of IS-IS collide. DEC needed a flexible routing protocol to route the new OSI-compliant DECnet Phase V. ISO had already developed the routed protocol used in the connectionless environment. So, DEC helped ISO develop IS-IS in the DECnet OSI (CLNP) environment.

IS-IS proved to be perfect for routing the OSI/DNA networks. ISO developed IS-IS as a quick, portable link-state routing protocol for CLNP. As a routing protocol, IS-IS fills the gap in the DECnet Phase V environment.

Because CLNP was OSI-based and connectionless by definition, IS-IS would be able to also route IP with minimal adaptation. Keep in mind that IP is also a connectionless protocol.

For a while there was some discussion (every once and a while it still comes up) about making CLNP the default protocol of the Internet. However, after a couple of years, it was clear that IP had a major chokehold on the Internet. Therefore, support for IP was added to IS-IS, completing the protocol.

IS-IS does not support IP by itself. When ISO started to tweak IS-IS to support IP, many people were still using it to route purely OSI protocols. To distinguish between the two implementations of IS-IS, the newer version was officially named *Integrated IS-IS*. Integrated IS-IS offers support for simultaneous multiple-routed protocols like CLNP and IP.

Let's look under the hood and see exactly how both IS-IS and Integrated IS-IS, as well as other link-state protocols, work.

IS-IS Link-State Routing

Routing protocols are separated into categories based on the algorithms they use to route data. One common category of protocol is link-state. Almost every router on the market today can use one of the many link-state protocols to move information around a network. Both IS-IS and Integrated IS-IS are link-state routing protocols.

Routers running link-state protocols update each other periodically. These updates, known as link-state advertisements (LSAs), let each router know the status (state) of every other router (link) in the environment. These updates have advantages and disadvantages; however, before we discuss them, let's define what sets IS-IS and other link-state protocols apart from other routing protocols.

Keep in mind that a *routing* protocol is the protocol used by routers and other connectivity devices to carry routed protocols across the network media. *Routed* protocols (such as IP and IPX) are used to encapsulate data for transmission to other devices.

All link-state protocols are bound by a number of common characteristics. The main characteristic is that they all work on a "shortest path first" basis. In other words, the main goal of any link-state protocol is to find the shortest route between two end systems. With that in mind, Figure 22.8 illustrates a network with multiple paths between two locations. A link-state protocol present with the scenario illustrated in Figure 22.8 might pick Path A as the shortest path between ES1 and ES2.

FIGURE 22.8

An example of a link-state protocol choosing the shortest path.

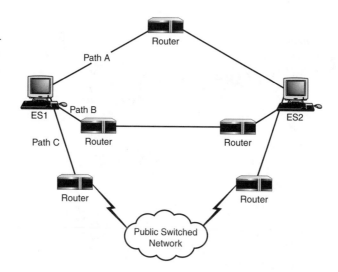

The term *shortest path* does not necessarily refer to the distance between two points. The shortest path can be the port with the most bandwidth, the cable that has the least amount of interference, the cheapest port to operate (as opposed to a leased line), or a combination of all these factors.

For example, a company has four offices across a large city. The buildings are connected by cables in order (Building A is cabled to Building B, which is connected to Building C, and so on). However, there is also an ISDN line directly connecting Building A to Building D. So data being routed from Building A to Building D has two paths to choose from: Either travel directly to Building D via the ISDN line, or be routed through Building B and through Building C to get to Building D.

Obviously the ISDN line is the shortest physical path, but it might not be the chosen path. It would most likely be terribly expensive to continually send routed data across the ISDN line, so IS-IS would likely choose the non-leased route. Figure 22.9 illustrates what link-state protocols might take into consideration when choosing a shortest path.

However, the protocols are called shortest path *first*, not shortest path *only*. If the actual shortest path from one system to another is not available, the protocol will open the next shortest path, and so on. By opening the shortest path between systems, link-state protocols reduce the amount of time required to move information from one PC to another.

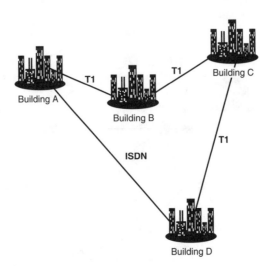

FIGURE 22.9

An example of the shortest physical path not being the chosen path.

However, referring to the example in Figure 22.9, the ISDN line connecting Building A with Building D would not sit around unused just because it is not the shortest path. If the amount of traffic on the shortest path begins to back up, causing delays and network latency, the speed of the ISDN line would outweigh the cost. The ISDN line would then become the shortest path until the traffic on the first shortest path once again becomes manageable. Then the bulk of the routed traffic would switch back to the non-leased line.

This form of load balancing makes most link-state protocols very attractive to administrators with multiple routes between destinations. Less expensive yet reliable lines can be assigned a lower cost, forcing IS-IS to choose it as a route over another comparable path, while more expensive leased lines can be given a slightly higher cost. These higher-cost leased lines can then be used by IS-IS when the less expensive lines become congested. This will keep data flowing in a smooth, economical manner.

When designers are choosing the protocols for their networks, several factors are considered. However, especially in larger networks, speed and cost are almost always at the top of the list. The obvious advantage to having a fast routing protocol is getting information from Point A to Point B in the shortest possible time. Fast routing protocols do have other advantages, though.

By moving data on and off the network as quick as possible, many network congestion-related problems (such as traffic jams and bandwidth over-usage) can be avoided. This will make for a clean, virtually error-free routing environment. Every network manager can appreciate not having to worry about the routers and the routing protocols.

Link-state protocols such as IS-IS offer an opportunity to route data quickly from Point A to Point B. Link-state protocols also have a disadvantage, however.

Link-state protocols go through a process known as *flooding*. While flooding, a router will send a large amount of LSAs across the network. The neighboring routers receive these advertisements, update their own tables, and send the updates back to their neighboring routers. Figure 22.10 shows an example of an LSA update.

FIGURE 22.10

A sample LSA update.

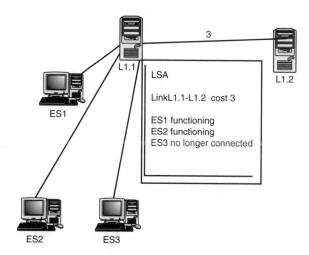

This flooding is the necessary process a link-state router goes through to build an accurate picture of the environment around it. The routers use the information contained within the LSA to create a dynamic table. The router then runs its routing algorithms against this table to calculate the shortest path for every packet. The amount of time an LSA flood lasts depends on the number of updates or changes in the routing environment and the convergence time.

However, flooding can cause traffic havoc on some networks. The heartiest networking environments might not feel the effects of a large-scale convergence, but most networks will notice some network latency during a flood. The environments that will be affected the most by a flood are larger networks that already have some bandwidth issues.

Larger networks with plenty of bandwidth and smaller networks with fewer routers might not have as much trouble during an LSA flood. These networks will either have plenty of available bandwidth to handle both LSAs and normal daily traffic, or there are not enough routers to generate a mass amount of advertisements.

In a network of any size, having enough available bandwidth before you implement IS-IS is one of the keys to getting through an LSA flood with no noticeable latency. If you are working on an existing network and are contemplating whether to implement IS-IS, make sure that you have the bandwidth to deal with LSA floods. This one factor will save you many headaches down the road.

Floods actually affect networks in two ways. The most obvious way is by drowning the network in LSA packets. The LSA updates cause a large amount of traffic, and normal network data might have trouble getting through. Keep in mind that every router on the network needs to tell its neighboring routers in the same area what changes were made to its table. Then, the routers that received the LSA information need to send out more LSAs telling the other routers about the changes they just received from the first round of LSAs, and so on until every router has the same picture of the network.

Another drawback caused by LSA flooding is evident in the amount of memory and processing power needed by the router to digest the updates. Depending on the number of LSAs on the network and the number of updates in each one, a router might devote the majority of its available memory and processor time to crunching LSAs in an attempt to converge as quickly as possible. LSA packets will always have processing priority over a routed protocol packet. Therefore, those network packets that do make it through the traffic jam of LSAs may not get processed.

The reason why a link-state router will always process an LSA over a routed protocol packet is simple. You want the environment to converge as quickly as possible, so the quicker an LSA can be processed and applied, the quicker a router can resume its normal daily function.

As far as protocol downsides go, this one really isn't that bad. Generally, link-state protocols have one of the quickest convergence times of all protocol types. Therefore, the network latency one would experience during a flood might not last very long. This is good news for administrators implementing IS-IS on a larger network with minimal bandwidth.

Controlling Link-State Floods

IS-IS has a few built-in mechanisms for controlling the amount of LSAs sent out during a flood. The first control is a *poison path*, which simply means that an IS-IS router can never send an LSA out on the same link it received it on. This keeps the same update information from looping infinitely between two routers. Figure 22.11 illustrates this concept.

Notice that Router A received an update from Router B on Port 1. L1A used that information to update its routing table and sent its own LSA to Router C on Port 2. However, Router A did not send its own updated information back out on Port 1 to Router B. Because Router B started the flood, and the only information in the update pertained to its own links, it didn't need to receive Router A's updated table information.

FIGURE 22.11

An IS-IS router send-ing and receiving LSA updates.

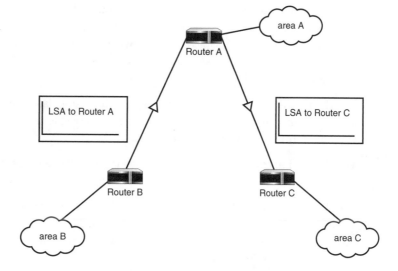

If we were to follow this scenario until the end of the update flood, we would see that Router C would then block, or poison the path between Router A and itself. Then, any router receiving an update from Router C would poison its ports as well. By poisoning (also known as killing) the link between two routers after an update has been sent, IS-IS ensures that the minimum amount of LSAs are flooded onto the network during an update.

You may already be thinking of a hole in this philosophy. Take a look at Figure 22.12, which illustrates a router with multiple ports receiving the same update. How would the router handle this information?

FIGURE 22.12

A router with multiple receiving ports.

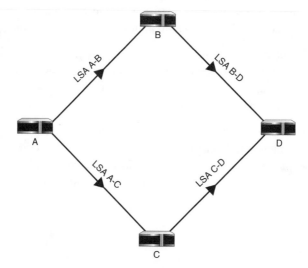

In this example, Router A sends its update to Routers B and C. Both of these routers are also connected to Router D. So, what will happen when Router D receives two LSAs on two different ports for the same update? Obviously, the router can only process one of the updates. But will it then send an LSA to the router that it didn't receive the update from first?

The short answer is that Router D will process the first update it receives, but not send an update to either. To understand why, let's take a look inside an LSA packet and see what kind of information is included in an update.

Two fields within the LSA control whether an IS-IS router can continue receiving updates, and if the updates are valid. These fields are Remaining Life and Sequence.

The Remaining Life field is a time setting used by the router after the LSA is processed. When the router examines the LSA, a timer is started that corresponds to the value indicated in the Remaining Life field. Until that timer expires, the router can not process any LSA pertaining to link(s) involved in the last LSA.

For example, in Figure 22.12, Router D receives an LSA from Router B stating that the link between Router A and Router B is down. Router D processes the LSA, starts the Remaining Life timer, and updates its table. However, before Router C receives the same update, it sends out its normal periodic LSA. This LSA (en route to Router D) still states that the link between Router A and Router B is fine.

Because the Remaining Life timer has not yet expired, Router D ignores the update, recognizing that the LSA pertains to an update that already occurred. Eventually Router C gets the updated LSA and convergence occurs. Also, the Remaining Life timer restricts Router D from sending any updates pertaining to the link between Routers A and B until it expires. In this way, routers do not needlessly receive conflicting information about a link's status, and they do not send out multiple LSAs for the same problem.

The second control field in an LSA packet is the Sequence field. The receiving router uses the Sequence field to identify the update contained within an LSA. A router will not process any LSA update that is out of sequence. By using the Remaining Life and Sequence fields, IS-IS can control the sometimes overwhelming LSA floods.

Another piece of good news for network administrators (who are adept at keeping network changes to a minimum) is that they can also control LSA flooding, to an extent. To limit the number of unnecessary floods on link-state protocols, administrators can simply keep the number of administrative network changes to a minimum.

While this will not eliminate floods altogether, it will minimize their frequency. LSA floods are sent out periodically to detect non-administrative changes, and they are triggered after a change. So, by reducing the administrative changes, the number of floods can be reduced. This may not be a very practical way to keep traffic down, but it is effective.

An administrator really has no authority over the periodic LSA updates; they are going to happen no matter what. However, the administrative updates are triggered by a change in the networking environment. This change could be the reassignment of a metric, a down line, or anything that would change a possible path for data. Figure 22.13 illustrates the events leading up to an LSA flood.

FIGURE 22.13

The life cycle of an LSA flood.

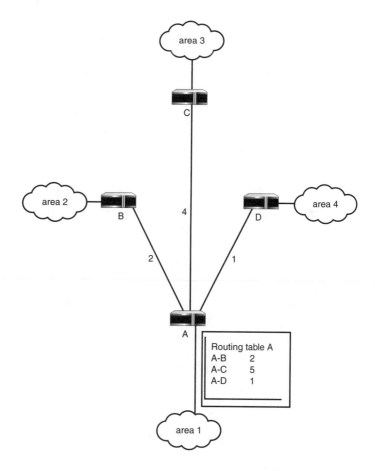

Notice that all the routers stayed online through the process shown in Figure 22.13, but an update was triggered anyway. What triggered the update was the changing of the metric assigned to the link between Router A and Router C. This arbitrarily administrator-assigned metric is the key calculation used by IS-IS's routing algorithm to figure out the shortest path between two objects.

IS-IS Metrics and Algorithms

The protocols installed on your router do not instinctively know the shortest route to every possible location on the network. Rather, they must consider certain elements of the environment. Then these elements must be acted upon to produce a definite result. By using metrics and algorithms, link-state protocols decide which path is the shortest to a particular destination.

Metrics are the network variables used in deciding which path is shortest. For link-state algorithms, these metrics are values assigned by a network administrator. Many routing protocols use multiple metrics, such as bandwidth, priority, cost, and other dynamic- or statically-assigned factors. However, IS-IS simplifies the process by using only one default metric—cost.

There are actually three other optional metrics that can be defined by the administrator for a line. However, the current implementation of IS-IS only recognizes the default metric of cost. The other metrics are as follows:

- Delay—The amount of delay on a particular line.
- Expense—The value associated with operating a particular line.
- Error—The relative amount of errors associated with a particular line.

Expressing values for these metrics will not effect your algorithm in any way. Future versions of IS-IS may make use of these values.

In an IS-IS environment, the most important job of an administrator is to assign a cost metric to every link emanating for every router. Figure 22.14 illustrates an IS-IS network with all the metrics assigned.

FIGURE 22.14

An IS-IS network showing all its assigned metrics.

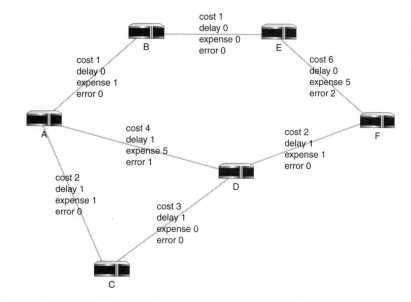

22

As far as an IS-IS administrator is concerned, the metric of cost is totally arbitrary. There is no formula or science to choosing a cost for a particular link. However, there are some guidelines to keep in mind when assigning a cost to a link:

- When IS-IS applies its algorithm to all the metrics on the network, the lowest metrics will form the shortest path.

- Reliable lines, such as those that are newer or not prone to interference (fiber-optic lines) should always have a lower cost.

- Less expensive lines such as those owned by the company installing the routers should always be assigned a lower cost than leased lines, such as ISDN.

- Higher bandwidth lines (like T3s) should be assigned a lower cost than a lower bandwidth line.

The assigned cost metrics, whatever you decide they should be, are going to govern what path that will be chosen as the shortest path between end points.

Before you assign metrics to all your links, be aware that there is a limit to the cost metric. A cost for a specific link cannot exceed 64. Therefore, any line assigned a cost of 65 will not be recognized as a valid path. However, there is no law against using duplicate values for different links. So, if you have a router with more than 64 ports, you might have to double up on costs.

Any two links with the same metric emanating from the same router will weigh equally when run against the algorithm. In this case, IS-IS will distribute packets over either link.

Another limit placed on the cost metric applies to the total cost of a path after being calculated by the routing algorithm. IS-IS will not route data over any path that has a total cost greater than 1024.

If the numbers 64 and 1024 sound familiar, they are a direct correlation to the amount of memory used by IS-IS to store the routing information.

Therefore, some planning is required before establishing your IS-IS costs, especially on a larger network. Fully map out your routes and links before you begin implementing your IS-IS routers. Then assign all your values on paper, add them up, and confirm that they are in line. Finally, you can implement your routers and let the algorithm take over.

Exploring IS-IS Addressing, Areas, and Domains

IS-IS, like every other protocol, addresses devices based on their location within an environment. IS-IS identifies devices by a two-part location identifier. These identifiers are the areas and domains a device can belong to. First, let's define the divisions of the IS-IS networks—the areas and the domains.

By dividing IS-IS networks into areas and domains, administrators have greater control over the flow of data in an environment. This concept can be better visualized in terms of a state road map.

Let's use the state of Texas as an example. There are hundreds of thousands of roads and highways in Texas. Each road has a name assigned to it, and each highway has a number. Because there are multiple cities in the state, road names can be reused and recycled in every city, and county highway numbers can be reused for every county.

The cities also serve as geographic markers within the counties, and the counties within the state. For example, if you are looking for a road in Dallas, not only do you immediately know what part of the county you need to be in, but you also already know the general part of the state as well. Counties and cities help keep the problem of finding geographic locations from getting out of control.

Now take away the cites and counties. Finding your way around the state becomes next to impossible. Not only does every city road and county highway need to be uniquely named, but you might never find them after you're done. If you are looking for a particular road and there are no cities or counties to reference, you would have to comb the entire state looking for that one road. Even if you had a road map, not knowing the general area to start in would make the task extremely daunting.

Apply this logic to networking and you have the reason behind assigning areas and domains to IS-IS environments. IS-IS domains are the equivalent to the counties in a state, whereas IS-IS areas are the cities. These areas and domains aid the router in finding ESes quickly, especially in large environments.

IS-IS Areas

An IS-IS area is a single subset of ESes and intermediate systems (ISes). A network of ESes and ISes that all share the same area number or ID is considered one area. Figure 22.15 illustrates an IS-IS area.

FIGURE 22.15
An IS-IS area.

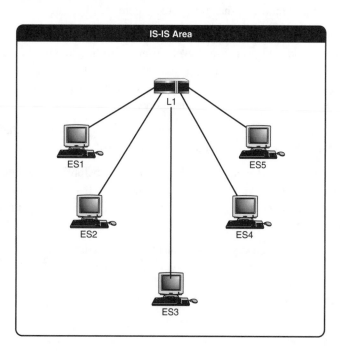

> The concept of IS-IS areas and domains is a direct reference back to the DECnet Phase IV architecture. All DECnet networks are also divided into areas.
>
> If you are familiar with IP networks and IP subnetting, IS-IS areas and domains will not be that hard to follow. However, areas and domains do not correlate directly to their IP cousins. It is more accurate to say that both IS-IS areas and domains together are equivalent to an IP subnet. IS-IS areas can be thought of as a subnet.

Areas tend to be fairly small and self-contained. A network architect would not necessarily design an area in the same fashion in which she would design an IP subnet. IS-IS areas are not as general as IP subnets. An area is very localized.

Routing within areas is accomplished by Level 1 routers. Just as in DECnet Phase IV, L1 routers are used for intra-area data routing. L1 routers are the major interior routing device of IS-IS areas. However, keeping true to their DECnet counterparts, L1 routers cannot route outside of their own local area. Therefore, a group of areas have greater routing requirements than the sum of their parts. In other words, just by putting a bunch of areas in a room, you are not guaranteeing that they will communicate with each other. In fact, they won't. For this reason, groups of areas are considered domains and have different requirements than the smaller, more localized areas.

A collection of related areas is known as a domain. In IS-IS terms, a *domain* is a group of areas bridged by a pair of Level 2 routers. To fully qualify this definition, only L2 routers can form a domain. One area with a L1 router connected to a L2 router that also bridges another area is not considered a domain. Figures 22.16 and 22.17 illustrate a correct and an incorrect IS-IS domain respectively.

Notice the two L2 routers with a backbone running between them. The presence of this L2 pair (with areas on either side) forms the IS-IS domain.

Having the correct area/domain layout on paper before you begin planning your IS-IS network can make all the difference in the world. If you inadvertently end up with an area/domain configuration like the one seen in Figure 22.17, your environment will not route correctly.

However, as with every protocol, just having the correct physical layout is not enough. The protocol address must correspond to the physical topology.

FIGURE 22.16
A correctly formed IS-IS domain.

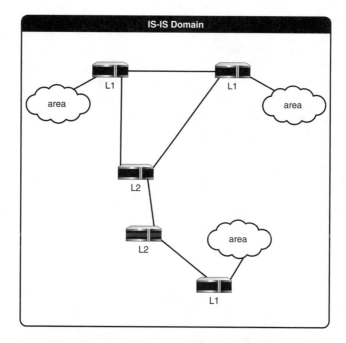

FIGURE 22.17
An incorrectly formed IS-IS domain.

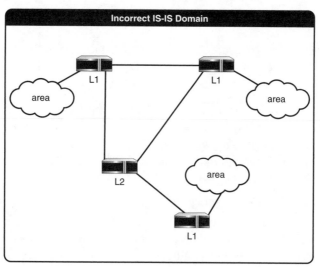

IS-IS Addresses

The address scheme of IS-IS is a mixture of pure OSI routing address conventions and the DECnet Phase IV area/node MAC addresses. This was not done by accident. Combining the two architectures was a necessary task for ensuring the interoperability of IS-IS and the DNA-based DECnet. This enables the protocol to easily route data on multiple platforms for multiple routed protocols. IS-IS addresses are also a key part of defining IS-IS areas and routing domains. Let's look inside an IS-IS routing packet to see how the addresses are defined.

Pure OSI protocols utilize an address known as an *NSAP (network service access point)*. The NSAP defines the location of an ES on a network, down to the area in which it's located. Because IS-IS is an OSI-compliant protocol, it also utilizes NSAP addresses. However, because IS-IS is not a *pure* OSI routing protocol, it interprets the address a little differently than other OSI protocols.

> The actual purpose of the NSAP is to address a specific point in the network layer of the OSI model on a specific device. Rather than arbitrarily assigning an address to a machine, the ISO chose to address the information entry point to the device.

Like most protocol addresses, an NSAP is divided into two parts to provide a more precise form of device location—an IDP and a DSP. The combination of these two parts identifies the point of entry for the device's network layer.

The *IDP (initial domain part)* is the portion of the address that refers to the domain-specific part of the device. The IDP itself also contains two parts, the AFI and the IDI. The *AFI (authority and format identifier)* specifies the authority assigning the address to the domain. The *IDI (initial domain identifier)* specifies general information about the domain and the DSP.

The second part of the NSAP, the *DSP (domain-specific part)* contains the literal address information. The DSP holds the address of the domain that a particular device belongs to. Although this is true for all pure OSI protocols, IS-IS is not a pure OSI protocol, and interprets the NSAP slightly differently.

IS-IS divides the NSAP address into two main portions: the area address and the system ID. (A third part attached to the end of the NSAP is the address selector and is almost always set to 0.) The *area address*, which incorporates the IDP of the NSAP, specifies the area within a domain to which the device belongs, and the *system ID*, much like a MAC address, addresses the actual device.

22

NSAP Area Address

The area address, comprised of the NSAP IDP, indicates the area a device belongs to. All devices in a specific area will have the same area address. The administrator assigns this address, comprised of at least one hexadecimal octet of data, at design time.

In an environment with multiple areas, the area address becomes very important to the routing of the network. All ESes and L1 routers in one area will have the same area address, enabling the correct identification of all systems in the area by extra-area devices.

NSAP System ID

The system ID identifies a system with an area. Just as the DECnet Phase IV systems use the area/node ID to modify the MAC address, IS-IS systems use a modified MAC address to create the system ID of the NSAP. The device-specific system ID will never be shared or duplicated on an IS-IS network. Therefore, the system IS stands as a reliable marker for locating a system in an area.

Examining IS-IS Packets

IS-IS routes data through the networking environment via IS-IS packets. These packets encapsulate the data that IS-IS is routing around the network. However, not all packets are meant for shuttling data. Some packets are for the internal use of IS-IS devices. These packets help IS-IS determine the configuration and topology of devices connected to an IS-IS environment.

There are three types of packets used in the IS-IS environment: hello messages, link-state packets, and sequence number packets.

If you were to dissect any type of packet, you would be able to divide it into three major sections: the header, the data, and the checksum. Figure 22.18 illustrates a typical packet.

FIGURE 22.18
A typical packet.

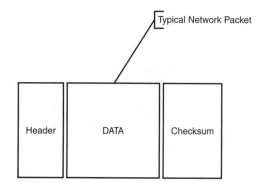

The header informs the device receiving the packet what kind of packet it is. Therefore, if a packet arrives at a device and the header information is that of an Ethernet packet, the remainder is presumed to be Ethernet data and treated as such. On the other hand, if the packet header indicates that the packet is a hello message, the receiving device would know that no user data was contained in the body of the packet and deal with it accordingly.

Most packet headers tend to be fixed in length, depending on the packet type. Although most packet headers found in Ethernet or IS-IS packets are 8 bytes long, others can vary. Therefore, there may be a header length indicator after the header. The header length indicator tells the recipient device how long the header is. This allows the device to easily determine where the header ends and the data begins.

The data portion of a packet is just that—the data that one system needs to send to another. This portion of the packet can vary in length depending on the amount of information being sent.

The checksum is usually the last part of a packet. The checksum tells the device what the total size of the packet is. A device can determine whether a packet is corrupt or incomplete by comparing how many bytes of data it received with the value in the checksum. All IS-IS packets follow the same basic format: a header, a data portion, and an extended data portion. Figure 22.19 illustrates an IS-IS packet.

FIGURE 22.19

An IS-IS packet.

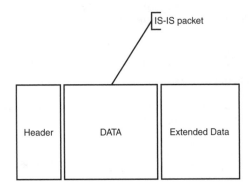

The 8-byte header is the part of the packet that we want to look at here. The header, regardless of the IS-IS packet type (hello message, link-state packet, or sequence number packet), is divided into eight 1-byte fields. These fields supply the recipient device with all the information it needs to process the packet correctly. Table 22.1 lists the eight fields of an IS-IS header.

TABLE 22.1 IS-IS Header Fields

Field	Purpose
Protocol Identifier	Identifies the packet as an IS-IS packet
Length	Holds the value equal to the length of the header
Version (1)	Specifies the version of IS-IS
ID Length	Specifies the length of the ID portion of the recipient's address
Packet Type	Designates the packet as either a hello message, a link-state packet, or a sequence number packet
Version (2)	Restates the version of IS-IS being used
Reserved	This field is reserved for future use
MAA (Maximum Address Area)	Specifies the maximum number of addresses in the current area

Figure 22.20 illustrates an IS-IS packet with header information.

FIGURE 22.20
An IS-IS packet with header information.

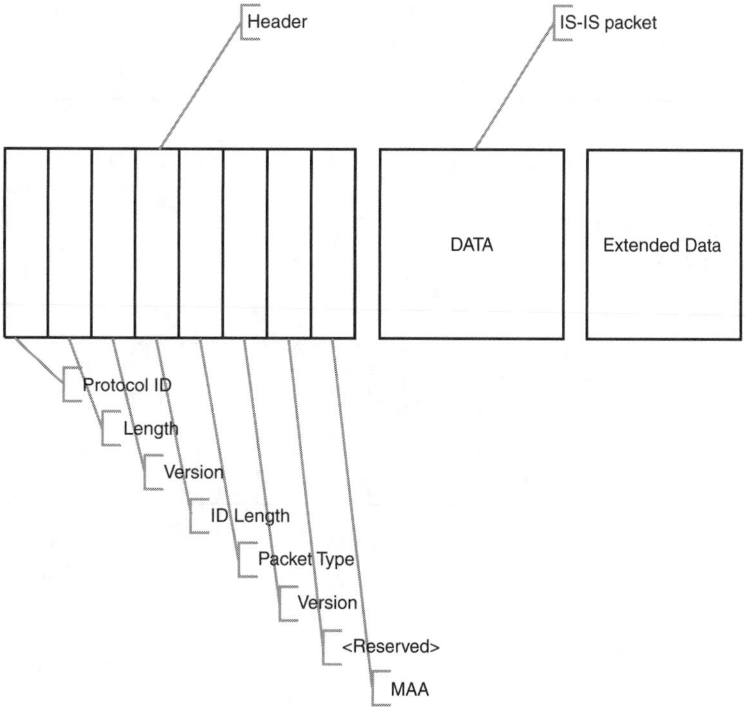

This packet format will be the same for every IS-IS packet. However, the fields following the header will change depending on the packet type. The fields after the header contain the actual data being sent from system to system.

Let's look at what these fields contain for the three types of IS-IS packets.

Inside IS-IS Hello Messages

Hello messages (HMs) are used by IS-IS devices to alert others as to their functional presence on the network. Table 22.2 lists the fields within the HM.

TABLE 22.2   IS-IS Hello Message Fields

Field	Purpose
Source ID	System ID of the device sending the message
Manual Address	The address of any manually-entered areas
IS Type	Indicates whether the IS sending the update is an L1 or L2 router
Priority	Indicates the administrator-assigned priority of the router
LAN ID	Specifies the LAN ID
Designated IS System ID	Indicates the system ID of the designated IS

Figure 22.21 illustrates a full HM packet with header information.

FIGURE 22.21

IS-IS hello message.

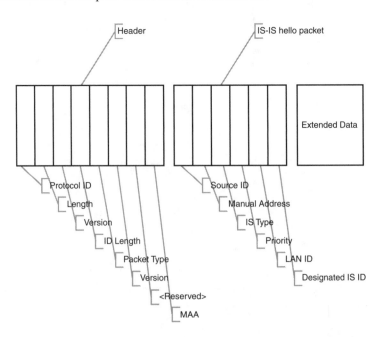

22

An IS will send out a HM periodically to inform the other ISes on the network that they are in a state to receive information. The packet also lets the recipient IS know the administrator-assigned priority, the IS type, and the address of the IS sending the HM.

When an IS receives a HM, it replies with a HM of its own. This confirms that both links are functioning, and that no changes have occurred in the networking environment. After the functionality of the link between the two devices has been confirmed, the two ISes add each other's information to their lists of neighboring ISes.

Uncovering Link-State Packets

Link-state packets (LSPs) are the cores of all link-state protocols. The LSP is the delivery device for all routing updates. During a link-state flood, all the ISes on a network will release LSPs to update the routing tables of the other routers in the environment.

Therefore, an LSP must contain all the pertinent information a router would need to correctly move data from one IS to another. Without correct and timely information, data released onto the network may never reach its intended recipient.

The fields within an IS-IS LSP are as follows:

- Source ID—System ID of the device sending the message.
- Manual Address—The address of any manually-entered areas.
- IS Type—Indicates whether the IS sending the update is an L1 or L2 router.
- System ID (with cost)—This field contains all the sending intermediate system's neighbors and their configured costs.
- Designated IS System ID—This value indicates the system ID of the designated IS.
- Static Adjacencies—This field contains all the statically configured ISes and their costs.

There are only two differences between the IS-IS HM and the IS-IS LSP. However, those two differences are the difference between an active routing network and a stagnant one. The LSP contains fields for routing table updates. When an IS receives a LSP, it inserts the sending device's system ID into its own routing table and appends to that entry the list of that intermediate system's direct neighbors and their costs.

Because L1 routers can only have knowledge of their local area, any foreign information received is discarded.

After the LSPs are received and digested, the IS runs the Dijkstra algorithm against the new data to calculate the new optimal paths. Figure 22.22 illustrates a LSP.

FIGURE 22.22

A link-state packet.

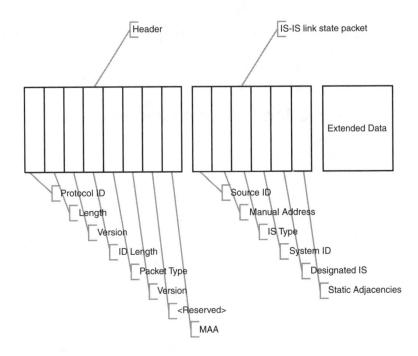

Sequence Number Packets

The purpose of the sequence number packet (SNP) is to ensure that every IS being updated by LSAs is getting the correct one. If an IS receives an SNP that is out of sequence, the accompanying link-state update is disregarded. The fields with an SNP are as follows:

- Remaining Life—Remaining life of the LSA (during this time the IS cannot accept any other updates).
- LSP ID
- SP Sequence #—Sequence number of the update.
- Checksum

These fields tell the receiving IS whether it has the correct update and for how long that update is valid. Figure 22.23 illustrates a sequence number packet with its header information.

Figure 22.23

A sequence number packet.

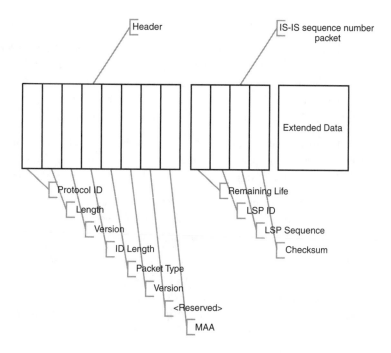

All the packets we have discussed thus far are crucial to the successful operation of an IS-IS environment. In the final portion of this chapter, we'll discuss how all these elements are combined to route data through an IS-IS network.

IS-IS Routing

Now that you know the history and the technology behind IS-IS, it's time to look into how it accomplishes its routing tasks. Routing in IS-IS is achieved through the successful and timely update of the topological information pertaining to the local IS-IS areas.

IS-IS requires some cohesiveness to route efficiently. That is to say, all the ISes on an IS-IS network cannot just run around doing what they please. They need to take direction from someone (or more realistically, something).

IS-IS, within its own areas and domains, elects one IS to be responsible for the actions of the environment.

The concept of a 'master node' to watch over the operations of a network is not new. If you are familiar with the master browser in Microsoft networking, or the active monitor in Token Ring, you've got the idea.

Designated IS

IS-IS nodes elect a *designated IS* to be the initiator during network events. The major job of the designated intermediate system is to send out LSPs that include LAN-wide information. After collecting the link-state updates for the network, the designated IS will generate an overall picture of the networking environment and send it to all other ISes on the LAN. This is done to control the number of redundant LSPs an IS may receive.

When an IS receives an LSP from the designated IS, all other LSPs are compared to it for accuracy. This also ensures that convergence will occur quickly. During an IS election to determine the designated IS, the ISes involved compare their priorities.

The IS priority is one of the administrator-assigned values. A network administrator will assign each IS a priority (an arbitrary numeric value, 1 being the highest). This value can be changed, and like the cost metric, is determined solely by the administrator.

The Priority field is also used in IS-IS hello messages to indicate the status of an IS. (In the event an intermediate system's priority changes, both an LSP flood and an election would take place. After all the ISes have compared their priorities, the IS with the highest priority is determined to be the designated IS. In the event that multiple IS are found to have equal highest priorities, the ISes have a second election, called an ID election.

The ISes with the highest priorities will then compare their MAC addresses. The IS holding the MAC address with the highest numerical value is then elected the designated IS. The designated IS will assume the job of collecting a distributing LSPs on behalf of the LAN as a whole.

If one IS has interfaces that span multiple LANs, it will be involved in the elections on all of them. In other words, elections occur based on the LAN an intermediate system is present on. If an intermediate system is present on more than one LAN, it will participate in more than one election. Therefore, there is a chance that an IS can be a designated IS for more than one IS-IS networking environment.

Examining IS-IS Pseudo-Nodes

After a designated intermediate system is chosen, the remaining ISes are grouped together into a *pseudo-node*. The pseudo-node is treated as one entity, when in reality it is a collection of the remaining ISes. IS-IS networks use these pseudo-nodes to receive information concerning the LAN as a whole.

The ISes in the pseudo-node accept LSPs from the designated IS. During an LSP flood, each IS will send an LSP to each IS it is connected to. (Obviously an IS can only send an update to a device that it is directly connected to.) This LSP (known as a *non-pseudo-node LSP*) contains all the information about an intermediate system's directly connected links.

For example, Figure 22.24 illustrates an LSP flood with four ISes. During this flood, Router A would receive an LSP from Router B stating that all of its links (Router C) are functioning properly.

FIGURE 22.24

Link-state flood with four nodes.

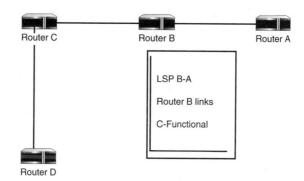

Router C Router B Router A

LSP B-A

Router B links

C-Functional

Router D

Therefore, Router A would note that Routers B and C are functioning properly in its routing table. However, it would have no way of knowing the state of Router D.

If every router were to send every other router the updates for the entire network, a neverending loop of updates would occur. Router A would receive updates about Router D from Routers B, C, and D. However, the concept of pseudo-nodes fixes this problem.

The designated IS collects all the update information and creates a master table of the network topology. The designated IS then sends one update to the pseudo-node. All the ISes in the pseudo-node process this information against the updates from their neighbors. This process keeps all the IS updates, and keeps the network free of update loops.

However, every intermediate system is addressed differently to be unique. Therefore, IS-IS has to make considerations for addressing a group of nodes as a pseudo-node. IS-IS accomplishes this through the use of *multicast addressing*. There are four Ethernet addresses that can be used for multicasting by IS-IS. These addresses are separated by destination. In other words, the address used depends on the group of devices being contacted. Table 22.3 shows the multicast addresses used by IS-IS and their intended destinations.

TABLE 22.3   Ethernet Multicast Addresses for IS-IS

Address	Use
0180C2000014	Used to contact all L1 routers only.
0180C2000015	Used to contact all L2 routers only.
09002B000005	Used to contact all ISes. This is also the address used to contact the pseudo-node.
09002B000004	Used to contact all ESes only.

All the nodes on an IS-IS network know how to process packets sent to the multicast addresses. Therefore, the designated IS only needs to send one update to the pseudo-node multicast address to have it processed by every device.

Routing in an IS-IS Environment

Routing in an IS-IS environment is accomplished in two different ways. L1 routers and L2 routers move data differently. The reason for this is simple: L2 routers have greater routing responsibilities than L1 routers. L2 routers are responsible for moving data on an area, domain, and LAN-wide environment, whereas L1 routers are responsible only for local areas. Let's look at the routing process through the eyes of an L1 router.

The source ES sends the packet to be routed to the nearest directly connected L1 router. Because the ES cannot move the data itself, it needs to go to either an L1 or L2 router. The L1 router now has some decisions to make based on the information in the header of that packet.

The router scans the header, looking for the destination address of the packet. The destination address holds two important pieces of information—the destination area and the destination system. When the router finds the destination address, it decodes the destination area.

The router then compares the destination area of the packet to its own. Remember that the L1 router will only have topographical knowledge of its own area, so if the destination area does not match its own, the router forwards the packet to the next router. After comparing the destination area to its own, the router can come to two conclusions: Either the packet should be routed within the local area, or it should be forwarded to a neighboring router.

By this time the router has already received an LSP, and the Dijkstra algorithm has been run against the updated information. Therefore, it can be assumed that the router is working from a complete and up-to-date picture of the network.

If the destination area is the local area, the router then rescans the header for the destination system. Also part of the destination address, the destination system will tell the router exactly which ES to forward the packet to. If the destination area matches the local area but the destination system is unknown to the router, the packet is dropped.

If the destination area is not the router's local area, it examines its routing table to find the neighboring router that can reach the intended area. The packet is then routed to the L1 router that governs over the destination area. If the destination area cannot be found, the packet is dropped. Figure 22.25 illustrates this process.

FIGURE 22.25

IS-IS L1 routing.

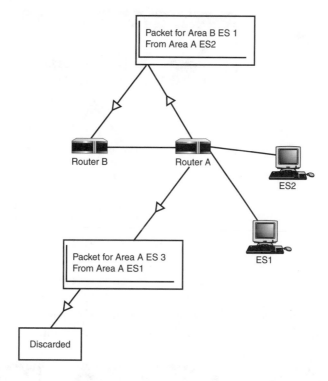

The routing process for L2 routers is slightly different. When an L2 router receives a packet, the first couple of steps in the routing process are the same. Because an L2 router can have directly connected areas, it determines the destination area and compares this to its own group of area L1 routers. If the destination area is one of the router's L1 neighbors, the packet is passed to the L1 router on the destination area. If the destination address does not match that of any of the L2 router's known areas, it then looks at the prefix information.

Areas that are not local to the L2 router are appended to a prefix in the router's routing table. This not only enables the router to differentiate between local and non-local areas, but it also helps the router determine where to send packets that are not local.

These local and non-local areas are known as *internal* or *external* routes. Typically, internal routes are *intra-domain*, meaning that only two L2 routers will be involved. External routes can span multiple domains and any number of L2 routers.

If the packet is destined for an internal route, it's forwarded to the appropriate L1 router. Figure 22.26 illustrates internal routing.

FIGURE **22.26**
Internal routing.

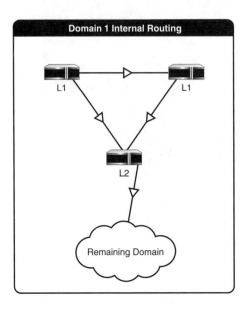

If the packet is destined for an external route, the router forwards the packet to its L2 router neighbor. Figure 22.27 illustrates external routing.

FIGURE **22.27**
External routing.

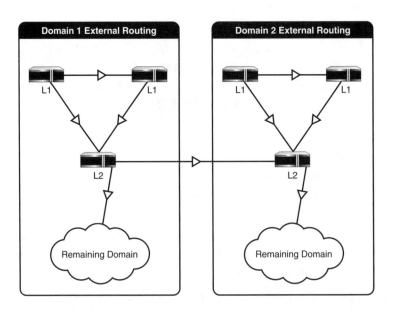

If the packet's destination area cannot be calculated, the packet is dropped.

Sample IS-IS Configurations

In what must be becoming a common configuration task, the first step in configuring IS-IS is to assign an area number:

```
Router(config)#router isis 45
```

The parameter 45 in this code sample represents the area number to route. After the isis command is executed, the net needs to be established. On a Cisco router, the net command assigns the network address to the router:

```
Router(config-router)# net 24.0001.001a.0000.0017.00
```

These two commands enable a Cisco router to participate in an IS-IS network on area 45. These are the only required commands for establishing an IS-IS-enabled router. One optional command that may prove useful is the is-type command. This is used to indicate whether the current router is an area router or a backbone router. When using the is-type command, a L1 router is an area router, while a L2 router is a backbone router:

```
Router(config-router)# is-type level-1
```

Summary

IS-IS is a routing protocol first developed for use on the DECnet system. The IS-IS protocol was later adapted for use with IP, and has become a high-end, robust routing protocol. As a link-state protocol, IS-IS uses the default metrics of delay, expense (cost), and reliability to calculate the best path. IS-IS is an efficient routing protocol that can move data rapidly from one hop to another. There are relatively few routing decisions that need to be made, and the separation of duties between L1 and L2 routers makes the process even easier by enabling the router to specialize on a specific area, without having to worry about the network as a whole.

Q&A

Q With the number of routing protocols that already exist for IP, why was IS-IS adapted from DECnet?

A IS-IS is one of the most robust link-state protocols in use today. IP networks were growing to a size and structure that the native IP routing protocols were having trouble keeping up with. Because the next version of DECnet was already leaning toward IP support, converting IS-IS seemed like the next logical step.

Quiz

1. How many default metrics are used by IS-IS?

2. Where are L2 routers found within the IS-IS domains?

3. What is the purpose of an SNP?

4. Which phase of the DECNet protocol provided the architecture for IS-IS?

Answers

1. Three—delay, expense, and reliability

2. The IS-IS backbone

3. A sequence number packet ensures that all the systems in an IS-IS environment receive the correct LSA.

4. Phase IV

Hour 23

Understanding BGP

One of the most popular and arguably most important routing protocols in use today is the Border Gateway Protocol (BGP). BGP is a very robust protocol that has become the backbone of the Internet. The main purpose of BGP is to advertise a network's presence and structures to other BGP routers on the Internet (more specifically, the routers of an ISP).

In today's routing landscape, engineers who are well versed in configuring and maintaining BGP environments are highly sought after. These routing experts literally make the Internet move.

The Internet is by nature a giant mesh of unrelated systems, architectures, and protocols. BGP has become the link that breaks the language barrier that exists between the dissimilar systems of the Internet. BGP enables systems and networks to recognize and be recognized by unrelated systems. Systems running BGP can advertise their routes and structures with other systems, regardless of the internal architecture of the networks involved.

The protocol commonly known as BGP is actually titled BGP4. The fourth incarnation of the Border Gateway Protocol is very different from all previous versions. However, BGP4 has become the most popular form of BGP after being adopted by Internet service providers, and is known simply as BGP.

As we have seen thus far, most routing protocols route data within a given networking environment. Protocols such as RIP are used to route data between internal networks and systems. This enables users on a network to exchange data with other users in the same area. BGP, on the other hand, routes data between different networks known as autonomous systems (ASes).

Each system logically has no inherent knowledge of any other system in the world. Because no system knows the topology (or for that matter the existence of) any other system, exchanging data between systems can be very difficult.

As a protocol, BGP enables systems with no knowledge of each other to communicate freely. However, if it were that simple, this would be the end of the lesson. BGP is an advanced topic for a reason. There are multiple variables and parameters that make BGP what it is.

Although BGP is best known for its capability to route between dissimilar ASes, it is actually comprised of two separate protocols: the *External Border Gateway Protocol (EBGP)*, and the *Internal Border Gateway Protocol (IBGP)*. EBGP is used to route data between autonomous systems, and IBGP is used to route data within a particular AS.

Defining BGP Autonomous Systems

Autonomous systems are the heart of BGP networks. The AS is the main routing unit of the BGP protocol. First let's look at how autonomous systems are physically formed, and how BGP differentiates between them.

An autonomous system can be a single network, or a group of related networks, such as a WAN.

An AS is a related group of systems. An AS is an environment, just like a LAN or WAN. Figure 23.1 illustrates a typical AS.

FIGURE 23.1

An autonomous system.

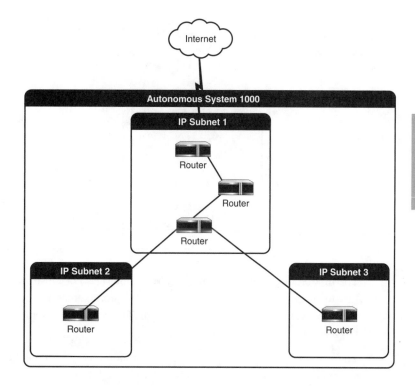

The network shown in Figure 23.1 is a fairly small LAN divided into several subnets. These subnets are in different geographical areas, and communicate back to the main office. The only outside access from the network emanates from the main subnet.

Because the small, external subnets do not have a separate connection to the Internet (they gain their connection through the central office), they are considered part of the same AS. All three subnetworks pictured in Figure 23.1 form one AS.

Autonomous systems can be even more basic than the one illustrated in Figure 23.1. A small Point of Presence (POP) network may have no more than one or two heavy-duty routers. Figure 23.2 shows a small one-router network as an AS.

The network in Figure 23.2, although small, is still a valid AS. The one router connecting the servers of the POP to the central office would qualify the POP as an AS.

Routers alone do not turn a network into an AS. If that were the case, almost every LAN, WAN, MAN, and SOHO in the country would be an AS, which is simply not true. Therefore, there are a couple of designators that determine whether a network is an AS.

FIGURE 23.2

A valid autonomous system with one router.

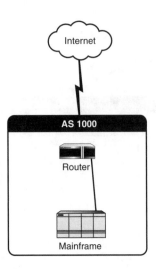

The first requirement is a connection to the Internet. For most companies, this means a link to an ISP. In order to implement effective communication between systems, there must be a carrier in place to connect them. This step is pretty logical and elementary, but it ties into the next requirement.

The second requirement for an AS is an autonomous system number (ASN). A network's autonomous system number is its identity on the Internet among other BGP systems. The ASN can range from 1 to 65535.

When you begin working with and designing large-scale environments, you might be faced with the task of obtaining and assigning an ASN for a BGP network. The process is not very difficult, but warrants some coverage here.

Obtaining an Autonomous System Number

An autonomous system number, like an IP network address, must be assigned to you by a governing body (assuming you will need to communicate to the outside world using EBGP). In most cases, your ISP will assign you an ASN as a subset of their own.

Because the range of autonomous system numbers is only 1–65535, there is a finite number of ASNs that can be assigned. Therefore, a smaller range of addresses has been set aside for private use.

The use and assignment of autonomous systems numbers is closely related to that of IP addresses. Both are assigned by governing bodies, both have public and private ranges, and both are (unfortunately) finite.

> In the United States, the governing body in charge of registering and releasing autonomous system numbers is the American Registry for Internet Numbers (ARIN). A list of the assigned autonomous system numbers and the entities who own them can be found at `ftp://ftp.arin.net/netinfo/asn.txt`.

Public Versus Private ASNs

Because there is a finite amount of public ASNs available, a number of addresses have been reserved for private use. Public autonomous system numbers range from 1 to 64511. These numbers are assigned to entities that require their network to be advertised to the Internet. Most often, ISPs and other large global companies are assigned these numbers.

Private ASNs range from 64512 to 65535. Like their IP counterparts, these numbers cannot be advertised to the Internet. Instead, these numbers are used for IBGP routing within a larger BGP network. The numbers in the private ASN range can be used freely by anyone.

To qualify for a public ASN, a network needs to supply proof of *multihoming*. Multihomed systems contain multiple links to external ASes. In other words, there are three classifications of ASes. Of these three, a network needs to be multihomed to obtain a public ASN. The three classes of autonomous systems are

- Stub
- Multihomed
- Transit

A stub AS is a network with only one connection to the Internet. Figure 23.3 shows a stub network attached to an ISP.

Stub ASes are usually treated as extensions of a larger AS. Because there is only one path to and from the stub AS, no further policies are required. It's not logical to host a massive list of BGP routes on a gateway with only one path to choose from.

> Most autonomous systems only qualify as stubs. However, a larger network might have stub sites that are attached to it, but are considered to be part of the same AS. These stub ASes do not require their own private ASNs. They can be considered part of the larger AS, and therefore share its ASN.

FIGURE **23.3**

A stub AS.

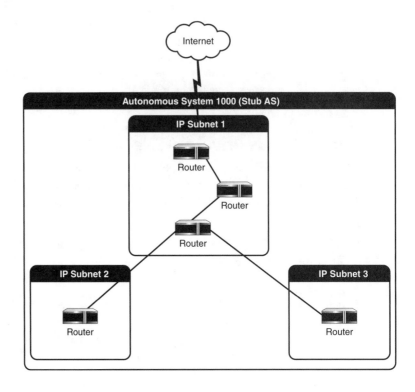

Multihomed systems are networks with multiple links to external ASes. The multihomed AS would accept routed information from all the systems linked to it, but it only routes internal data. Figure 23.4 illustrates a multihomed AS.

In Figure 23.4, the AS 1000 is multihomed because it connects to both AS 2000 and AS 3000. However, a multihomed AS will only route internal data, so AS 2000 would not be able to send information to AS 3000 through AS 1000. AS 1000 will only accept and route data bound for its internal network. For AS 2000 to communicate with AS 3000, it would need to have its own link to AS 3000.

The third type of autonomous system is a transit AS. Transit ASes are multihomed systems that accept and route information from other external ASes. If the multihomed AS in Figure 23.4 were a transit AS, AS 2000 would be able to send data to AS 3000 via AS 1000.

> The uses and ranges pertaining to autonomous system numbers are outlined in RFC 1930.

Figure 23.4

A multihomed AS.

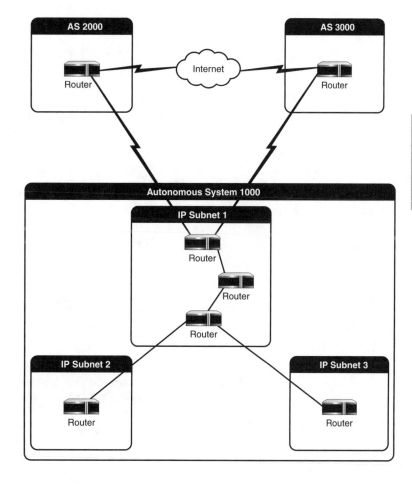

ASNs and IP

The link between ASes and IP addresses goes deeper than just the regulations on how the two are utilized. IP plays a big part in the operation of BGP and the formation of ASes.

An ASN is directly linked to the IP addresses of the AS it belongs to. In other words, an ASN needs to be associated with the IP address segments of the network to which it is attached. This will ensure that the proper traffic gets routed to the proper AS.

Only IP addresses specifically assigned to the ASN will be routed from the gateway. Having the proper IP address configured for the correct ASN will ensure that any external ASes route the correct data to your border gateways. If you leave out a subnet or change schemes without modifying your ASN, your network will not correctly receive data bound for it.

Autonomous System Terms

Now that we've discussed what ASes are, we can dive into how they work. The three major parts to an AS are the BGP speaker, the border gateway, and the BGP peer.

BGP Speakers

All routers with an AS that are configured for BGP are known as *BGP speakers*. A BGP speaker needs to be configured with the ASN of the AS to which it belongs. If the AS is comprised of more than one IP subnet, all the IP networks need to be associated with the ASN.

If a BGP speaker in an AS has an IP address from an IP address scheme that is not associated with the ASN, the speaker will not be able to participate in the AS. Consequently, any other systems or BGP speakers that are behind the non-participatory speaker will not receive data from the rest of the AS. Figure 23.5 illustrates an AS with one speaker that is not a member of the assigned IP scope.

FIGURE 23.5

An AS that is not fully functional.

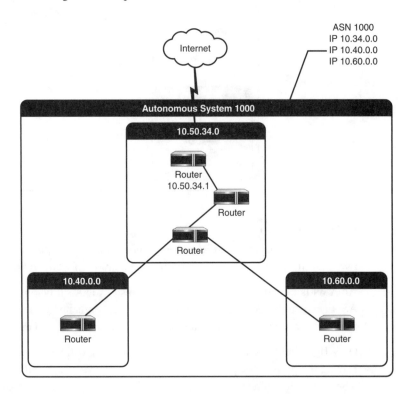

The two BGP speakers (and the end systems linked to them) located behind speaker
10.50.34.1 would not be able to participate in the AS. Even though the IP address
schemes that they belong to are associated with the ASN of the system, no data would
pass through speaker 10.50.34.1.

Border Gateways

BGP speakers located between two or more ASes are known as *border gateways*. Figure
23.6 illustrates an AS with a border gateway.

23

FIGURE 23.6

*An autonomous
system with a border
gateway.*

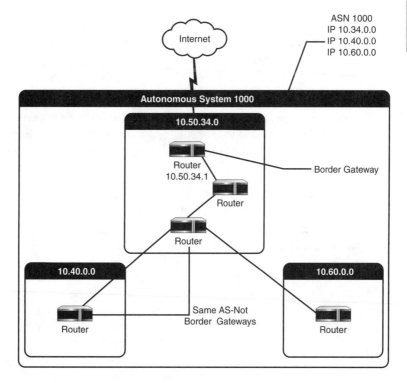

ASes do not necessarily need a border gateway. A border gateway is needed only if the
AS will be using EBGP to communicate with other ASes on the Internet. Conversely,
any single AS can have multiple border gateways.

If an AS interfaces with more than one external AS on more than one BGP
speaker, the AS will have multiple border gateways.

The job of the border gateway is to advertise the AS and any other routes that it has knowledge of to any external BGP speakers that it can contact. This might seem like a broad job description, but it will make more sense after we look at the Exterior Border Gateway Protocol.

BGP Peering Sessions

Like all other routing protocols, BGP works by sharing routing information among the network's participants. Every BGP speaker in an environment needs to exchange topographic and metric routing information with other BGP speakers to successfully route network data.

This exchange of routing information takes place during BGP *peering sessions*. When a BGP router is ready to exchange routing data with another BGP speaker, it opens a BGP peering session with the second speaker. The two BGP speakers involved in the peering session are now BGP peers.

For BGP to function correctly, BGP speakers must be BGP peers with all other speakers in their AS. They need to form a logical routing mesh. Depending on the amount of BGP speakers in your AS, this mesh can get rather large, becoming hard to control and keep track of.

The BGP peers do not need to be directly connected to each other, but they do need to communicate if they're using EBGP (all IBGP peers require a physical connection). Therefore, a standard path of communication must exist between the two BGP speakers for them to initiate a peering session.

> BGP can establish a peering session between two routers that are not directly connected. This is known as *EBGP multihop peering*. Using the external peering capabilities of EBGP, a BGP speaker can initiate a peering session with speakers that are multiple router hops away.
>
> However, the most common (and least complicated) form of peering is between two directly connected speakers.

Upon initiating a peering session, BGP speakers exchange their entire routing tables. This can make the process of achieving convergence rather lengthy. Depending on the number of advertised routes on any given router, the initial update exchange can be very intensive. BGP routers can hold hundreds of thousands of advertised routes. During the first update for a new BGP speaker, each one of these routes needs to be transferred.

If two BGP speakers are not physically linked, they need to also run an IGP. In other words, any BGP speakers that do not share a common link can only communicate with each other through the use of a protocol such as IGRP.

23

However, all future updates between existing BGP peers will consist of only changes made to the routing table. Therefore, the longer a router is functioning in the AS, the less intensive the table exchanges are.

BGP peers will exchange full routing tables whenever they peer for the first time. This includes restarts. Every time a router is restarted, it will exchange full copies of its routing tables with all its peers. Minimizing the number of router reloads will alleviate the burden placed upon the network by the heavy traffic of full BGP table exchanges.

After a BGP speaker has its routing configuration, it is ready to begin sending and receiving data. Depending on the needs of the network, the speaker will use one of two protocols: IBGP or EBGP.

Routing with the Exterior Border Gateway Protocol (EBGP)

EBGP is used to establish communication between BGP speakers in different ASes. Situations in which EBGP is used include communication between an ISP and a POP, or a large enterprise with multiple communications vendors. Functionally, there are few differences between EBGP and its counterpart IBGP; however, the differences are profound enough to warrant separate discussions.

BGP routers learn about their surroundings from other BGP routers. During peering sessions, BGP routers tell each other about the routes they know. These routes are the backbone of BGP operation, especially for speakers in different ASes. The key to the smooth and quick operation of the Internet is BGP's capability to communicate and exchange routes with speakers in dissimilar networks.

For any BGP speaker outside of your AS to be able to successfully route data to you, it needs to be aware of your location and what address you represent. However, a route can mean more than the addresses of the networks within your AS. Often a BPG speaker will advertise routes it knows to other ASes (that is, paths to ASes other than its own).

A BGP route simply states "I know how to get information bound for XXX.XXX.XXX.XXX from here to there." The routes specify an IP network address, and (if the network is not within the sending device's AS) a next hop router address. The next hop router address is the location of the border gateway that must be used to reach the destination. This information enables BGP speakers to advertise routes they are not directly connected to, thus enabling data from different ASes to reach virtually anyone.

One unfortunately common error in BGP route advertising is advertising a route incorrectly. For example, if an administrator keys in a network incorrectly and ends up advertising someone else's IP, traffic will not flow to the advertised network.

The BGP router advertising the route would receive all the traffic meant for the address. However, because the router does not actually know how to send data to the address (and no one within the AS actually matches the address), all information received would be discarded. Conversely, all data bound for routes that the router is correctly advertising would be distributed without interruption.

When a BGP speaker has information about a route that needs to be sent as an update to other internal or external BGP speakers, it advertises the route. Advertising is a way for one speaker to offer routes or routing updates to other speakers. Other BGP speakers then receive these routes as routing updates.

The most common form of BGP route advertisement is *BGP route redistribution*. Let's take a look at how BGP route redistribution works. Figure 23.7 illustrates four ASes connected through EBGP (in Figure 23.7, the ASes are designated by their ASN, so AS 1000 is ASN 1000).

Router 2000 advertises to ASes 3000 and 4000 that it knows to route all traffic for IP network 10.34.0.0 to AS 1000, and all traffic for IP network 10.60.0.0 goes to AS 2000 (itself). It will also advertise to Router 1000 that it can route all traffic for IP networks 10.80.0.0 and 10.35.0.0 to ASes 3000 and 4000, respectively. Router 2000 will then redistribute the knowledge of these routes to Router 1000, Router 3000, and Router 4000.

Now, if Router 3000 receives any data for the IP network 10.34.0.0, it knows that by forwarding the data to Router 2000, the information will get to the intended recipient (AS 1000).

FIGURE 23.7

Four ASes connected with EBGP.

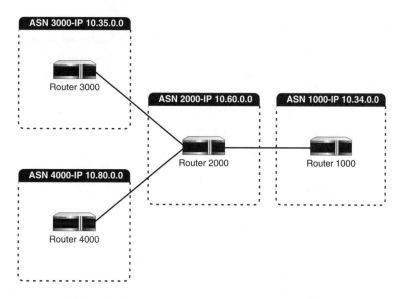

This form of route advertisement helps BGP speakers learn about each other and the networks they represent. Routes advertised by BGP speakers can be either dynamic or static.

A *dynamic* BGP route is one that the speaker learns about through IGP updates with other routers. In Figure 23.7, the route that Router 3000 and Router 4000 learn through their updates with EIGRP are considered dynamic routes. These routes, and their redistribution, can be controlled with the use of route maps.

BGP Route Maps

BGP route maps are used to filter the redistribution of BGP routes from AS to AS. Imagine the number of BGP routes that are exchanged on the Internet every day. If every BGP speaker redistributed every path it discovered, that traffic alone would bring the Internet to a halt. Route maps give you a way to determine what discovered BGP routes you want your speaker to redistribute to the Internet.

Route maps only work on the update level. Any route maps that might be in place will affect only routes being sent from the router, not those being received.

A route map can consist of a list of criteria that will permit or deny the advertisement, or reset a particular metric of the route. For example, using the networks from Figure 23.7 as our guide, an administrator could create a route map on Router 2000 that states: "Do not redistribute any routes learned from AS 2000." (The actual technical language of the route map will vary on the brand of router being used.)

With this route map in place, Router 1000 would still receive updates from Router 2000. However, it would run the route map against it and determine that it should not redistribute that route to Router 3000 or Router 4000.

However, let's say that AS 3000 was also connected to AS 1000, as illustrated in Figure 23.8.

FIGURE 23.8

Four interconnected ASes.

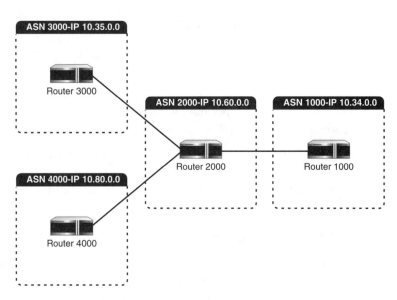

After all the BGP updates have been processed, Router 3000 will have two possible routes to select from for sending data to AS 1000: Send the data through Router 2000, or send it directly to Router 1000. When faced with a choice like this, the routing algorithm would decide which route to use based on the lowest cost or metric value.

The administrator of AS 2000, knowing that Router 2000 was one of the possible paths to AS 1000, could create a route map that would ensure that the direct route (Router 3000 to Router 1000) would be used before the indirect route (Router 3000 to Router 2000 to Router 1000). Assuming that the route updates from Router 1000 are sent out with a default metric of 4, the route map on Router 2000 could say: "Redistribute any routes learned from Router 1000 with a metric of 10."

After Router 3000 has received all its BGP updates, it would have two choices for sending data to the AS 1000: Send the data directly to Router 1000 for a cost of 4, or through Router 2000 for a cost of 10. Ninety-nine times out of 100, the routing algorithm will go with the direct route.

Conversely, if your site has the biggest and best in technology and you want your BGP border gateway to be the preferred route to another AS, you can create a lower metric value. By implementing a route map that changes another autonomous system's metric to a lower value, you will almost ensure your site as a preferred path to that AS.

This might be valuable during an acquisition of a company. If one company purchases another and wants the larger site to be the preferred route to the smaller one before actual network changes can be made, it can implement a route map.

Sometimes the preferred network described in a BGP route is no longer available. Network outages, power failures, and other interruptions are not uncommon in computer communications. Routes that describe such networks are said to be *flapping*. BGP has a feature for dealing with such occurrences called flap dampening.

BGP Route Flapping and Flap Dampening

If a BGP speaker fails to connect to any of the routers in its BGP table through a peering session, the route is said to be *flapping*. That is, if Router A learns about Router B (illustrated in Figure 23.9) through a dynamic BGP route redistribution and cannot open a peering session to it, the route to Router B is flapping.

Flapping can result in a loss of data due to packets not reaching their destination. In some cases, the BGP carrier can take networks offline if it detects that a router is flapping. Such occurrences can complicate network packet delivery and cause multiple routing updates, using needless amounts of bandwidth.

FIGURE 23.9

A flapping route.   Router A

Router B

The cause of a route flap could be anything from a T1 line becoming temporarily dislodged, to an entire network going belly-up. Either way, route flaps can be a processor-clogging hassle. If one route were to flap, and every BGP speaker connected to that route continued to redistribute it around the Internet, a lot of information going nowhere would clog the routers.

Therefore, a failsafe was put into place known as *flap dampening*. Flap dampening works by "blacklisting" any route that flaps for a specified amount of time (usually to BGP updates). When a route is dampened, it is removed from its peers' BGP route tables. Any further updates would not include the route. The consequence of this is the erasure of the route from the collective conscience of the Internet.

> Many times routes that are down temporarily must wait a certain amount of time after coming live again before they can be re-advertised, resulting in a longer downtime than necessary. This is one of the down sides of flap dampening.

Flap dampening is not something that needs to be configured by an administrator. It is simply a feature of the protocol. However, understanding that it exists is important to understanding BGP as a whole.

It is always best to check with your provider if you suddenly lose connectivity. Many times a problem on the provider's side (a cable coming loose) can cause the routes to your site to be dampened, making your site invisible for a few hours.

Some BGP Metrics and Attributes

Like most routing protocols, BGP relies on the use of metrics to aid in the route decision process. We have already discussed how the use of route maps enables an administrator to change a metric to a higher or lower value, depending on the desirability of a particular route. In BGP, these metrics are known as *attributes* and are very important in deciding how data is routed.

BGP Headers

There are four different BGP headers that can be attached to a BGP message. Each header contains information specific to the type of message being delivered. However, a common header precedes each of the four message headers. The BGP common header introduces the message and indicates to other systems that it is intended for BGP routers.

The *BGP common header*, also known as the BGP protocol header, will be found on all packets sent from a BGP router. The common header designates the packet as BGP, and indicates what type of information is contained within. Figure 23.10 illustrates the fields of the BGP common header.

FIGURE 23.10
The BGP common header.

16 Bytes	2 Bytes	1 Byte	Variable
Marker	Length	Type	Variable Data

The four fields of the BGP common header are the Header Marker, Length, Type, and Variable Data. The Header Marker is a 16-byte field that indicates the message is a BGP message. A receiving BGP router uses an internal calculation to predict what the marker field should be. If the router receives a packet and the Header Marker field is different from the field it predicted, then the router knows that the packet is being sent out of sequence and should be discarded.

The Length field, consisting of two bytes, is the total length in bytes of the BGP packet (not the length of the header).

The third field is the Type field. This single byte field indicates whether the following message is of the type open, update, notify, or keep alive.

Finally, the Variable Data field is the message itself. A message-specific header precedes the data in the Variable Data field. This field can vary in size, depending on the type of message.

An open message is sent between routers when a BGP session is established. After the routers establish a session using TCP, they exchange open messages to formally begin the session. Figure 23.11 illustrates the fields of an open message header.

FIGURE 23.11
An open message header.

1 Bytes	2 Bytes	2 Bytes	4 Bytes	1 Byte	4 Bytes
Version	AS	Hold-Time	BGP ID	Optional Param Length	Optional Params

The first field of the open message header is the 1-byte Version field. This field indicates which version of BGP the sender is using. Indicating versions of BGP helps the routers determine whether they are using compatible protocols.

The second field is the AS Indicator. This 2-byte field is the ASN of the router sending the message.

The next field is the Hold-Time field. The sending router uses the Hold-Time field to determine whether the recipient is online. If the router that sends the open message does not receive a reply within the time indicated by the Hold-Time field, the recipient is assumed to be offline.

The BGP Identifier is a 4-byte field that refers directly to the sender of the message. The BGP Identifier usually consists of the sending router's MAC address and its ASN.

The remaining two fields are optional. The first is the Optional Parameters field, which contains any parameters that the sending router wants to pass on to the recipient. Currently BGP has only one optional parameter that can be sent in an open message. The Authentication Information parameter is used in cases where the packet must be authenticated before use. The second optional field is the Optional Parameter Length field. This 1-byte field simply contains the length of the Optional Parameter field. If the optional parameters are not set, this field is set to 0.

An update message is distributed between BGP routers to amend the routing table information. A header with five fields precedes these messages within the variable data portion of the common BGP header. Figure 23.12 illustrates the fields of the update message header.

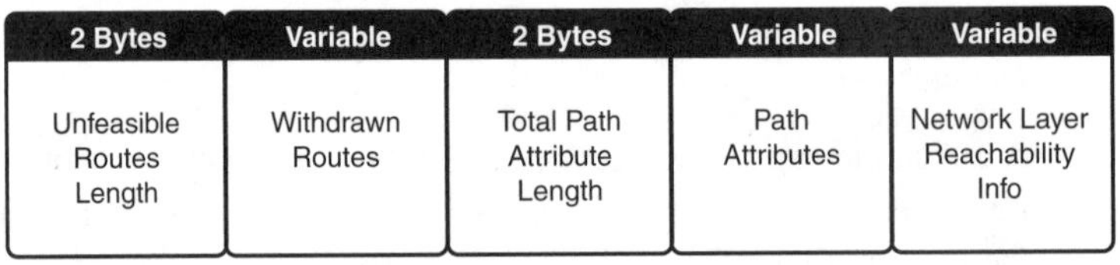

FIGURE 23.12

A BGP update *message header.*

2 Bytes	Variable	2 Bytes	Variable	Variable
Unfeasible Routes Length	Withdrawn Routes	Total Path Attribute Length	Path Attributes	Network Layer Reachability Info

The first two fields in the update message header concern any paths that should be removed from the recipient's routing tables. These paths are known as *withdrawn routes*. The first field of the header is Unfeasible Route Length. This 2-byte value indicates the length of the withdrawn routes field. If there are no withdrawn routes, the Unfeasible Route Length is set to 0.

The Withdrawn Routes field is a variable length field that contains the IP prefixes of any routes that should be deleted from the routing table.

The third field in the update message header is the 2-byte Total Path Attribute Length field. The field that immediately follows is the Path Attribute field. The Path Attribute field contains the metrics used by BGP to assign values to particular paths.

The final field in the update message header is the Network Layer Reachability information. This variable length field contains the IP prefixes of the paths that are to be added to the routing table.

The BGP `notify` Message and `keep-alive` Message

A BGP notification message is a message exchanged between BGP routers when an error occurs. When one router experiences a problem, it sends a 3-field notification message and disconnects any open sessions. The three fields are comprised of an error code, an error subcode, and the error data.

A `keep-alive` message is sent when a hold-time is about to expire. The `keep-alive` message is comprised of one field that lets the recipient know not to expire any hold-timers.

AS-Path/AS-Set

The AS-path is an attribute that is attached to a BGP route update. The AS-path indicates a cumulative account of the ASes a BGP update passed through before reaching its destination. To illustrate this, let's look at the BGP environment in Figure 23.13.

FIGURE 23.13

An AS-Path cycle.

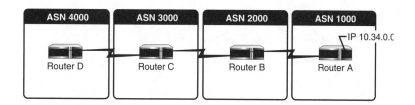

Router A advertises that "The path `10.34.0.0` belongs to ASN 1000." When Router B processes the update, the AS-path that the update came from is added as a prefix to the update. The update now says "AS 1000 says that the path `10.34.0.0` belongs to ASN 1000."

Next, Router B advertises the same route to Router C. After Router C processes the update, the path would read "ASN 2000 says that ASN 1000 says that path `10.34.0.0` belongs to ASN 1000." Finally, when the update reaches Router D, the AS-path would include the AS-set of "ASN 3000 says that ASN 2000 says that ASN 1000 says that path `10.34.0.0` belongs to ASN 1000."

A complete AS-path is known as an *AS-set*.

Now when Router D has a message for IP network `10.34.0.0`, it just needs to look at the AS-set on the update. The AS-set will give the router the AS-path to the destination. In our example, Router D would forward any data for `10.34.0.0` to the first AS-path (ASN 3000). Router C would forward that data to ASN 2000 (what it sees as the first AS-path), and so on until the information reaches ASN 1000.

Next Hop

The Next Hop attribute functions similarly to the AS-path; however, it specifies the IP address of the router port used to reach a particular AS. Using our previous example, just telling Router D that the AS-path for data going to `10.34.0.0` is ASN 3000 doesn't do it any good if Router D doesn't understand how to get to ASN 3000. Therefore, the Next Hop attribute on Router D needs to be set to the IP address of the physical router port that Router D can use to access Router C (ASN 3000).

Origin

The Origin attribute indicates where a particular update came from, or better yet, *how* it came. BGP will route data somewhat differently, based on whether the path is internal (IBGP) or external (EBGP). Therefore, BGP needs a way to quickly determine a route's origin.

The origin can be one of three values:

- IGP
- EGP
- Incomplete

> Do not confuse IGP and EGP with IBGP and EBGP. Although IBGP and EBGP are specific protocols, *IGP* and *EGP* are designators that stand for *Internal Gateway Protocol* and *External Gateway Protocol*, respectively. These protocols do not necessarily need to be IBGP or EBGP. In fact, oftentimes you will find other protocols being used to aid in the transportation of BGP data. Protocols such as *IGRP* and *EIGRP* (*Interior Gateway Routing Protocol and Enhanced Interior Gateway Routing Protocol*) can be used to route IBGP data. Therefore, the BGP origin is specifying generally which type of protocol the route was forwarded on.

An origin of IGB indicates that the route was learned from an internal protocol, such as IBGP. The BGP speaker can then assume that any path with an origin of IGP is within its own AS.

An origin of EGP indicates that the route was learned through an external update. This would cause the BGP speaker to use EBGP to reach any route with this origin.

Finally, an origin of Incomplete means that the route was obtained through a process other than internal or external update. In most cases, an incomplete origin represents a route that was obtained through route redistribution.

Local Preference

Local Preference is a metric used to determine the desirability of one path over another when there are two paths to a particular destination. When a router is presented with two seemingly equal paths to the same destination, it will compare the Local Preference attribute of the paths to determine which to use.

The higher a path's Local Preference is, the more likely it is to be used. If no Local Preference is defined, the default value is 100.

Interior Border Gateway Routing

As shown in the preceding sections, BGP operates by opening a peering session between two routers on specific physical and logical IP ports. BGP peering sessions will always be established between two routers on IP port 179, on which the physical Ethernet port (IP address) is defined.

In EBGP, this process poses one problem. If the specified physical port is unavailable, the peering session cannot be established. IBGP fixes this problem by using a loopback address.

A *loopback address* is an IP address that represents a cluster of physical router ports. By representing more than one physical port, a loopback address ensures that a BGP neighbor will still gain connectivity, regardless of the availability of the physical ports.

Loopback addresses are only found in IBGP because of the reachability of the routers. More often than not, routers connected through EBGP are only connected on one physical port, whereas routers connected by IBGP normally share an entire networking environment.

BGP Confederations

As we discussed earlier in this lesson, all BGP speakers in an IBGP AS need to be fully meshed to communicate successfully. This means that every BGP speaker that's running IBGP in a specific AS needs to have a physical connection to every other IBGP speaker. Figure 23.14 illustrates a large, fully meshed AS.

It is quite obvious from the example that as the number of IBGP speakers increases, the number of physical connections increases exponentially. Utilizing, tracking, and administering such a large number of connections can be trying even for the most seasoned of network professionals.

One method for reducing the number of physical router connections without limiting the number of IBGP speakers is to configure multiple BGP confederations.

23

FIGURE **23.14**
A fully meshed AS.

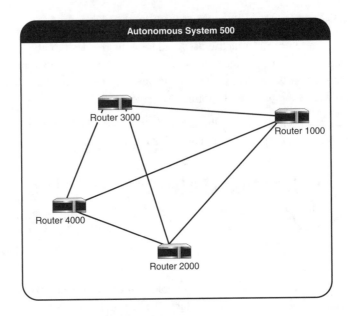

A *BGP confederation* is a sub-group within an AS. One larger AS can be divided into multiple smaller ASes while retaining the same ASN, yet reducing the number of physical connections between speakers. The function of BGP confederations can be compared to that of IP subnets. Whereas IP subnets break down the physical size of IP networks while retaining their identity as a larger entity, confederations create smaller sub-ASes that retain all the outward characteristics of the original, larger AS.

To divide an AS into several confederations, you need to do a bit of planning. Map out on paper where your confederation borders will be. This will help you visualize how you should configure the speakers within the confederations. After you have decided where you will be dividing the AS into confederations, you need to assign confederation identifiers to the new AS sub-groups. A *confederation identifier* is a number assigned to a confederation that distinguishes it from other confederations within the same AS. Confederation identifiers act, and follow the same conventions as ASNs.

Keep in mind that a confederation is a small AS. In other words, IBGP peers within a confederation need to be fully meshed. However, the IBGP peers within a confederation do not need to be fully meshed with the IBGP peers of another confederation, even if they are within the same AS. This lack of meshing between confederations creates a more manageable environment. After the confederation identifiers have been assigned, the inter-confederation physical links can be broken down.

You now have completely self-contained confederations with an AS. However, how do the confederations communicate with each other? To enable intra-confederation communication, and thus create a fully functional AS, you need to define IBGP confederation peers.

Confederation peers are routers that communicate from confederation to confederation. They act as BGP speakers for the individual confederations. Defining confederation peers can be confusing because of one small aspect of the process: Confederation peers speak to each other in EBGP.

Because confederations each have their own confederation identifier, EBGP speakers are needed to enable communication between two or more confederations. However, because these EBGP speakers are contained within an IBGP environment, they follow all the rules of IBGP speakers. Therefore, confederation peers share routes like IBGP peers and not EBGP speakers, even though they are technically running EBGP.

After the confederation peers are defined, connecting all the confederations within your AS by a single physical link will give you a fully functional group of confederations that appear as one large AS from the outside world. Figure 23.15 illustrates an AS divided into multiple confederations.

FIGURE 23.15

A group of confeder-ations.

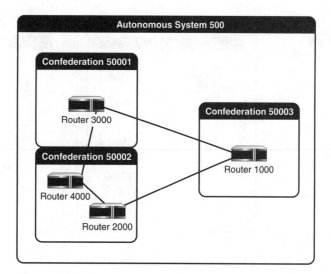

BGP Synchronization

Within a BGP environment, you might have more than one protocol being run through your routers. That is, all routers not running BGP should be running another routing protocol to facilitate the delivery of packages. BGP is a Border Gateway routing protocol, and your environment needs an Interior Gateway Protocol to route data through the rest of your network.

Your routers might be running OSPF, IS-IS, or any other IGP on the remaining portions of the network that are not serviced by BGP. The IGP that your remaining routers are running will communicate with and supply table information to the local BGP speakers. The information received from the IGP's tables will be used within BGP's own routing updates. The BGP speakers will update each other with the table information to provide a status report of the network's overall condition.

However, running two or more routing protocols simultaneously can pose a big problem. Each protocol is going to run its own routing updates. The problem is that if one router is running both IGRP and BGP, both of which receive routing table updates from different sources, which protocol's updates take precedence?

BGP synchronization helps the router determine what updates to include in its routing table and pass on to other BGP routers. Through BGP synchronization, a BGP router can hold its BGP updates until all routers have reported receiving updates from the IGP.

For example, the network in Figure 23.16 shows two ASes. Each AS is running both BGP and OSPF. Notice that some routers are running both protocols, while others are running only OSPF.

FIGURE 23.16

An AS running two routing protocols.

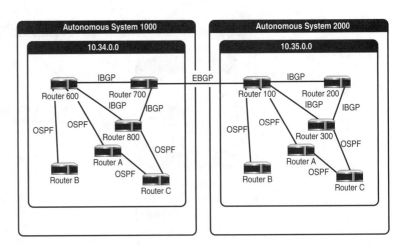

Before the BGP can begin its routing updates, it needs to wait for each router to receive an OSPF update. This will ensure that each router is receiving the most accurate information.

BGP Route Reflection

As we have discussed, all IBGP peers must be fully meshed within an AS. One of the reasons for this is that an IBGP peer cannot distribute routes learned from one IBGP peer to another.

IBGP peers will only propagate updates that relate directly to their own routes. This enables IBGP routers to send out updates that the routers know about first hand, reducing the number of incorrect or outdated routes. However, the obvious problem is that every IBGP peer must be physically linked to every other IBGP peer. The solution to this problem is BGP route reflectors.

IBGP peers can be configured as *BGP reflectors*. IBGP peers that are route reflectors can distribute, or reflect, routes learned from one BGP peer to another BGP peer. In other words, a BGP router can send an update to another BGP router without being physically meshed to that router. Figure 23.17 illustrates route reflection.

23

FIGURE 23.17

An AS with a route reflector.

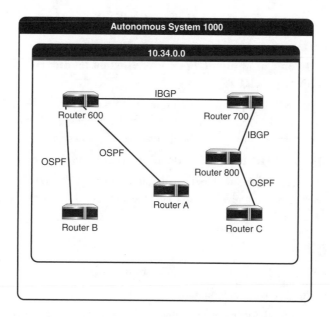

In this example, Router 700 can reflect routes from Router 600 to Router 800.

Route reflectors are a great tool administrators can use to help reduce the number of physical links needed between IBGP peers. However, the use of route reflectors does require more router overhead than a standard BGP router.

Summary

BGP is an exterior gateway protocol (EGP) used for large networks like ISPs. Today's current version of BGP is BGPv4, but most notation continues to refer to it as BGP.

BGP networks are called autonomous systems (ASes), and are designated by an autonomous system number (ASN). ASNs are supplied by a governing body such as ARIN, and can range from 1 to 65535. Every BGP AS publicly viewable from the Internet must have a unique ASN.

One unique feature of BGP is known as flap dampening. Flap dampening allows BGP to discontinue the forwarding of packets to areas it suspects are down. This keeps the number of lost packets on a BGP network to a minimum.

BGP offers other tools, such a route reflection, that can aid in the securing of a BGP network.

Q&A

Q If I don't want my BGP AS advertised on the Internet, do I still need to get an ASN from ARIN?

A No. ARIN has provided a number of ASNs for private use. These numbers range from 64512–65535. If you do not need to receive BGP information directly from an external source, you should use one of these numbers.

Q If I use BGP as my EGP, do all my routers need to run the same IGP?

A No. BGP allows routers to maintain different IGPs and IGP routing tables. BGP will ensure that every router gets the correct information through BGP synchronization.

Quiz

1. What BGP feature keeps packets from being forwarded to routes that are flapping?
2. What is a BGP confederation?
3. What are the three origin values for a BGP update?
4. What type of session is used by BGP peers to communicate with each other?
5. What is a BGP path's default local preference?

Answers

1. Flap dampening
2. A sub-autonomous system
3. IGP, EGP, and Unknown
4. Peering session
5. 100

Hour 24

Basic Router Security

Router security is not an easy topic to cover in a one-hour lesson. There are routing professionals who devote their entire careers to the subject of securing networks through the use of routers. We will not cover all of the various security methods in this lesson, but you will learn about the major points of concern within the most effective choices.

> You will also be introduced to two specific forms of routing security, NAT and access lists (covered in more detail in Appendix A, "Using NAT," and Appendix B, "Access Lists," respectively).

Knowing how to secure a router is as critical to learning how to use routers as knowing the protocols. A router is generally the first line of defense on a network. All traffic into and out of a network will pass through a routing device. For this reason, routers are capable of implementing strong security policies. You do not want all of your hard work configuring and implementing a full routed network to fall victim to a network attack.

Router security can take many forms. You can implement hardware security, rules-based security, or (preferably) a combination of the two. A good security policy will include provisions for hardware-based security, as in physical router protection and physical port protection, as well as software-based security, including port blocking, password protection, NAT, and access lists.

Hardware-Based Router Security

Many professionals tend to downplay the importance of physical router security, focusing solely on attacks originating from external networks. In fact, many malicious network attacks come in the form of corporate espionage. These attacks almost always occur from the inside.

Because routers are literally the gateways to networks, controlling the router equals controlling the network. The main goal of any hardware-based router security policy is to ensure that the wrong people cannot physically access the router, and if they do, ensuring that they cannot do anything to the router's configuration or equipment.

There are two basic forms of hardware-based security that you will learn about in this hour. They are

- Physical router security
- Physical port (cable) protection

Do not confuse *physical* port protection with *logical* port protection. You will learn about logical port protection (also known as port blocking) in the appendixes. Logical port protection blocks access to protocol-based ports in the router's memory.

These two forms of security can go a long way toward ensuring the protection of your network. Physical port protection is used to keep people from accessing the router's memory and operating system through unused interfaces. Physical router security, on the other hand, outlines policies for securing the location where a router is stored.

Physical Router Security

In short, physical router security involves restricting access to the router's hardware. The primary configuration point on any router is direct access to the hardware. If you can access the router's hardware, you can gain access to the direct configuration point.

> The *direct configuration point* on any router is normally a terminal that is attached to the router itself. Indirect router configuration points include telnet clients and HTML clients.

Many engineers and administrators assume that a potential network attacker is merely looking to gain access to points beyond the router, as in data from a central database, or information from an e-commerce Web server. Therefore, the external interfaces of the router are secured and the network is set in place.

However, it is not uncommon for the router itself to be the direct target of a network attack. Routers hold one very important piece of information within their memory—the routing table. The routing table holds information pertaining to the location and address of every device on your network, and the gold at the end of a cracker's rainbow—any other network you share routing information with. In many cases, your network may not even be the focus of an attack, but your router may hold the keys to access it.

To minimize the potential of anyone extracting information directly from the router, it needs to be placed in a secure location. The two most common solutions to providing a secure location for a router are a locked closet and a locked hardware rack.

Many companies implement both by placing all critical routing equipment into lockable hardware mounting racks, then placing those racks in a locked and secure room. This solution, while not foolproof, minimizes the equipment's exposure to uninvited guests.

If an intruder does gain access to the routing hardware, you need to take measures to prevent him from accessing as much information as possible.

Physical Port Security

Once an intruder has access to the router's hardware, his job is not finished. He still needs to find ways into the router's memory. The intruder will generally use a secondary device, such as a laptop or palmtop, and directly attach it to the router and access the router's memory through a telnet or terminal session.

One easy way to prevent such events is to password-protect all of your logical, terminal, and telnet lines on the router. Although the number and type of logical lines will vary from router to router, they all have a form of password protection.

Setting the passwords on the terminal lines once is usually not a safe option, however. To keep the router's assets as safe as possible, you should change the router's passwords on a regular basis. The passwords you assign to the router's lines should also consist of a mixture of upper and lower case alphanumeric digits. By doing so, the passwords are harder for an intruder to guess.

24

If your router has more than one interface that's being used, you might want to consider another form of port protection. Most routers provide a mechanism for internally disabling any interface not in use. By disabling any of your open (unused) interfaces, an intruder cannot simply plug into the interface for router access. Although this does not prevent the intruder from unplugging an existing (used) interface to gain access (as that interface cannot be disabled while it is in use), it does limit his possibilities.

> Many routers that carry highly sensitive data, like those used by government agencies, use specialized cables and interfaces that can immediately shut down if the cables are tampered with. These specialized cables are shielded with a pressurized layer of air. If the cable is unplugged or otherwise tampered with, the router's interface will detect the change in air pressure and automatically switch off the interface.

Software-Based Security for Routers

When most people think of router security, the first thing that comes to mind is software-based "hacker protection." While protecting your router's hardware from physical tampering is an important part of any router security plan, you still need to be familiar with the many software-based security options that exist.

Although there are many options for securing your router from external attacks, the two we will focus on are NAT and access lists. Combining both NAT and access lists can produce a simple, yet fairly secure environment.

Introduction to NAT

NAT (Network Address Translation) is usually implemented on gateway routers, or routers with a direct external connection, like the Internet. The concept behind NAT is that one routable IP address (or a pool of addresses) is assigned to one interface of the gateway router. Another interface of the router is configured with a non-routable IP address that corresponds to the addresses of the local network. NAT then translates non-routable IP traffic to routable IP traffic.

NAT is good for basic security because the router performs an address translation, making it exceedingly difficult for crackers to "piggyback" on IP traffic into and out of networks. NAT works hand-in-hand with another basic security tool, IP access lists. NAT is covered in detail in Appendix A.

Introduction to Access Lists

Access lists should be an everyday part of routing maintenance. Looking back through most of the lessons in this book, a majority of the protocols used by routers operate through the use of access lists. There are two types of access lists: IP access lists, and IPX access lists. In Appendix B, we will be examining the structures and concepts behind IP access lists.

Access lists provide a mechanism for the administrator to allow or deny routed protocol traffic based on certain criteria. These criteria can range from the port that the incoming traffic is using to the originating address.

Summary

The two major forms of router security are hardware-based and software-based. Hardware-based security options include placing your router hardware in a locked location. Software-based security options include NAT and access lists.

24

Q&A

Q Does every network need to implement router security?

A While I am a big believer that you can never be too safe, not every network needs the types of security options described in this hour. Many smaller networks will be perfectly secure with just a password-protected router, while others may require even more elaborate solutions.

Q Is physical router security really important?

A Physical router security is one of those subjects that is so basic it is often overlooked. Many companies either do not physically secure their routers at all, or subscribe to some form of group security (whereby all the network equipment is secured in the same physical location). Take the time to evaluate your router's physical security needs and compare those against the needs of your company.

Quiz

1. What does NAT stand for?

2. What should you password-protect on your router?

3. What is a direct configuration point?

4. What is the purpose of an access list?

Answers

1. Network Address Translation

2. All telnet and terminal lines

3. Any terminal directly connected to a router

4. Access lists provide a mechanism for the administrator to allow or deny routed protocol traffic based on certain criteria.

PART IV
Appendixes

A   Using NAT

B   Access Lists

APPENDIX A

Using NAT

One tool that you will encounter on almost every network is Network Address Translation (NAT). NAT is a way of mapping routable public IP addresses to private, non-routable, addresses. From the larger Web-based enterprise environments to the smallest SOHO networks, NAT can be found mapping addresses to keep information flowing. Even remote network technologies such as broadband cable use NAT to protect themselves and their clients.

NAT started as a simple way to help extend the shelf life of the dwindling IP addresses. By using NAT, a company could limit the number of public IP addresses needed within the environment. A large number of private addresses could all be mapped to a single public address. All information sent to and from the address network would pass through this single address.

What began as a way to limit IP address consumption quickly turned into a viable security solution. One great advantage to translating between IP addresses was that crackers and other reverse engineers found it nearly impossible to sneak into a network by "piggy-backing" on legitimate IP traffic.

All the configuration examples used throughout this appendix are taken from a Cisco router. These examples will allow you to better visualize the process of using and configuring NAT in various production environments.

Behind NAT: The Concepts and the Technology

NAT is a tool that allows gateway routers to map external IP addresses to internal IP addresses. This tool is most often used on gateway routers that control access to the Internet. Because of the growing shortage of IP addresses, many network administrators choose to implement local IP schemes that consist of public IP addresses. The problem with public IP addresses, however, is that they cannot be routed over the Internet.

Using NAT, one private IP address is assigned to the gateway router. This router then performs address translation on all incoming and outgoing traffic. This ensures that the outgoing traffic is tagged with the private address, and the incoming traffic is correctly referred to the proper public address.

NAT is an effective security tool because the translation process changes the source and destination addresses of each packet, making it harder for crackers to access networks through IP services. NAT also relies on IP access lists (covered in Appendix B, "Access Lists") to secure the translation process.

Like access lists, NAT works on the concept of inside and outside traffic. To fully configure NAT on most routers, you need to define the inside and outside characteristics of the affected interfaces. On a gateway router, it is assumed that at least one interface will be addressed for the internal network, and one interface will be addressed to the Internet (or another external network). The internal interface will be configured with an inside NAT rule, and the external interface will have an outside rule.

The first step in configuring NAT is to define the interfaces as being either inside or outside. This process is accomplished from interface configuration mode. In the following code sample, Interface Ethernet 0 is configured as an inside interface, and the ISDN port is configured as the outside interface:

```
Router(config)#interface ethernet 0
Router(config-if)#ip nat inside
Router(config-if)#interface bri 0
Router(config-if)#ip nat outside
```

Within a Cisco environment, the interface command is used to specify which physical interface you want to configure. In the example, the first line states that the following line is a configuration command for the first Ethernet interface. The third line of the example indicates that the final line is a command for the first ISDN interface (bri 0).

The next step in configuring NAT is to ensure that each interface has a proper IP address. In other words, the inside interface must have a public address, and the outside interface must have a private address. In scenarios similar to this, your ISP will generally provide you with an address to define the outside interface.

```
Router(config)#interface ethernet 0
Router(config-if)#ip address 198.65.1.1 255.255.0.0
Router(config-if)#interface bri 0
Router(config-if)#ip address 186.91.108.1 255.255.0.0
```

The interfaces of this router are configured for NAT. However, the router still does not know what to do with this information. A pool of translatable addresses needs to be established for the router to map to. In other words, the router needs to be told what addresses are available to translate the inbound data into.

Forming NAT address pools is done from the global configuration mode of the router. The syntax for forming a NAT pool is

```
#ip nat pool <name> <address range> netmask <subnet mask>
```

The code below illustrates the creation of a NAT address pool:

```
Router(config)#ip nat pool my_pool 198.65.1.1 198.65.254.254 netmask 255.255.0.0
```

This command created an address pool named my_pool for NAT to use when translating addresses. This particular pool uses the addresses from 198.65.1.1 to 198.65.254.254. Because the pools are named, different interfaces can use different address pools.

To configure NAT to use the pool named my_pool, we need to first create an access list detailing how to deal with the addresses in the pool. NAT can then be configured to use the pool address in accordance with the rules established in the access list. The access list must simply "permit" traffic to the addresses in our pool.

```
Router(config)#access-list 1permit 198.65.0.0 0.0.255.255
```

The final step is to associate this access list with the NAT pool. This last step will complete the NAT configuration process:

```
Router(config)#ip nat inside source list 1 pool my_pool
```

This command states that all inbound NAT traffic that meets the rules of Access List 1 can be translated to my_pool. After the rules are established, the router is ready to run. Any inbound packets not permitted by the access list are never translated by NAT and dropped.

APPENDIX B

Access Lists

As a form of security, access lists can be used as "router guard dogs." Access lists control protocol traffic into and out of routers. This appendix focuses on how access lists work and how to use them. You will be introduced to sample access list configurations, and you will view Cisco-based access list rules.

There are many types of access lists that can be implemented on a router. Each type of list corresponds to the protocol that it works in—IP access lists, IPX access lists, and so on. This appendix focuses primarily on IP access lists.

The primary goal of an access list is to monitor both incoming and outgoing traffic. Access lists are actually sets of rules that determine how certain protocol packets are treated as they enter or leave the router. The packets (data traffic) flowing through the router are compared against the access lists. Depending on the function of the list and the protocol of the packets, different operations are then performed on the packets.

You can use access lists to perform simple tasks, such as to permit or deny traffic based on the source or destination of the packets involved. If written correctly, access lists that use such rules are very effective in protecting networks.

Access lists can also be configured to perform more complex tasks, such as changing the metrics of packets to shape the flow of traffic across a network.

Examining IP Access Lists

While this appendix will only focus on two access lists, there are 11 different kinds that can be configured within Cisco routers. The following list illustrates the different access lists available to Cisco users:

- Standard IP
- Extended IP
- Protocol type-code
- DECnet
- XMS
- Extended XNS
- Appletalk
- MAC (Media Access Layer)
- Standard IPX
- Extended IPX
- IPX SAP
- Extended MAC
- IPX summary address

As with most routers, configuring a Cisco router to utilize access lists is a two-step process. The first step is to configure the actual access list. In other words, create a general rule that dictates how the router will deal with particular packets. The second step is to apply that access list to an interface. The process of binding access lists to particular interfaces allows different lists to be bound to different interfaces.

Each access list is identified by a number. The number assigned to an access list is partially dictated by the type of access list being configured. Each type of access list is assigned a range of 100 addresses (meaning there are 100 of each kind of access list that can be configured). Table B.1 features the address ranges available to each kind of access list.

TABLE B.1 Access List Numbers

Access List	Access List Number Range
Standard IP	1–99
Extended IP	100–199
Protocol type-code	200–299
DECnet	300–399
XNS	400–499
Extended XNS	500–599
Appletalk	600–699
MAC (Media Access Layer)	700–799
Standard IPX	800–899
Extended IPX	900–999
IPX SAP	1000–1099
Extended MAC	1100–1199
IPX summary address	1200–1299

Standard IP access lists will always have a number between 1 and 99, while extended IP access lists will range from 100 to 199. These are the two types of access lists we will be focusing on for the purposes of this appendix. To configure an access list on a Cisco router, use the access list command. The following code sample shows the creation of a standard IP access list:

```
Router(config)#access-list 1 permit 198.42.16.1
```

The syntax for using the access list command to configure a standard IP access list is

```
#access-list <access-list number> <action> <source address>
➧<optional address mask>
```

The syntax of the access list includes an optional address mask. If this mask is omitted, the router assumes it to be 0.0.0.0. A mask of 0.0.0.0 (using wild-card bits) tells the router to include all hosts matching the address specified.

The access list configured in the previous example simply states, "Permit traffic from IP address 198.42.16.1." The other option Cisco provides for the <action> parameter is to deny traffic from an IP address. To create a standard IP access list that denies traffic from 10.36.149.8, you would use the following code:

```
Router(config)#access-list 1 deny 10.36.149.8
```

Standard access lists are ideal for smaller environments, where an implicit allowance or denial of one or two addresses can secure a network. Standard access lists allow a user to create blanket rules, where all traffic from an address is either permitted or denied. However, standard access lists offer little else in the way of flexibility and customization.

Extended access lists give you more control over the rules behind the type of packets that are allowed or denied. The syntax for creating extended IP access lists is as follows:

```
#access-list <access-list number> <action> <protocol> <source address>
➥<destination address> <port>
```

There are more options for configuring extended access lists than there are for standard access lists. These extra options allow routers to filter traffic based on source, destination, protocol, or port. For example, to deny IP telnet traffic from 10.98.12.1–10.99.36.5, you would use the following example:

```
Router(config)#access-list 100 deny IP host 10.98.12.1 host 10.99.36.5 23
```

Telnet traffic runs over IP port 23. Table B.2 illustrates the more common IP services and their related port assignments.

TABLE B.2   Common IP Ports

Service	Port
SSH	22
Telnet	23
SMTP	25
HTTP	80
LDAP	389
MS NetMeeting	1024, 1503
HTTPs	443
SOCKS	1080
MS NetShow	1755
MSN Messenger	1863
Mirabilis ICQ	1024
AOL Instant Messenger	5190
AOL ICQ	5190,
AOL	5190–5193
Dialpad.com	5354, 7175, 8680–8890, 9000, 9450–9460

TABLE B.2 Continued

Service	Port
pcAnywhere	5631
VNC	5800+, 5900+
Netscape Conference	6498, 6502
Common IRC	6665–6669
Real Audio & Video	7070
VocalTec Internet Conference	22555
MSN Gaming Zone	28800–29000
DirectX Gaming	47624, 2300–2400

This access list example uses the keyword host before the source and destination addresses. If a user wanted to make a much broader statement, such as disabling HTTP traffic for the entire network, the any keyword is used.

```
Router(config)#access-list 147 deny IP any 10.0.0.0 0.255.255.255 any
➡0.0.0.0 255.255.255.255 80
```

This example blocks all of the local users on network 10.0.0.0 from accessing any Web sites on the broadcast range 0.0.0.0–255.255.255.255 on port 80. Using the any keyword can be dangerous, though. Services and users that legitimately need access to a particular destination may be blocked. Design your access lists carefully.

The two different types of access lists, standard and extended, can be combined in any configuration to filter traffic in almost any way administrators see fit. However, simply creating the access list is only half the equation; the access list still has to be implemented. The rules within the access list need to be applied to a particular interface.

To apply an access list to an interface, the access group keyword of the IP command is used from within the interface configuration mode. The IP command only allows one parameter, in/out. This parameter indicates whether the rule is to be applied to incoming or outgoing packets. The following code will establish one standard and one extended access list. These access lists will then be bound to the router's interface, Ethernet 0.

```
Router(config)#access-list 13 permit 128.53.12.1
Router(config)#access-list 108 deny IP host 198.26.13.118 host 128.53.12.1 80

Router(config)#interface ethernet 0
Router(config-if)# ip address 198.26.13.115
Router(config-if)# ip access-group 108 out
Router(config-if)# ip access group 13 in
```

In this code sample, two access lists were created. The first access list permits incoming traffic from the source address 128.53.12.1, while the second access list states that all IP HTTP traffic from 198.26.13.118 to host 128.53.12.1 should be denied. This is an effective way to keep the user at address 198.26.13.118 from viewing the Web pages at 128.53.12.1 80, yet still allowing services from that site to access the local network.

One very important thing to keep in mind about access lists is the rule of implicit deny. If an access list is created and a packet does not match the rules established in the access list (regardless of whether the access list was set to permit or deny), the packet is denied.

INDEX

A

Access lists, 353, 361-365
addresses
  Class A (IP), 94
  Class B (IP), 94
  Class C (IP), 95
  DECnet. *See* areas
  IPX (Internetwork Packet
    Exchange), 140-142
  loopback (IP), 343
  MAC addresses, 286
  NSAP (network service
    access point)
    area addresses, 309
    DSP (domain-specific
      part), 308
    IDP (initial domain
      part), 308
    system ID, 309

protocol addresses versus
  system addresses, 73
public IP (Internet
  Protocols) addresses,
  130
reserved (IP), 93
AFI (authority and format
identifier), 308
algorithms
  Dijkstra's algorithm, 275
  distance vector, 35-36
  DUAL (Diffusing Update
    Algorithms), 231-232
  link state, 36, 242
  routing, 31-34, 155
    distance vector algo-
      rithms, 35-36
    IS-IS (Intermediate
      System-to-
      Intermediate
      System), 304
    link state algorithms,
      36, 242

application layer (OSI), 17
architectures, ATM
  (Asynchronous Transfer
  Mode), 255-257
areas
  DECnet, 286-287
  IS-IS (Intermediate
    System-to-Intermediate
    System), 305-306
  NSAP addresses, 309
ARIN (American Registry
  for Internet Numbers),
  327
AS-path (BGP), 341
AS-set (BGP), 341
ASes (autonomous sys-
  tems), 219, 244-246
  ASN (autonomous system
    number), 326-329
  BGP (Border Gateway
    Protocols), 324-325

BGP gateways, 331
BGP peering sessions,
    332
BGP speakers, 330
multihomed ASes, 328
stub ASes, 327
transit ASes, 328
multihoming, 327
NSSAs (not-so-stubby
    areas), 240-241, 247
route redistribution, 247
stub areas, 240, 247
**ASN (autonomous system
numbers), 326-329**
**ATM (Asynchronous
Transfer Modes)**
end systems, 258
networks
    architectures, 255-257
    ATM end systems, 258
    ATM switches, 258
    PNNI (Private
        Network to Network
        Interface), 253-254,
        263-272, 280
    public/private net-
        works, 257-258
    UNI (User Node
        Interface) signaling
        protocol, 259-263
switches, 258
ATM Forum, 253-254
**autonomous system
numbers. *See* ASN**
**autonomous systems. *See*
ASes**
**AvCR (Available Cell
Rate), 273**
**AW (Administrative
Weight), 273**

B

**bandwidth (IGRP metric),
222**
**basic rate interface ISDN.
See BRI ISDN**
**BBS (bulletin board sys-
tem), defining, 9**
**BGP (Border Gateway
Protocol), 323**
ASes (autonomous
    systems), 324-325
    ASN (autonomous
        system numbers),
        326-329
    gateways, 331
    multihomed ASes, 328
    peering sessions, 332
    speakers, 330
    stub ASes, 327
    transit ASes, 328
attributes
    AS-path, 341
    AS-set, 341
    BGP headers, 338-340
    keep-alive messages,
        341
    Local Preference, 343
    Next Hop, 342
    notification messages,
        341
    Origin, 342
common headers, 338
confederations, 343
    confederation identifier,
        344
    confederation peers,
        345

dynamic BGP routes, 335
EBGP (External Border
    Gateway Protocol), 324
    multihop peering, 332
    routing, 333-334
gateways, 331
headers
    common headers, 338
    open message headers,
        339
    protocol headers. *See*
        BGP common head-
        ers
    update message head-
        ers, 340
IBGP (Internal Border
    Gateway Protocol), 324
    route reflection,
        346-347
    routing confederations,
        343-345
    routing
        synchronization,
        345-346
metrics, 338
open message headers,
    339
peering sessions, 332
protocol headers. *See*
    BGP common headers
route distribution, 334
route maps, 335-336
route reflection, 346-347
routes
    flap dampening, 338
    flapping, 337
speakers, 330
synchronization, 345-346
update message headers,
    340

BRI ISDN (Basic Rate Interface ISDN), 168
burned-in addresses. *See* MAC addresses

C

caches, routing, 292
carrier networks (X.25), 179
CDV (Cell Delay Variation), 273
CIDR (Classless Inter-Domain Routing), 46, 99, 133-137
circuits
    point-to-multipoint (UNI signaling protocols), 261
    point-to-point (UNI signaling protocols), 260-261
    virtual, 56
Cisco Web site, 145, 175
Class A addresses (IP), 94
Class B addresses (IP), 94
Class B IP (Internet Protocol) licenses, 114
Class C addresses (IP), 95
Class C IP (Internet Protocol) licenses, 114
classful IPs (Internet protocols), 44-45, 130-132
classful protocols, 44-45, 129
Classless Inter-Domain Routing. *See* **CIDR**
classless IPs (Internet protocols), 45

classless protocols versus classful protocols, 44-45
CLNP (Connectionless Network Protocol), 293
CLR (Cell Loss Ratio), 273
complex network routing, 82-83
confederation identifiers, 344
confederation peers, 345
configuring
    IPX (Internetwork Packet Exchange) routers, 143-144
    ISDN (Integrated Services Digital Network), 174-177
connection-oriented protocols versus connectionless protocols, 41-44
connectionless network protocols. *See* **CLNP**
connectionless protocols versus connection-oriented protocols, 41-44
convergence, 68, 86
cost fields. *See* Metric fields
crankbacks (PNNI), 279

D

data circuit terminating equipment. *See* DCE
Data field (IP protocol header), 77

data link connection identifiers. *See* DLCIs
data link layer (OSI model), 22, 27
data packets, 64, 78, 156
data terminal equipment. *See* **DTE, 181, 192**
DCE (data circuit terminating equipment), 181
DCE (data circuit terminating equipment) switches, 191
DECnet (Digital Equipment Corporation), 283-284
    areas, 286-287
    DRP (DECnet Routing Protocols), 291-292
    nodes, 287
        L1 routers, 288, 291
        L2 routers, 289-291
        Phase V, 292
DECnet routing protocol. *See* **DRP**
demultiplexers. *See* multiplexers/demultiplexers
designated IS (Intermediate System), 316
Destination Address field (IP protocol header), 77
Dijkstra's algorithm, 275. *See also* link-state algorithms
direct configuration points, 351
distance vector algorithms, 35-36
DLCIs (data link connection identifiers), 193-195

DRP (DECnet Routing Protocols), 291-292

DSP (domain-specific part), 308

DTE (data terminal equipment), 181, 192

DUAL (Diffusing Update Algorithms), 231-232

dynamic BGP (Border Gateway Protocol) routes, 335

dynamic route updating. *See* **routing updates**

dynamic routes, 102

dynamic routing, 155-158
troubleshooting, 159-161
versus static routing, 153-154

E

E protocols (ISDN), 171

EBGP (External Border Gateway Protocol), 324
multihop peering, 332
routing, 333-334

EIGRPs (Enhanced Interior Gateway Routing Protocols), 218
configuring, 234
DUALs (Diffusing Update Algorithms), 231-232
multiprotocol routing, 232
neighbor discovery, 233-234

enabling/disabling
hold-down timers (IGRP), 225-226
split horizons (IGRP), 225-226

encapsulating
ethernet, 145-148
IPX (Internetwork Packet Exchange), 144
protocols, 46-47

encapsulation method (Frame Relay), 194

end systems. *See* **ESes**

enhanced interior gateway routing protocols. *See* **EIGRPs**

ESes (end systems), 287, 291-292

ethernet, encapsulating, 145-148

external border gateway protocols. *See* **EBGP**

F

fields
Flags field (IP protocol header), 76
Flags field (RIP routing tables), 202
Remaining Life field (LSA controls), 300
Sequence field (LSA controls), 300

Flags field (IP protocol header), 76

Flags field (RIP routing tables), 202

flap dampening, 338

flapping, 337

flash updates (IGRP), 223

flooding, 239

floods
link-state, 272, 298-300

Fragment Offset field (IP protocol header), 76

frame relays, 189-190
configuring, 194
DCE (data circuit terminating equipment) switches, 191
DLCIs (data link connection identifiers), 193-195
DTEs (data terminal equipment), 192
LMIs (local management interfaces), 193
multiplexers/demultiplexers, 192-193
PVCs (permanent virtual circuits), 193
QoS (Quality of Service), 192
static maps, configuring, 195
subinterfaces, 194
SVCs (switched virtual circuits), 193

G – H

gateways, 218-220

GCAC (Generic Call Admission Control), 274

hardware-based router security, 350-351

Header Checksum field (IP protocol header), 77

headers

common headers, 338

open message headers, 339

protocol headers. *See* BGP common headers

update message headers, 340

hello messages (OSPF), 243. *See also* **HMs, 291-292**

hello packets, neighbor discovery (EIGRP), 233-234

HMs (hello messages)

DRP (DECnet Routing Protocol), 291-292

IS-IS (Intermediate System-to-Intermediate System), 312

hold-down timers, 206-207, 225-226

hop count limit (RIP), 203-204

hubs, 113

I

I protocols (ISDN), 171

IBGP (Internal Border Gateway Protocol), 324

BGP (Border Gateway Protocol)

confederations, 343-345

route reflection, 346-347

synchronization, 345-346

ICMP (Internet Control Message Protocol), 104-105

ping utility, 106-107

traceroute utility, 108

Identification field (IP protocol header), 76

IDI (initial domain identifier), 308

IDP (initial domain part), 308

IEEE (Institute of Electrical and Electronics Engineers), 180

IETF (Internet Engineering Task Force), 237

IGP (Interior Gateway Protocols). *See also* **RIPs (Routing Information Protocols)**

OSPF (Open Shortest Path First), 237-238

ASes (autonomous systems), 244-247

ASes (autonomous systems), NSSAs (not-so-stubby areas), 241, 247

ASes (autonomous systems), stub areas, 240, 247

configuring, 248-250

link-state algorithms, 242

updates, 242-244

IGRP (Interior Gateway Routing Protocols), 217

configuring

enabling/disabling hold-down timers, 225-226

enabling/disabling split horizons, 225-226

modifying update timers, 224

flash updates, 223

metrics

bandwidth, 222

Internetwork delays, 221

loads, 222

reliability, 222

routing updates, 223

versus RIPs (Routing Information Protocols), 218

interdomain routing, 218

interfaces

router, 102-104

serial, 192-194

interior gateway routing protocols. *See* **IGRPs**

intermediate system-to-intermediate system. *See* **IS-IS**

Internet, history, 8-10

Internet Control Message Protocol. *See* **ICMP**

Internet Header Length field (IP protocol header), 76

Internet Protocol Routing. *See* **IP (Internet Protocol) routing**

Internet Protocols. *See* **IP
(Internet Protocols)**
**Internetwork delays (IGRP
metric), 221**
**Internetwork Packet
Exchange.** *See* **IPX**
IP (Internet Protocols), 92
addresses
Class A addresses, 94
Class B addresses, 94
Class C addresses, 95
legal addresses, 102
loopback addresses,
343
public IP (Internet
Protocols) addresses,
130
reserved addresses, 93
addressing schemes, 113
classful IP (Internet
Protocols), 130-132
classless IP (Internet
Protocols), 45
fields
Data, 77
Destination Address,
77
Flags, 76
Fragment Offset, 76
Header Checksum, 77
Identification, 76
Internet Header
Length, 76
Options, 77
Protocol, 77
Source Address, 77
TOS (Type of
Service), 76
Total Length, 76

TTL (Time to Live),
77
Version, 75
licenses, 114
networks, 99, 112-122
routing, 112, 125-126
subnet masks, 95-98
**IPX (Internetwork Packet
Exchange), 140**
addresses, 140-142
encapsulation, 144
ethernet encapsulation,
145-148
router configuration,
143-144
routing, 149-150
**IS-IS (Intermediate
System-to-Intermediate
System) protocols, 283**
addressing, 304-308
CLNP (Connectionless
Network Protocol), 293
DECnet (Digital
Equipment
Corporation), 283-284
areas, 286
ares, 287
nodes, 287
routers, 288
routing, 291-292
designated IS
(Intermediate System),
316
examining IS-IS packets,
309-314
link-state routing, 294-302
metrics, 302-303
multicast addressing, 317
routing, 315, 320
algorithms, 304
pseudo-nodes, 316-318

**ISDN (Integrated Services
Digital Network), 167,
172-173**
BRI ISDN (Basic Rate
Interface ISDN), 168
configuring, 174-177
lines, 57
NT1 (Type 1 network
termination equipment),
170
NT2 (Type 2 network
termination equipment),
170
PRI ISDN (Primary
Rate Interface ISDN),
168-169
protocols, 171
reference points, 171
TAs (terminal adapters),
170
TE1 (Type 1 terminal
equipment), 170
TE2 (Type 2 terminal
equipment), 170
**ISDN PSNs (public
switched networks),
frame relays, 189-190**
configuring, 194
DCE (data circuit termi-
nating equipment)
switches, 191
DLCIs (data link connec-
tion identifiers), 193-195
DTEs (data terminal
equipment), 192
LMIs (local management
interfaces), 193
multiplexers/demultiplex-
ers, 192-193

PVCs (permanent virtual circuits), 193

SVCs (switched virtual circuits), 193

ITU-T (International Telecommunication Union-Telecommunication Standard Section, 180

J – K – L

keep-alive messages (BGP), 341

L1 routers (DECnet), 288, 291

L2 routers (DECnet), 289, 291

LAN (local area networks), 11

LAPD (Link Access Protocol D) protocols, 171

legal addresses. *See* **IP (Internet Protocols) addresses**

Level 1 routers. *See* **L1 routers**

Level 2 routers. *See* **L2 routers**

lines

ISDN (Integrated Services Digital Network) lines, 57

T1 lines, 58

link-state acknowledgements (OSPF), 244

link-state advertisements. *See* **LSAs**

link-state algorithms, 36, 242

link-state floods, 272, 298-300

link-state protocols

Dijkstra's algorithm, 275

IS-IS (Intermediate System-to-Intermediate System), 283, 294-302

addressing, 304-308

CLNP (Connectionless Network Protocol), 293

DECnet (Digital Equipment Corporation), 283-288, 291-292

designated IS (Intermediate System), 316

examining IS-IS packets, 309-314

metrics, 302-303

routing, 315-320

routing algorithms, 304

OSPF (Open Shortest Path First), 238

ASes (autonomous systems), 244-247

ASes (autonomous systems), NSSAs (not-so-stubby areas), 241, 247

ASes (autonomous systems), stub areas, 240, 247

configuring, 248-250

link-state algorithms, 242

updates, 242-244

PNNI (Private Network to Network Interface), 254, 263

configuring, 280

metrics, 273

NSAP (Network Service Access Points) addressing, 265-270

PGs (peer groups), 264

routing protocols, 270-272

link-state requests (OSPF), 243

link-state updates (OSPF), 244

LLC (Logical Link Control) sub-layer (data link layer (OSI model), 24

LMIs (local management interfaces), 193

load balancing, 222

loads (IGRP metric), 222

local management interfaces. *See* **LMIs**

Local Preference (BGP), 343

Logical Link Control sub-layer. *See* **LLC (Logical Link Control) sub-layer**

loopback addresses (IP), 343

LSAs (link-state advertisements), 294, 297

fields

Remaining Life field, 300

Sequence field, 300

flooding, 239, 298-300

LSPs (link-state packets), 313

M

MAC (Media Access Control) addresses, 286

MAC sub-layer (data link layer), 23

mapping networks, 26

maps

BGP (Border Gateway Protocol) route, 335-336

static maps, configuring, 195

masks, subnet masks (IP), 95-98

MaxCR (Maximum Cell Rate), 273

MaxCTD (Maximum Cell Transfer Delay), 273

Media Access Control sub-layer. *See* **MAC sub-layer**

Metric fields (RIP routing tables), 202

metrics, 64, 74, 85

BGP (Border Gateway Protocol), 338

IGRP (Interior Gateway Routing Protocols), 221-222

IS-IS (Intermediate System-to-Intermediate System), 302-303

multicast addressing, 317

multihomed ASes (autonomous systems), 328

multihoming, 327

multiplexer/demultiplexers, 192-193

multiprotocol routing, 232

N

NAT (Network Address Translation), 352, 357-359

neighbor discovery (EIGRP), 233-234

neighbors, 202

network address translation. *See* **NAT**

Network fields (RIP routing tables), 201

network layer (OSI model), 21-22, 27

networking, gateways, 218-220

networks

ATM (Asynchronous Transfer Mode) networks architectures, 255-257

ATM end systems, 258

ATM switches, 258

public/private networks, 257-258

UNI (User Node Interface) signaling protocol, 259-263

complex network routing, 82-83

connecting

ISDN (Integrated Services Digital Network), 57

T1 lines, 58

convergence, 68

IP (Internet Protocols)

subnetting, 112-122

supernetting, 99

ISDN (Integrated Services Digital Network), 167-168, 171-174

BRI ISDN (Basic Rate Interface ISDN), 168

configuring, 174-177

E protocols, 171

I protocols, 171

NT1 (Type 1 network termination equipment), 170

NT2 (Type 2 network termination equipment), 170

PRI ISDN (Primary Rate Interface ISDN), 168-169

Q protocols, 171

reference points, 171

TA (terminal adapters), 170

TE1 (Type 1 terminal equipment), 170

TE2 (Type 2 terminal equipment), 170

LAN (local area networks), 11

mapping, 26

metrics, 74, 85

PSNs (public switched networks), 53, 189

frame relays, 190-191

versus private networks, 54

segmented, 111-112, 122-124

simple network routing, 79-82

subnetting, 96-98

VPNs (virtual private networks), 12

WAN (wide area networks), 11

Next Hop (BGP), 342

Next Hop fields (RIP routing tables), 201

next hop router addresses, 334

nodes, pseudo-nodes (IS-IS), 316-318

nodes (DECnet), 287

L1 routers, 288, 291

L2 routers, 289-291

not-so-stubby areas. *See* **NSSAs**

notification messages (BGP), 341

NSAP (network service access point) addresses

area addresses, 309

DSP (domain-specific part), 308

IDP (initial domain part), 308

PNNI (Private Network to Network Interface), 265-270

system ID, 309

NSSAs (not-so-stubby areas), 240-241, 247

NT1 (Type 1 network termination equipment), 170

NT2 (Type 2 network termination equipment), 170

O

open message headers, 339

open shortest path first. *See* **OSPF**

Open Systems Interconnection models. *See* **OSI models**

Options field (IP protocol header), 77

Origin (BGP), 342

OSI (Open Systems Interconnection)

model, 16, 72-73

application layer, 17

data link layer, 22-24, 27

network layer, 21-22, 27

physical layer, 24-25, 28

presentation layer, 18

router/protocol interaction, 25

session layer, 20

transport layer, 20

protocols,

CLNP (Connectionless Network Protocol), 293

NSAP (network service access point) addresses, 308-309

OSPF (Open Shortest Path First), 237-238

ASes (autonomous system), 244-246

NSSAs (not-so-stubby areas), 241, 247

route redistribution, 247

stub areas, 240, 247

configuring, 248-250

link-state algorithms, 242

updates, 242

database descriptions, 243

hello messages, 243

link-state acknowledgements, 244

link-state requests, 243

link-state updates, 244

P

packet assembler/disassembler. *See* **PAD**

packet layer protocols. *See* **PLPs**

packet-switching exchange. *See* **PSE**

packets, 156

hello packets, neighbor discovery (EIGRP), 233-234

IS-IS (Intermediate System-to-Intermediate System)

examining, 309-312

LSPs (link-state packets), 313

SNPs (sequence number packets), 314

LSPs (link-state packets), 313

SNPs (sequence number packets), 314

PAD (packet assembler/ disassembler), 181
peer groups. *See* **PGs**
permanent virtual circuits. *See* **PVCs**
PGs (peer groups), 264
physical layer (OSI model), 24-25, 28
physical port security, 351
physical router security, 350-351
ping utility, 106-107
PLPs (packet layer protocols), 185-187
PNNI (Private Network-to-Network Interface), 253-254, 263
  configuring, 280
  crankbacks, 279
  metrics, 273
  NSAP (Network Service Access Points) addressing, 265-270
  PGs (peer groups), 264
  routing protocols, 270-272
  signaling protocol, 275-276
point-to-multipoint circuits (UNI signaling protocols), 261
point-to-point circuits (UNI signaling protocols), 260-261
poison paths (link-state flooding), 298
ports, physical port security, 351
presentation layer (OSI model), 18

PRI ISDN (Primary Rate Interface ISDN), 168-169
primary rate interface ISDN. *See* **PRI ISDN**
private ASNs (autonomous system number), 327
private networks
  versus PSNs (public switched networks), 54
  X.25, 179
Protocol field (IP protocol header), 77
protocols
  classful IP (Internet Protocols), 129-132
  CLNP (Connectionless Network Protocol), 293
  data packets, 78, 156
  DECnet, 283-284
    areas, 286-287
    DRP (DECnet Routing Protocols), 291-292
    nodes, 287-291
    Phase V, 292
  DRP (DECnet Routing Protocols), 291-292
  E protocols (ISDN), 171
  EBGP (External Border Gateway Protocol), 324
    multihop peering, 332
    routing, 333-334
  EIGRPs (Enhanced Interior Gateway Routing Protocols), 218
    configuring, 234
    DUALs (Diffusing Update Algorithms), 231-232
    multiprotocol routing, 232
    neighbor discovery, 233-234

  encapsulating, 46-47
  headers, 74-77
  I protocols (ISDN), 171
  IBGP (Internal Border Gateway Protocol), 324, 343-347
  ICMP (Internet Control Message Protocol), 104-105
    ping utility, 106-107
    traceroute utility, 108
  IGP (Interior Gateway Protocols), 237-250
  IGRPs (Interior Gateway Routing Protocols), 217
    bandwidth, 222
    configuring, 223-226
    flash updates, 223
    Internetwork delays, 221
    loads, 222
    reliability, 222
    routing updates, 223
    versus RIPs (Routing Information Protocols), 218
  IP (Internet Protocols), 92
    addresses, Class A, 94
    addresses, Class B, 94
    addresses, Class C, 95
    addresses, reserved, 93
    subnet masks, 95-98
  IS-IS (Intermediate System-to-Intermediate System)
    addressing, 304-308
    CLNP (Connectionless Network Protocol), 293
    DECnet (Digital Equipment Corporation), 283-292

designated IS
(Intermediate
System), 316
examining IS-IS
packets, 309-314
link-state routing,
294-302
metrics, 302-303
routing, 304, 315-320
LAPD (Link Access
Protocol D), 171
link-state
IS-IS (Intermediate
System-to-
Intermediate
System), 283,
293-320
OSPF (Open Shortest
Path First), 238-250
PNNI (Private to
Private Interface),
254, 263-273, 280
multiprotocol routing, 232
OSI (Open Systems
Interconnection) model,
16, 72-73
application layer, 17
data link layer, 22-24,
27
network layer, 21-22,
27
NSAP (network ser-
vice access point),
308-309
physical layer, 24-25,
28
presentation layer, 18
router/protocol inter-
action, 25
session layer, 20
transport layer, 20

PLPs (packet layer proto-
cols), 185-187
PNNI (Private Network
to Network Interface),
253-254, 263
configuring, 280
metrics, 273
NSAP (Network
Service Access
Points) addressing,
265-270
PGs (peer groups),
264
routing protocol,
270-272
signaling protocol,
275-276
protocol addresses versus
system addresses, 73
Q protocols (ISDN), 171
RIPs (Routing
Information Protocols),
197-199, 202
configuring, 211
hold-down timers,
206-207
hop count limit,
203-204
multiple versions,
213-214
route poisoning,
204-205
routing tables, 200-201
routing updates,
209-211
setting timers, 212-213
split horizon, 205-206
versus IGRPs (Interior
Gateway Routing
Protocols), 218

routed
classful versus class-
less protocols (IP),
44-45
connection-oriented
versus connection-
less protocols, 41-44
defining, 39-40
IPX (Internetwork
Packet Exchange),
140
IPX (Internetwork
Packet Exchange)
addresses, 140-142
IPX (Internetwork
Packet Exchange)
encapsulation,
144-148
IPX (Internetwork
Packet Exchange)
router configuration,
143-144
IPX (Internetwork
Packet Exchange)
routing, 149-150
routers, interacting with,
25
routing, 61-65, 74
BGP (Border Gateway
Protocol), 323-347
DRP (DECnet Routing
Protocols), 291-292
dynamic routing,
155-158
dynamic routing,
troubleshooting,
159-161
dynamic routing
versus static routing,
153-154

EBGP (External Border Gateway Protocol), 324, 332-334

EIGRPs (Enhanced Interior Gateway Routing Protocols), 218, 231-234

IBGP (Internal Border Gateway Protocol), 324, 343-347

IGRPs (Interior Gateway Routing Protocols), 217-218, 221-226

IS-IS (Intermediate System-to-Intermediate System), 283, 293-320

loops, 199-200

RIPs (Routing Information Protocols), 197-214, 218

routing algorithms, 31-34

routing algorithms, distance vector algorithms, 35-36

routing algorithms, link state algorithms, 36

static routing, 161-162

static routing, troubleshooting, 163-164

static routing versus dynamic routing, 153-154

scalable, 198

specialized, defining, 25

TCP (Transmission Control Protocols), 91-92

UNI (User Node Interface) signaling protocol, 259-263

point-to-multipoint circuits, 261

point-to-point circuits, 260-261

upper-layer protocols, 190

WAN (Wide Area Network), 51-52

frame relays, 189-194

PSNs (public switched networks), 56-58

routing versus switching, 54

PSE (packet-switching exchange), 181

pseudo-nodes (IS-IS), 316-318

PSNs (public switched networks), 53, 56-57

frame relays, 189-190

configuring, 194

DCE (data circuit terminating equipment) switches, 191

DLCIs (data link connection identifiers), 193-195

DTEs (data terminal equipment), 192

LMIs (local management interfaces), 193

multiplexers/demultiplexers, 192-193

PVCs (permanent virtual circuits), 193

SVCs (switched virtual circuits), 193

ISDN (Integrated Services Digital Network), 167, 172-173

BRI ISDN (Basic Rate Interface ISDN), 168

configuring, 174-177

E protocols, 171

I protocols, 171

NT1 (Type 1 network termination equipment), 170

NT2 (Type 2 network termination equipment), 170

PRI ISDN (Primary Rate Interface ISDN), 168-169

Q protocols, 171

reference points, 171

TAs (terminal adapters), 170

TE1 (Type 1 terminal equipment), 170

TE2 (Type 2 terminal equipment), 170

networks, connecting, 57-58

versus private networks, 54

public ASNs (autonomous system number), 327

public IP (Internet Protocols) addresses, 130

public switched networks. See PSNs

public/private ATM (Asynchronous Transfer Mode) networks, 257-258
PVCs (permanent virtual circuits), 182-184, 193

Q – R

Q protocols (ISDN), 171
QoS (Quality of Service), 192, 273-274

reference points, 171
reliability (IGRP metric), 222
Remaining Life field (LSA controls), 300
replacement routes, 231
reserved addresses (IP), 93
RIPs (Routing Information Protocols), 197-199, 202, 208
  configuring, 211
  hold-down timers, 206-207
  hop count limit, 203-204
  multiple versions, 213-214
  route poisoning, 204-205
  routing
    tables, 200-201
    updates, 209-211
  split horizon, 205-206
  timers, setting, 212-213
  versus IGRPs (Interior Gateway Routing Protocols), 218
route
  poisoning, 204-205
  redistribution, 247
  removal timers (RIP), 202
  timeout timers (RIP), 202

routed protocols
  classful versus classless protocols (IP), 44-45
  CLNP (Connectionless Network Protocol), 293
  connection-oriented versus connectionless protocols, 41-44
  defining, 39-40
  IPX (Internetwork Packet Exchange)
    addresses, 140-142
    encapsulation, 144
    ethernet encapsulation, 145-148
    router configuration, 143-144
    routing, 149-150
routers
  configuring (IPX), 143-144
  convergence, 68, 86
  defining, 25
  direct configuration points, 351
  interfaces, 102-104
  L1 (DECnet), 288, 291
  L2 (DECnet), 289-291
  neighbors, 202
  next hop router addresses, 334
  protocols, interacting with, 25
  routing tables, 26
  security, 349
    hardware-based, 350-351
    software-based, 352-353, 357-365
  segmented networks, placing, 122-124
  serial interfaces, 192

routes
  BGP (Border Gateway Protocol)
    flap dampening, 338
    flapping, 337
    route maps, 335-336
  dynamic, 102
  route maps (BGP), 335-336
  static, 103
routing
  algorithms, 155
    distance vector algorithms, 35-36
    IS-IS (Intermediate System-to-Intermediate System), 304
    link-state algorithms, 36, 242
  caches, 292
  complex network routing, 82-83
  defining, 10-12
  gateways, 218, 220
  interdomain routing, 218
  IP (Internet Protocol), 112
  IPX (Internetwork Packet Exchange), 149-150
  loops, 199-200, 205-206
  multiprotocol routing, 232
  protocols, 61-65, 74
    BGP (Border Gateway Protocol), 323-343
    DRP (DECnet Routing Protocols), 291-292
    dynamic routing, 153-161

EBGP (External Border Gateway Protocol), 324, 332-334

EIGRPs (Enhanced Interior Gateway Routing Protocols), 218, 231-234

IBGP (Internal Border Gateway Protocol), 324, 343-347

IGRPs (Interior Gateway Routing Protocols), 217-218, 221-226

IS-IS (Intermediate System-to-Intermediate System), 283-288, 291-320

PNNI (Private Network to Network Interface), 270-273

RIPs (Routing Information Protocols), 197-214, 218

static routing, 153-154, 161-164

replacement routes, 231

simple network routing, 79, 81-82

tables, 26, 84-85, 200-202

updates, 65-68, 161, 209-211

versus switching, 54

routing information protocols. *See* **RIPs**

routing update timer (RIP), 202

S

scalable protocols, 198

security, routers, 349

hardware-based, 350-351

software-based, 352-353, 357-365

segmented networks, 111-112, 122-124

Sequence field (LSA controls), 300

serial interfaces, 192-194

service profile identification number. *See* **SPID**

session layer (OSI model), 20

signaling protocols

PNNI (Private Network to Network), 275-276

UNI (User Node Interface), 259, 263

point-to-multipoint circuits, 261

point-to-point circuits, 260-261

simple network routing, 79-82

SNPs (sequence number packets), 314

software-based router security, 352

Access lists, 353, 361-365

NAT (Network Address Translation), 352, 357-359

Source Address field (IP protocol header), 77

specialized protocols, defining, 25

SPID (Service Profile Identification Number), 175-176

split horizons, 205-206, 225-226

static

maps (frame relay), configuring, 195

routes, 103, 125-126

routing, 161-162

troubleshooting, 163-164

versus dynamic routing, 153-154

stub areas (ASes), 240, 247

stub ASes (autonomous systems), 327

subinterfaces, 194

subnet masks (IP), 95-98

subnets, 96-98, 125-126

subnetting, 112-122

supernets, 99

SVCs (switched virtual circuits), 193

switches, ATM (Asynchronous Transfer Mode), 258

switching versus routing, 54

system addresses versus protocol addresses, 73

T

T1 lines, 58

tables, routing, 84-85, 200-202

TAs (terminal adapters), 170

TCP (Transmission Control Protocols), 91-92

TE1 (Type 1 terminal equipment), 170

TE2 (Type 2 terminal equipment), 170

Time to Live field. *See* TTL (Time to Live) field

timeout. *See* TTL (time-to-live)

Timer field (RIP routing tables), 202

timers
  hold-down timers, 206-207, 225-226
  RIP (Routing Information Protocol) timers, setting, 212-213
  route removal timers (RIP), 202
  route timeout timers (RIP), 202
  routing update timers (RIP), 202
  update (IGRP), 224

TOS (Type of Service) field (IP protocol header), 76

Total Length field (IP protocol header), 76

traceroute utility, 108

transit ASes (autonomous systems), 328

Transmission Control Protocols. *See* TCP (Transmission Control Protocols)

transport layer (OSI model), 20

troubleshooting
  dynamic routing protocols, 159-161
  static routing protocols, 163-164

TTL (Time to Live) field (IP protocol header), 77

TTL (time-to-live), 107

Type of Service field. *See* TOS (Type of Service) field

UNI (User Node Interface) signaling protocol, 259, 263
  point-to-multipoint circuits, 261
  point-to-point circuits, 260-261

U – V

update timers (IGRP), 224

update triggers, 210

updates
  database descriptions (OSPF), 243
  hello messages (OSPF), 243
  link-state acknowledgements (OSPF), 244
  link-state requests (OSPF), 243
  link-state updates (OSPF), 244
  routing, 65-68, 161, 209-211

upper-layer protocols, 190

utilities
  ping utility, 106-107
  traceroute utility, 108

Version field (IP protocol header), 75

virtual circuits, 56

VPNs (virtual private networks), 12

W

WAN (Wide Area Network) protocols, 51-52
  defining, 11
  frame relays, 189-190
    configuring, 194
    DCE (data circuit terminating equipment) switches, 191
    DTEs (data terminal equipment), 192
    multiplexers/demultiplexers, 192-193
  ISDN (Integrated Services Digital Network), 167-168, 172-173
    BRI ISDN (Basic Rate Interface ISDN), 168
    configuring, 174-177
    E protocols, 171
    I protocols, 171
    NT1 (Type 1 network termination equipment), 170

NT2 (Type 2 network termination equipment), 170

PRI ISDN (Primary Rate Interface ISDN), 168-169

Q protocols, 171

reference points, 171

TAs (terminal adapters), 170

TE1 (Type 1 terminal equipment), 170

TE2 (Type 2 terminal equipment), 170

PSNs (public switched networks), 56-58

routing versus switching, 54

X.25, 180

    carrier network, 179

    DCE (data circuit terminating equipment), 181

    DTE (data terminal equipment), 181

    LAPBs (link access procedures, balanced), 185

    PAD (packet assembler/disassembler), 181

    PLPs (packet layer protocols), 185-187

    private networks, 179

    PSE (packet-switching exchange), 181

    PVCs (permanent virtual circuits), 182-184

SVCs (switched virtual circuits), 184

Web sites

    Cisco, 145, 175

    Webopedia, 192

Webopedia Web site, 192

Wide Area Network protocols. *See* **WAN (Wide Area Network) protocols**

X – Z

X.25, 180

    carrier networks, 179

    DCE (data circuit terminating equipment), 181

    DTE (data terminal equipment), 181

    LAPBs (link access procedures, balanced), 185

    PAD (packet assembler/disassembler), 181

    PLPs (packet layer protocols), 185-187

    private networks, 179

    PSE (packet-switching exchange), 181

    PVCs (permanent virtual circuits), 182-184

    SVCs (switched virtual circuits), 184

Hey, you've got enough worries.

Don't let IT training be one of them.

Get on the fast track to IT training at InformIT,
your total Information Technology training network.

 | **www.informit.com** | **SAMS**

■ Hundreds of timely articles on dozens of topics ■ Discounts on IT books
from all our publishing partners, including Sams Publishing ■ Free, unabridged
books from the InformIT Free Library ■ "Expert Q&A"—our live, online chat
with IT experts ■ Faster, easier certification and training from our Web- or
classroom-based training programs ■ Current IT news ■ Software downloads
■ Career-enhancing resources